Patti Miller was raised on Wiradjuri land in central western New South Wales and now lives in Sydney. She is the author of *Writing Your Life* (Allen & Unwin, 1994, 2001); *The Last One Who Remembers* (Allen & Unwin, 1997); *Child* (Allen & Unwin, 1998); *Whatever the Gods Do* (Random House, 2003); *The Memoir Book* (Allen & Unwin, 2007); the award-winning *The Mind of a Thief* (UQP, 2012); *Ransacking Paris* (UQP, 2015); *Writing True Stories* (Routledge, 2017); and *The Joy of High Places* (NewSouth, 2019). She has also taught memoir and creative non-fiction for many years around Australia and in Fiji, Bali, Paris and London.

Praise for *True Friends*

'Told with courage, wisdom and grace, Patti Miller has restored female friendship to its rightful place at the centre of the interwoven narratives of women's lives. This brave and beautiful book explores what friendships give to and take from us on our life journeys, while also contemplating the mercurial nature of memory.' **Ceridwen Dovey**

'Miller dissects the anatomy of friendship as delicately as a surgeon, laying bare its heart. *True Friends* is at once a visceral and tender exploration of friendship's consolations and risks, the mysteries of connection and the creative life. In its raw depth and honesty, the story reveals as much about Miller as it does about relationships and the creative life – and the tensions that spark between them.' **Kristina Olsson**

'Warm and welcoming, *True Friends* is full of candid insights about the threads of friendship that weave through our lives – and what it means when a friendship is lost. Reading it, I felt connected to – and enlarged by – a whole new circle of friendship. I loved it.' **Kathryn Heyman**

'Miller's honest and self-revealing account of a lifetime of difficult and intense female friendships captures the aching vulnerability of rejection, misunderstanding, regret, remorse and guilt ... *True Friends* explores the often mysterious alchemy of affection between women.' **Caroline Baum**

True Friends

Patti Miller

First published 2022 by University of Queensland Press
PO Box 6042, St Lucia, Queensland 4067 Australia

University of Queensland Press (UQP) acknowledges the Traditional Owners
and their custodianship of the lands on which UQP operates. We pay our
respects to their Ancestors and their descendants, who continue cultural and
spiritual connections to Country. We recognise their valuable contributions to
Australian and global society.

uqp.com.au
reception@uqp.com.au

Cover design by Alissa Dinallo
Cover photograph by Shutterstock
Author photograph by Sally Flegg
Typeset in 12/16.5 pt Bembo Std by Post Pre-press Group, Brisbane
Printed in Australia by McPherson's Printing Group

University of Queensland Press is assisted
by the Australian Government through
the Australia Council, its arts funding and
advisory body.

A catalogue record for this book is available from the National Library of
Australia.

ISBN 978 0 7022 6554 9 (pbk)
ISBN 978 0 7022 6679 9 (epdf)
ISBN 978 0 7022 6680 5 (epub)
ISBN 978 0 7022 6681 2 (kindle)

University of Queensland Press uses papers that are natural, renewable and
recyclable products made from wood grown in well-managed forests and other
controlled sources. The logging and manufacturing processes conform to the
environmental regulations of the country of origin.

A true friend is a sweet thing / He searches the depth of your heart to know your needs.

—La Fontaine

I do not wish to treat friendships daintily, but with roughest courage. When they are real, they are not glass threads or frostwork, but the solidest thing we know.

—Ralph Waldo Emerson

For
Merril Shead
1948 – 2021

'Do you mind being in my book?' I asked.

I wasn't asking for her permission and didn't mean that I would leave her out if she did mind. I just wanted to know how she felt.

'That's not me. That's only your construction of me,' she said. 'Whatever you have written of me, it is not me.'

It is only my construction.
Of my friends.
Of myself.

Even so, some names and a few details have been altered in the interests of privacy.

One

It's hard to know exactly when the friendship with Gina ended. It could have been when the sudden text message from her arrived, or it could have been a slow slide out of favour that I willed myself not to see. What matters is that it did end, and I don't know why.

The beginning was clearer. I knew from our first meeting in a café in Balmain that we would be friends. I don't recall the name of the place, but it was in Darling Street on the left-hand side heading towards the ferry wharf, perhaps Café Berlin which I did use a few times for meetings. I could say it doesn't matter which one, but that would be trying to cover my blurriness about long ago events. Every detail matters, whether I use it or not.

I do remember the square table, the content and quality of our conversation, its intensity, and the delight we both took in each other. We had met to discuss a book I'd written a few years earlier. Gina had picked it up in a bookshop, drawn by the image of choral singers on the cover, and then realised she knew my name through my older son, Matt. She had directed him in a play when he was a teenager, *Mad Forest*, I thought it was; Caryl Churchill's exploration of the downfall of Ceauśescu and the Romanian revolution of 1989. It was a fascinating play about repression and liberation, but I mostly remember watching my gold-red haired son.

I may have seen Gina at the opening night – I have an outline memory of being introduced to a vibrant younger woman that evening – but that image might have been made retrospectively. Memory is a tricky conjurer; its sleight of hand, planting images from anywhere into any historical context, is impressive. I have a memory of the carpet, stairs and corridors in the foyer of the Seymour Centre in Sydney, and of milling parents and excited young actors – which could have come from any number of visits – and I'm shaking hands and saying thank-you to the Director who has a lively air and a tossing mane of dark hair. Her shape in memory has the slightly 'neat fit' feeling of being inserted, so it possibly wasn't Gina.

Then one morning in the Blue Mountains where I lived with my partner, Anthony, and younger son, Patrick – Matt had already started his life in films in Sydney – I answered the telephone and an unknown woman's voice greeted me. It was 2003 and people were still ringing as often as emailing or texting, so I wasn't as startled as I would be now, but I was surprised, and then pleased as she explained why she was calling.

The woman introduced herself as Gina, saying she had directed Matt in a play and that he'd mentioned at the time that his mother was a writer. She still had his home telephone number, so she assumed that it was mine, and had rung in the hope of talking to me about writing a play based on a book I had written. She apologised for taking advantage of having my phone number and hoped I didn't mind. I was thrilled and didn't really listen to any of her background explanation.

The book told the story of my friend – I called her Dina in the book – who, after a brain haemorrhage, had suffered in the immobile prison of her body for thirteen months, and then died, leaving her three-year-old son motherless. She had been a singer, and when she died I looked after her little boy and learnt how to sing.

'I'd like to work with you,' Gina explained. 'Meet with you and discuss the characters.'

'That sounds wonderful,' I said, 'but I'm going to Paris to live for a year. I'm leaving soon, in three weeks, so I can't really commit to anything.' The farm girl inside me was embarrassed at the casual mention of Paris. 'I could meet with you once before I leave, if you like?'

'That's all right,' she said. 'I'll come to Paris too.'

I know that's exactly what she said because we often laughed about it afterwards; that I had offered a compelling reason why I couldn't work with her and that she had jumped over it in a second. I remember being impressed by her determination, and then feeling rushed into it, then worried that I didn't know her. I wondered if I wanted to commit to working with an unknown woman on her project when I had another book to write.

But I was excited. This bold stranger wanted to write a play from my book!

'Oh, that was a sudden decision,' I laughed. 'How about we meet before I leave and we'll see how it goes.'

After I put the phone down, I felt doubtful.

~

3

I knew who Gina was as soon as I walked into the café because she had a copy of the book about Dina resting on the table. She was younger than I was, perhaps ten years younger, with remarkably smooth, pale skin and the thick auburn hair I thought I'd remembered; striking looking, but plainly dressed. A little white shirt comes to mind, but it was June, winter in Sydney, so perhaps a long-sleeved white tee. Light, rather than strong colours, anyway.

I felt shy and excited, like a child. We both smiled.

A waitress came over and we ordered coffee. While we waited for it, she explained again that she was an actor and occasionally, a director, which was how she had met Matt. 'He's a lovely actor, just the loveliest young man.'

I nodded and smiled again. Of course he was.

She said she had wanted to write a play for some time and my book had given her the narrative.

'I have to say it doesn't seem very theatrical to me. It's so internal,' I said.

'Oh, but it is!' She looked surprised. 'There's a mother who was a singer, she is dramatically damaged and trying to stay alive; there's a motherless child; and then there's this other woman trying to become his mother, even learning to sing like the real mother. I can see it very clearly on the stage.'

Then she told me part of her story. She had been rehearsing a play several years before – it was a dress rehearsal so she was in costume, a long dress, bonnet and knee-high lace-up boots – when a heavy cabinet full of books had fallen on her feet and lower legs, crushing them.

'The ambos told me my dainty boots had held my mangled feet in shape and saved them. Otherwise they wouldn't have been able to fix them. I wouldn't have been able to walk,' she said.

I sat there not knowing what to say, fascinated by the image of her pretty, fitted boots holding her limbs in shape. Was there blood seeping out through the eyelets? I didn't want to imagine, but the thought slid into my mind. How curious to have been crippled, almost, while playing someone else, dressed in a fictional character's clothes.

'I know Dina's story is not the same – she died and I lived – but there's something more for me.' Gina told me then, quietly, that she had an illness inherited from her grandmother. She didn't suffer from it yet, but she would, most likely, die from it. She wanted to write about living under a death sentence.

'We're all living under a death sentence.'

'Exactly. And what do we do? It's just that I *know* it. And so did Dina.'

There was such a quality of openness in her that none of this was too much for a first meeting. I have heard many stories of great pain because of the work I do with people writing about their lives, but in those situations I'm working on the words with them – I am not helpless. I separate myself from their pain so that I can ruthlessly say, 'You need to build that scene of your sister's breakdown,' without flinching. In ordinary conversation, I often feel overwhelmed and useless in the face of suffering. But not this time. It was as if I were being invited into a generous and thoughtfully arranged room where dramatic and life-changing things happened, but where I would not be in danger.

Like a theatre, I think now.

'Dina wasn't her real name,' I said. 'It was Dolly.' Although it wasn't conscious, I see now that I wanted to establish that Dolly was real, and, in a sense, Dina was invented, made by me. Dolly had existed as a separate immutable self in the breathing world, forever who she was, unaffected by anything Dina said or did.

Gina talked then about the structure of the play she had in mind, the same short series of scenes I had used in the book, the projection of a video on the back wall, the use of songs, a dramatic device for representing the small child, perhaps the mother could also play the child? I started to see how it could exist in a three-dimensional way, that the theatre could recreate the internal world, that perhaps theatre with all its sound and colour and action could do a better job of it than words on a page.

We were both glowing by now, the physical heat that comes from a creative work coming into being was coursing through us. My worry about a stranger taking up my time had dissolved in the warmth. When I spoke, Gina listened attentively; when she spoke, I heard every word. We were delighted with each other.

It was clear Gina had read every sentence, every phrase, every word of the book. To meet a real reader, a reader who sees what you hoped was there and then more, is a rare and delicious experience. It's the same as someone gazing at you with love and recognition. It's the recognition that warms you, makes your (my?) anxious soul unfurl and blossom, lets you become that glowing writer-self that is both tiny and unlimited. Friends and certainly family can't be bothered with it – rightly – because they know your ordinariness and your multitude of flaws, and if they see it at all, they know that the storyteller in the book barely exists in the outside world. Even readers care little for the storyteller herself, only the story. It was most likely different in the old days when the storyteller was there in person, standing in front of her listeners, feet planted on the ground, breathing between phrases, spinning the story out in front of her audience. But once she disappeared onto the page, or at first, onto a clay tablet, she was no longer noticed. No-one knows who wrote the first stories pressed into the earth itself. She wasn't observed as she performed her patient work, and no-one would have asked her over dinner, 'How is it going, this book you are working on?'

The glowing storyteller doesn't sit down to dinner, or clean the bathroom, or argue with telecommunication companies, or drink coffee in cafés. But this day in the café, because of Gina's detailed attention, I became that glowing being in the real world.

Two decades have passed since then, yet I believe I have an accurate recall of that first meeting. The emotional quality of it seems exact, unchanged from the day it happened, although there is no historical record for emotions so nothing can be proved. Regarding factual details, on the other hand, I have belatedly researched an online database and found Gina did not direct *Mad Forest* at any time. All I can say now as verifiable fact: my older son was in a play directed by Gina somewhere, sometime, before we met in Balmain. I don't know what other inadvertently falsified details I might have drawn from the questionable vault of memory.

~

Given the gaps and errors in memory even thus far, it seems necessary to say something about the way it creates stories about other people. Memory or Mnemosyne, in Greek mythology,

7

is the mother of all the Muses, of every creative spirit, so she can't be left out of anything. Zeus, the king of the gods, was their father, but I'm not so interested in his thunder and lightning. Mnemosyne is not a tyrannical or dramatic mother, rather she is more like one of those loose, creative, sloppy mothers who forgets to wash your school clothes but presents you with a glorious bunch of waratahs she stole when she was out walking.

Memory has to be part of this story. How can I know any friend except through my perception of her, which then becomes a memory the instant it has happened? And what I remember, what stays with me past the moment it happened, must be shaped not just by perception but by my personality and temperament, and by my own past. The buried memories of long-ago childhood friendships shape and colour who I am drawn to, even now. And then there is also the science of memory itself, how it actually works in the brain – what is perceived, what is recorded, how it is stored.

Apparently – and I'm going to say 'apparently' a lot because I am not a scientist and have to take their word for it – science currently divides memory into three parts. Our sensory memory gathers information – sights, sounds and smells – in the moment and lasts less than a second. Short-term or working memory enables me to remember what just happened, hopefully, and lasts for from thirty seconds to two minutes. Long-term memory enables me to remember my childhood friends, the knowledge of the discovery in Nineveh of the first story written on clay tablets, and the date and place of Montaigne's birth, 1533 AD near Bergerac in south-west France. It is stored around the brain in specific sites and can last a lifetime.

Before that process, how a moment of experience gets to the brain in the first place, and then becomes a memory, requires a transformation of religious proportions. It translates experience from one order of being to another, from physical to representational, from the three-dimensional world to an electrochemical network. How flesh and blood is able to enact such transubstantiation is impressive and elegant science.

Apparently, during the original experience, the senses are activated by the smell of coffee, the feel of a china cup, the eyes of an auburn-haired woman, and messages are passed to the brain where the seahorse-shaped hippocampus puts them together into a story – I am having coffee in a café with a new friend. When the almond-shaped amygdala, the 'emotion receptor', is excited, senses and emotions are linked making the memories more likely to last. The next time – and for years afterwards – when my senses are activated by any one of these elements, there is a kind of video replay of the original events. A curious editing can happen though. If something else occurs while I am recalling the memory, say a woman in a white shirt walks past, the white shirt can be edited into the original memory – and I won't even notice. The next time I remember, Gina will be in the café wearing a white shirt. Or directing *Mad Forest*.

This, of course, is the barest outline of the body's magic trick – turning life into electrical circuitry via a seahorse and an almond in the brain. It all sounds so unlikely and yet it forms a sense of self. Without the seahorse and the almond, I would have no memory and no consciousness of being and there could be no books, no poetry, no theatre, no painting, no clay tablets inscribed with wedge-shaped cuneiform script, no storytelling, no friendships.

~

Friendships begin early, although not at home. I'm not counting any of my seven brothers and sisters as friends even though my connections with them contain many of the same elements as friendship. According to Montaigne, whose entire writing output came from the need to distract himself after his dear friend died: 'In friendship there is no traffic or commerce, but with itself.' Common genes and upbringing create a great deal of highly tangled traffic, and friendships are complicated enough without the shared blood, rooms, parents and battles of childhood.

My first friendship, or at least, alliance, started in kindergarten at Suntop, a one-teacher school in the corner of a paddock, twenty kilometres from the small town of Wellington, at that time a day's drive north-west of Sydney. The school consisted of one classroom and a porch, a separate weather shed and toilets, a large open playground and eucalypts, pepper-trees and wattles. All the students, seventeen of us, were from local farms, and when I began, three of them were my brothers.

Sue Bestwick (the name is forever one unit, Suebestwick) and I were the only two girls in kindergarten so our friendship wasn't a matter of choice. I can't remember the content of the earliest years of our friendship, even what we played – although there is a faint memory of making houses under the wattle trees, but I do remember sitting in the classroom waiting impatiently as she stumbled over the words in the Dick and Dora reader. In the schoolyard there was no pairing off with individual friends, it was more the comings and goings of a swirling noisy flock of cockatoos. Because there were so few of us, everyone had to play together to have enough for team games – prisoners' base, rounders and soccer – although inherited prejudice between Catholics and Protestants occasionally erupted into war.

Then, when I was ten years old, some of the fathers fixed

the school tennis court and Sue and I played with and against each other, belting the ball back and forth even in the searing heat, practising to win the Walmer Shield against the other small schools. We were fiercely competitive when we played singles, even though I knew Sue's backhand would always defeat mine, but in doubles we were unified and unbeatable.

Sue was also a fast runner and won all the blue ribbons at the inter-school sports days. She was determined and focused and I knew she would always run faster than I did no matter how hard I tried. She did well in class, too, working methodically and studying for exams. I was struck by the fact that she studied. I had never even imagined doing such a thing – I thought you just sat down and wrote what you remembered from class. When we did maths together, I worked out how to do the problem and she did the actual sums.

On weekends we visited each other's ramshackle farmhouses. Hers was tidier and better furnished than mine with a pretty lounge, a television and a carpet. I envied her nice things, especially the furry zip-up dog which sat on her bed and contained her pyjamas. One visit, we played in a small grove of Tree of Heaven down the hill from her house and Sue confessed afterwards she hadn't played there before because she thought the trees were boring. I remember being aware they were uninteresting, but fascinated by their name. One day when she stayed at my place, I organised for us to map and name every twist and turn of our dry creek – Emerald Isle for the rough outcrop in the middle of the gully, Cape Argentina for a longish 'headland'. I loved that game but Sue didn't see the point of naming things.

We met at the tin church on Sundays in our best dresses and hats – Sue's always matching her little sister's – and I wished

I could have clothes like hers. They were flowery – one had red flowers on it, gathered at the waist – and always had frills; my mother didn't like frills. But our mothers were friends. I watched them standing outside the church, talking and laughing as the men stood around, pushing their hats back and remarking about the weather. Her mother had curly blonde hair and my mother often remarked that she was the prettiest woman in the district, but I only remember noticing that she smoked, the smell of it, and that she drove the family car. My mother did neither. Sitting in the Bestwicks' car and smelling the cigarette smoke was the first time I registered the strangeness of physical proximity with friends' parents.

I have tried to remember what Sue and I talked about when we were children, but it's difficult to find any detailed conversations in the dark of memory. From observing girls now, I know we must have discussed the games we played and television shows, our lessons and the other kids, but probably not our families. We did discuss the unfortunate Furner kids, unfortunate because being new to the school they didn't have uniforms, enough to damn them in the closed society of Suntop school. The three Furner kids were placed at the bottom of our small hierarchy and were dissected every day until they left a few months later. I sensed that the oldest girl, Susan, was someone I might like to talk to in another world, but I could not risk stepping out of my own.

As well as flowery dresses, Sue had soft brown hair and striking hazel eyes. I saw that boys liked her and finally – I don't recall when – I realised she was pretty. Once, I organised a 'kissing' where Chris, the teacher's younger son, kissed Sue while all the rest of us watched from around the corner. I directed them, insisting they kiss on the mouth. I had forgotten until I started writing this, that I also liked Chris at that time, so it appears now a strangely voyeuristic performance.

I was involved in Sue's romantic life as a teenager, too. She was going out with a boy who had left school and worked as a mechanic at a local garage. After the first date, she invited me over on the weekend and told me she didn't know what to talk to him about. I was sitting on her bed and she was looking in her dressing-table mirror, trying to see what her lips looked like when she pursed them to kiss.

'What can I talk about? You always know what to talk about.' She flopped back on her bed.

I was flattered. I took a piece of paper and with much discussion and added instruction, wrote a list of topics and questions – I wish I could remember them now – which she folded up and put in her purse. This Cyrano de Bergerac effort must have worked because later on she married the mechanic. Sue asked me to be her bridesmaid and I think they lived happily ever after.

When Sue said she was going to leave school as soon as she could and get a job at the local bank, I knew we were fundamentally different. She had studied and achieved high marks but she had no desire to finish school and go to university and was happy to stay in Wellington. It was a contentment I could not fathom. Why would she want to stay in this going-nowhere town? I tried to argue with her, and then tried to mock her lack of desire for anything more, but she just shrugged. 'I hate schoolwork,' she said. 'I don't want to do it anymore.'

These conjured fragments of childhood memories feel like wooden puppets suddenly jerking into a semblance of life inside me, like the characters in Beckett's *Endgame* who move only when someone thinks of them – we each exist momentarily, two small girls who believe they are friends. A synapse has fired and the seahorse and the almond have spliced a series of short stories together for my entertainment. In the three-dimensional world, there could be records, photographs, school reports, possibly even a website where I could check facts, although that's unlikely, but I want to see what constructions memory has made. It's not so much the evidence that creates reality, it's what memory tells us. Memory is the first storyteller.

~

I've been wondering why, compared to romantic love, the love of friends is not much written about. Philosophers – Plato, Aristotle, Montaigne, Emerson – have explored friendship, and there are memoirs and novels and films, but it is only a small percentage compared to the narratives of passion and romance. It seems an odd imbalance because the oldest written story ever discovered is a story of friendship.

No-one knows who the storyteller was, but *The Epic of Gilgamesh* was inscribed on twelve clay tablets found in the library of King Assurbanipal in Nineveh, an ancient Assyrian city in present-day northern Iraq. The tablets, found by Ottoman Empire scholar, Hormuzd Rassam, and an English archaeologist, Austin Henry Layard, caused a nineteenth-century storm in the Western world because they pre-dated the Bible and recounted a story from which the Bible had clearly borrowed. Recent research has identified early Sumerian fragments of The Epic in the third millennium BC, up to two thousand years before Homer penned the *Iliad* and the *Odyssey*, although like Homer's stories, it may have existed as a spoken tale long before someone thought to carve it into clay tablets. The most complete version of The Epic, written in the contemporary language of Akkadian, was put together by Assurbanipal's scholars in the seventh century BC.

I can't read Akkadian, but in English translation the story goes like this: Gilgamesh was the physically beautiful but self-absorbed ruler of the Sumerian city-state of Uruk. His people hated him, not least because he insisted on using his right to bed any bride, or groom, the night before their wedding. The gods decided to humble Gilgamesh by creating the wild man, Enkidu, to confront him.

Enkidu lived with the animals and was accepted by them – he could run as fast as a gazelle – but one day a woman, Shamhat, was sent to seduce him from the wild with her sexuality and human wisdom. They had sex for 'six days and seven nights' and afterwards the animals shunned him 'for wisdom was in him and the thoughts of a man were in his heart'. Shamhat persuaded Enkidu to go to the city and meet Gilgamesh, but first she taught him the ways of civilisation, how to eat bread and drink wine.

Enkidu went to the city of Uruk saying, 'I have come to challenge the old order because I am the strongest here.' Gilgamesh and Enkidu had a physical fight and Gilgamesh won, but because they recognised each other's strength and each had longed for a comrade who understood his heart, they embraced and became best friends.

But soon Enkidu was heartsick – oppressed by idleness. Gilgamesh, too, began to think of the futility of existence, that 'our occupations are a breath of wind'. To make his name endure forever, he decided to set out with Enkidu to defeat the ferocious god-monster, Humbaba, who guarded the Land of the Cedars. With Enkidu's help and advice, the guardian of the forest was felled, the mountains and hills trembled, and Gilgamesh cut down the cedars all the way to the Euphrates.

Afterwards, he washed his long locks, cleaned his weapons and put on his royal robes. The goddess Ishtar saw him and desired him. 'Grant me the seed of your body, let me be your bride,' she said, but Gilgamesh refused. He knew that each of her former lovers had a horrible fate, either death or being transformed into an animal – a harried wolf or a sightless mole. She fell into a rage and sent the bull of heaven to destroy him.

Gilgamesh and Enkidu killed the bull and as soon as Ishtar learnt of it, she cursed both of them. Enkidu sickened and died, feeling the meaninglessness of everything that had happened, the pointlessness of glory and fame. But before he died, he told Gilgamesh the dream that had come to him:

> The sombre faced bird man
> led me down the road from which there is no coming back.
> There is the house whose people sit in darkness;
> Dust is their food and clay their meat,
> They are clothed like birds with wings for covering,
> They see no light, they sit in darkness
> I entered the house of dust and I saw the kings of the earth,
> Their crowns put away for ever.

Gilgamesh was grief-stricken by the loss of his friend and in despair, because Enkidu had revealed the pointlessness of power and success. Now alone, Gilgamesh set out on a journey to find the man who had survived the Babylonian flood and knew the secret of everlasting life. He toiled over the Mountains of Mashu where no human had been before, through twelve days of thick darkness.

After many dangerous travels, grieving the loss of his friend every day, Gilgamesh finally found the man who had survived the flood by obeying a dream that had instructed him to build a boat. He told Gilgamesh there was no permanence, even for kings and princes. But then the man promised to tell Gilgamesh the secret of eternal life if he passed the test of staying awake for six nights. Gilgamesh failed. The gods pointed out that none of the great or good, no matter how strong, would ever come again, that everlasting life was not the lot of man.

As compensation for failing to attain immortality, Gilgamesh was given a plant that restored youth and beauty, but, on the way home, it was stolen from him by a serpent. (You have to watch serpents.) He accepted the loss, returned to Uruk, and engraved on stone the story of his friendship and his vast journey, thereby attaining the immortality of all who live in stories.

It is very appealing that the first written story tells of a friendship, but what is even more striking is that, finally, it is about the immortality bestowed by stories. Right near the end of The Epic, it says: 'He went on a long journey, was weary, worn out with labour, and returning engraved on a stone the whole story.' We know of Gilgamesh and Enkidu *only* because a story was written about them. We can only live on in stories. It is almost unbelievable, that *this*, the story of why we must tell stories, is the oldest written one ever found. It seems too perfectly made-for-purpose to be true.

Not only does achievement, power and beauty end, says the oldest story, but so does the deepest love and friendship. Everything and everyone ends up in the 'house of dust'. No matter how much we cry, how bravely we face the terrors of existence, how long we quest for the secret of eternal life, no matter what tests we endure, what prayers we utter, what dear friends we make, what we think we remember, the only thing that lasts is the story of our quest – and even more precisely, the story that is written down.

Two

Gina arrived in Paris some time before her Bastille Day birthday. We exchanged emails about her playwriting project over the months after our meeting in Balmain, but it's still difficult to establish an accurate timeline for a couple of reasons.

A few years ago, in an impulse towards simplicity and clarity – and thinking I wouldn't need them anymore, I deleted all emails dated ten or more years earlier. It means there's no email record of our exchanges during that time. And then, in the book I wrote about living in Paris, I altered the sequence of some events so that now I'm not sure of the correct order. In fact, I lived there twice, once for six months, and then, after a year back in Australia to save more money I returned again for twelve months – and blended those two sojourns to write an account of one year. There was no intention to deceive, merely to correct the clumsy gaps and bunching of the natural rhythm of events, but it has made it difficult to establish when anything really happened. The written word tends to trump electrochemical memory, but I don't suppose the time sequence is crucial. What matters is that our friendship came into being in Paris. That it happened there in that city of endless stories was the defining element.

It's easy to recall the Bastille Day birthday. It was Gina's fortieth, one of the most significant of decade birthdays. It's only a date, a number, but in the ritualistic way that we order our lives, it has weight and power. It's a turning point when some things are still possible, still hopeful, but others are probably not going to happen. You could still hit the big-time in your career, although time is running out; and you can still hope to fall in love and live happily ever after. But there is a statistically low chance of running in the Olympic Games, singing at the New York Met, having a baby. I don't know if Gina wanted any of the things that might have been slipping out of reach, I don't even know if she wanted a baby – we didn't talk about babies – but I know she felt this birthday was a turning point, a time to shed old ways, even old friends.

She told me that her friends in Australia were upset that she didn't want to celebrate with them but, she said, she wanted to break free of their expectations of her.

'I don't want to be held to anyone's idea of me,' she said a couple of weeks before her birthday. 'That's their need, not mine. I'd rather be here, working with you.'

Perhaps I should have been warned, but I was filled with admiration for her steely clarity – and deeply flattered. I felt as if I, a newcomer, had without even trying, won the prize of Gina's friendship against the serried ranks of a powerful established order. I'd never had that experience before, had never had the charm to win a friendship battle. I'd lost one before though.

At Suntop school, I had a position, a place, without being aware of it. I wasn't the leader, there was an anarchic shifting mob dynamic with four or five of us older ones leading the charge, but I did have a sense of belonging – and of power. I had punched the teacher's older son on the nose and put a dead blue-tongue lizard in his desk, and his father had humiliated me by cleaning my dirty fingernails in front of the whole school – but he still awarded me Dux of the school over his son. I was dirty and brainy and utterly innocent of the brutal power plays I've seen teenage girls engage in so many times since, ill-prepared for the epic complications of high-school friendship.

During my first year at St Mary's High, I was unexpectedly an outsider. In the classroom, with thirty other students instead of two, I was still the brainiest – I knew what to do, how to behave in class – but outside in the school grounds I was adrift. I have a clear image of walking along the school veranda on the first day, and another of walking into the quadrangle some weeks later, and in each memory I am approaching a solid group of girls, aware of fear and isolation, the anxiety of not belonging. My second-hand uniform was too big and I wore a bra for the first time; cotton, unfilled, uncomfortable, and my limbs would not move naturally. I didn't know where I should put myself.

Sue was there, but she attached herself on the first day to a group of other girls, one of whom was her cousin. Then Cathy tried to befriend me – she gave me holy cards and whispered to me in class – until several girls from the powerful group, led by Julie-Anne, let me know that it was not a good idea to be friends with Cathy. She was Greek, had a thick, old-fashioned plait, and, I was told, she smelled. In the severe hierarchy of teenage girls, she had been given the role of class pariah and by association the same judgement would be handed down to me. After the warning, I didn't return her notes and didn't sit with her at lunchtime. I knew it was wrong and admitted it as a sin in the confessional, but still, I left her to her preordained fate.

Afterwards I swirled around on the edge of the powerful girls, awash, not able to get any kind of toehold. Although I was the same age as they were, I felt much younger. I had been used to spending every lunchtime playing and didn't yet know how to make conversation. Some of the girls would talk to me for a while, but when we sat in a long line along the wall of the quadrangle at lunch, I was always at the outer end. Whenever I was outside the classroom I was alone in a dangerous sea.

In class, I talked to one of the boys, Michael, who had red hair like me. We both enjoyed learning and whispered and laughed and exchanged notes about our schoolwork, causing the other girls to say, 'Oh, you like Michael Bird.' But there was no possibility I could sit with him, talk to him out in the school grounds. It was unimaginable to be friends with a boy outside of the classroom, outside of schoolwork.

For a while I hung around Lyn, who wore her uniform looped over her belt to make it as short as possible. She was not yet a bad girl, but her older sister who also wore her uniform looped and drove around with her boyfriend in his FJ Holden, showed which way Lyn would go. And she lived in a Housing Commission house.

'Have you seen Lyn's house?' one of the powerful girls asked, disparagingly. When I did see it, part of a row of identical Commission houses, I was grateful that I lived on a farm out of town where no-one could see what our house was like. Lyn's house was much better than our tin and fibro place. I had to be careful. I continued to bump from Lyn to the powerful group and sometimes to Sue's friends, clinging to the illusion of being included.

And then halfway through the year, Peta became my friend. She was by far the prettiest in the class, with large brown eyes, brown skin and a spiky cap of hair, the shortest I had ever seen on a girl. But she was not powerful or central because she was a boarder and kept herself apart. There were only a handful of boarders, perhaps a dozen across the whole school, who lived at the convent with the nuns. They had their own friendship group, apart from the rest of us.

I realised immediately that she had become my friend because she had a crush on one of my older brothers, Tim, who was two years above us. Tim was good-looking with thick blond hair and blue eyes, but he wore glasses and was quiet and shy. He would never make the first move. It wasn't the last time that a girl befriended me because of one of my five brothers, but I didn't mind. I had someone to sit with in the playground.

'Let's go and sit away from the others,' Peta said. She took me behind the Infant de Prague Hall where we were forbidden to sit – forbidden only because the nuns couldn't see us there. We sat on the edge of the concrete steps and swung our legs and talked. I remember sunshine and her smooth brown legs, her ease, my awkwardness. I enjoyed doing something forbidden and it was thrilling to have the attention of the prettiest girl in the class. It was a kind of romance, from my side at least. Whenever I see a pretty teenage girl with a plain acolyte, I understand.

Peta came from a huge station out west between Bourke and Brewarrina, one of those properties so vast it was marked on maps of New South Wales. It was the kind of place I wanted to come from, a proper station and homestead with horses for everyone. She was lighthearted and enjoyed being able to tell me things I clearly had no idea about. Because she lived with the older boarders, she knew all about sex. My only knowledge had come from a sex education booklet called *Youth Looks Ahead*, written by a nun and given to me by my mother when I started to menstruate. Sue had been given the same book and we read it together hiding in the wheat shed, neither of us wanting to be seen with it even though our mothers had given it to us. I couldn't pretend to know anything more about sex than the nun's booklet told me.

'My favourite film is *La Dolce Vita*,' Peta said one day with a naughty, knowing look on her face. I knew it was an 'immoral' film about sex but had no clear idea what that meant. It's one of those memories when I remember exactly where I was – memory imprinting is geographical, it turns out. Each memory is attached to the place where it was laid down, an exact location in the physical world, with trees, buildings, furniture, a precise quality of sunlight. We were walking, the two of us, up across the bitumen school quadrangle towards the central steps that led onto the veranda, on a very bright day.

'Isn't that a sinful film?' I exclaimed in surprise. Sin was a word that used to be easy to use. I can see the knowing look on Peta's face, and in her eyes a glint of pleasure in breaking the rules. She seemed to have everything I could want; so pretty, so knowledgeable and nonchalant about things that were obviously important.

But I did have something Peta wanted; inside knowledge of my brother, and I began to relax into the role of the intriguer. I could feed her any amount of information about my sweet brother.

One day a patrolling nun found us sitting behind the Infant de Prague Hall and we were sent back to the quadrangle. Giggling, we found a bench away from the others and continued to talk and laugh. I was getting better at it.

But then Julie-Anne saw us. She was lively and forceful with dark wavy hair, sparkling eyes and had the kind of charm that makes the recipient feel they are among the chosen. She listened, paid attention, laughed easily. She had the confidence of coming from a substantial grazing family, not well off anymore but still part of the aristocracy of country towns. She was captain of the basketball team and class captain, and as head of the powerful group, had the largest circle of friends.

Julie-Anne began to focus on Peta. She chatted to her as we stood in line to go into class, sent notes and laughed with her during lessons, and then, within a week or so, right before my eyes she had stolen her away. Peta was placed in the centre of her group, her closest confidante. She lavished attention on Peta, asked her questions, teased her, shared her cake from the tuckshop, made her laugh, put Peta's head in her lap while she played with her hair.

Watching that last scene – head in lap, Peta smiling up at Julie-Anne – I remember thinking, I have no chance. It was a thought without anger. I was drawn to Julie-Anne myself, I wanted her to like me, to lavish attention on me, but I was aware of powerlessness. And of hurt. I had lost the battle before I could even imagine any other outcome.

A childhood loss of friendship is a long way from Paris and Gina's birthday, but that's part of the way memory operates. In spiralling loops, some tiny, connecting moment to moment, some vast, connecting an abandoned twelve-year-old girl at a country high school to a woman beginning a friendship on the other side of the world nearly forty years later. The Storyteller knows the woman will later be abandoned too, but at this moment even she does not know why. The spiral will loop again, I'm sure of it.

How do I remember Peta's laughing face in Julie-Anne's lap and recall the pang of hurt and jealousy – and forget anything else that happened that day? I can remember the place, the wooden benches in the quadrangle, but no other events. Even though memory itself is attached to particular places, the images of my friendship seem arbitrary and disconnected. I want to understand the science of it, the biology and chemistry of it. It doesn't encompass the whole truth – science never mentions love or spiritual union, admiration or laughter – and it uses chilly Latin and Greek words – but I like its valiant search for understanding. It is one way of seeing what is happening when I hold someone in my mind.

First, there is memory at the cellular level. I imagine it working something like messages sent in Morse code; the original words are changed into dots and dashes and sent over a telegraph wire as a pattern of electrical impulses, which are then reassembled into words at the other end. It strikes me as an image of how a message can be translated from one medium to another, from word to sign to electrical wave and back again, a kind of magical transformation.

Morse code machines have a tapping arm that stops and starts the electric current; neurons have dendrites, feathery branches for receiving messages and a long single thread, an axon, for sending messages. Between them is a tiny gap, a synapse. A message begins with the light from Peta's smile hitting my eye, which is then encoded as an imbalance of ions between the inside and outside of the cell. The imbalance creates a rapid flow along the axon and once it reaches the end, tiny chemical bubbles of neurotransmitters are released across the gap and received by the dendrites of the next neuron. Peta's smile is encoded in chemistry floating between an axon and a dendrite, waiting to be decoded one day.

If I don't see her smile often enough, the coded message will disappear. If groups of neurons fire together often enough, they become linked. 'Neurons that fire together wire together,' is what the cool neuroscientists say. The hippocampus, the Morse code headquarters, is where all the small fragments of information are put together to make one story in the brain, an engram, or memory trace. The more I recall Peta's smile and the quadrangle and the sunlight, the stronger the connection becomes and the more likely it is to last.

My memories of my friendship with Sue and Peta and everyone who is to come, are mere electrochemical reactions in my brain, encoding the Infant de Prague Hall and a bitumen quadrangle along with fragments of long-ago conversations and smiles and hurt feelings, and all of it stored as changed brain chemistry. It makes it easier to accept that, even at the verifiable level of scientific fact, my knowledge of others is a weirdly airy, but convincing, construction. Each friend, everyone I know, has been made in my brain out of momentary impressions, imperfectly recorded, giving the illusion of continuous beings.

It doesn't feel like a reduction or an evisceration of their flesh and blood. In fact, it creates in me a frisson of delight, a dreamy sensation, as if I am looking at a vibrant painting and another one has come shimmering into being underneath it like one of those patterned pictures where, if you blur your eyes, another distinct 3D image of a dolphin or a face, emerges. Both pictures exist, both are real; what you see depends on how you look at the picture.

~

After the loss of Peta, I was plunged back into the high-school hell of having no particular friend. The rest of the first year I bobbed awkwardly from group to group, sometimes trailing around in the wake of Julie-Anne's glorious train, sometimes hanging onto the edges of Sue's group, occasionally talking to Lyn. I didn't sit alone but hovered uncertainly on the edges of eddying circles of girls, constantly anxious about not belonging anywhere.

That year so long ago has meant that whenever I am in a situation where I have to approach a group of people alone, my neural pathways activate feelings of awkwardness. It's not paralysing – and doesn't happen if I have a defined role to play, but when I have no particular function it dissolves the adult woman into a clunky twelve-year-old girl, an outsider in an ill-fitting uniform and a scratchy cotton bra.

Perhaps because of being on the outside, the exact composition of each group of girls in that year is sharply imprinted in my neurons. Even today, decades later, I could take out a pencil and map them with flawless accuracy, a detailed landscape of feminine friendships. Each girl and her friends, the one who is central, the ones who are on the fringe, the pretty and the plain, first names and surnames linked and remembered for a lifetime – Julie-Annekelly, Suebestwick, Cathydantrinos, Petahorton, Lynorourke. Memory is sometimes perfect.

In the oldest written story, women do not have friendships with each other and, in fact, do not relate to each other in any way at all. They each relate only to men. They have important functions, they are goddesses and prostitutes and mothers, but the story is not about them, it's about the friendship between two men. The goddess, Aruru, creates Enkidu – she is obviously a key player – she makes him out of 'the stuff of Anu', the firmament, water and clay, to be the equal of Gilgamesh, to be 'as like him as his own reflection, stormy heart for stormy heart', but it's not her story. What matters is that she creates a friend for Gilgamesh.

It's clear that the friendship between Gilgamesh and Enkidu was grounded in their likeness, that they shared a restless passion. Common wisdom says we are attracted to those who are not like us, but perhaps the opposite is true in friendship. Perhaps the joyful feeling in friendship is seeing your inner self recognised and reflected, and perhaps that is true whether the friendship is between men or between women, or between men and women, a non-gendered reflection of equals. Maybe, as the gods understood all along, I recognised myself in Gina, was drawn to the best of myself in her. Montaigne, writing in his sixteenth-century tower room in south-west France about his dear friend Étienne de la Boétie, felt it was a meeting of equal and like minds; 'Not only did I know his mind as well as I knew my own, but I would have entrusted myself to him with greater assurance than to myself.'

For Gilgamesh and Enkidu, as you might expect of men, the first meeting is a battle of physical strength. They did meet before in a dream. Gilgamesh dreamed that a meteor fell from the heavens, and that it held for him the attraction of the love of a woman. In the dream, his mother said the meteor was his brother. Afterwards, the court's dream interpreter said the dream meant he would meet a friend who would never desert him.

When Enkidu first came to the city of Uruk, he stepped in front of Gilgamesh to prevent him from 'taking' a bride on her wedding night. He knew it was his job to stand up to Gilgamesh and would not let him pass. The crowd remarked on their similarity, 'He's the spit of Gilgamesh,' and noted one was shorter than the other, but the other was bigger of bone. I can just see them watching and gossiping. The two men battled until they shattered the doorposts of the bride's house and the walls shook. Gilgamesh threw Enkidu to the ground, defeating him, but immediately his fury died. They embraced and their friendship was sealed.

Does it mean male friendship begins with some sort of test? I know men who have begun a friendship with me by testing, sparring, almost needling, checking my mental strength and agility – and I often participate in the test because I don't know what else to do, but I resent it. Why must I show I can be clever? Why pass your test? I wonder if my friendships with men have all been a mind connection rather than an emotional one, always about ideas, a meeting of true minds.

Perhaps men can only find equality in battle. Instead of wrestling in the street and knocking down doorposts, in these civilised days they engage in sport, or sparring conversations, and then, when the contest is done, head out on adventures, crossing seas and climbing mountains together. For Enkidu and Gilgamesh, their adventure was to defeat the ferocious god-monster who guarded the Land of the Cedars. It was to escape boredom, to distract from a futile life and death, to make their mark, and finally, to have stories sung about them.

~

After the Balmain café meeting with Gina, I had felt not tested, but exposed. I had undressed in public as I do when I write. She had seen my blotchy naked mind and heart, or rather she had already seen it in my book and there I was in real life, still unclothed. A total stranger had seen the messy insides of my gut, the green shadows in my brain. When I meet a reader in life, I usually feel an uncomfortable three-part split into the Storyteller who has done the writing, the self I have constructed on the page, and the ordinary woman who is standing there in front of them, awkwardly, in pieces. I shuffle a bit, I try to hold eye contact, I try to speak as if conversation comes naturally.

But with Gina it was different. In that first meeting I was not divided. Everything in me was subsumed into the Storyteller. The Storyteller was the only one who breathed, the only one who spoke, and the relief of being whole was like a drug-rush, warm and flowing and opening my heart. In that whole state I glowed, knowing without question that Gina saw my best self. I spoke every sentence with passion and clarity and even humility. I was a vessel.

But afterwards as I waited for her to arrive in Paris, I was afraid again. What if that was a one-off, what if I would be split as usual when we met again? She would see the clunky country girl, the awkward shuffling woman, instead of the glowing one. She would wonder what the hell was going on. I sat in my fifth-floor eyrie in the rue Simart and worried. I put it aside. I wrote, I shopped at the markets, I practised French, I sang in a choir, I worried.

But I need not have. Gina's delight in being in Paris swept all before it in a warm, dissolving wave. A decade or so earlier she had lived there for a year herself, studying physical performance at an acting school in the rue du Faubourg Saint-Denis, so that coming back was a return to the centre of her practice and her passion as an actor. She was as thrilled as I was to be in this mythical place, which mostly existed inside our own heads. We shared, friends share, a construction, a common interpretation of the world, a common gaze.

Where did we first meet up there? I can't remember which café, or was it in our apartment in the rue Simart, where she would also have met Anthony for the first time? In any case we all knew each other by Bastille Day when Anthony and I decided to take her out to dinner for her birthday.

We booked a table for three at Bofinger, a brasserie near Place de la Bastille. It seemed the right address for the Fourteenth of July. Bofinger is a nineteenth-century extravagance with mirrors, wood panelling, flamingo columns, palms and a huge vase of artificial wisteria under an elegant glass-domed ceiling. Our table was at the black leather banquettes and Gina and I were seated together on one side looking outwards towards the other tables. Anthony sat looking at us both and able to see the whole brasserie reflected in the mirror behind us.

We were dressed up, Gina in an elegant black dress with a wide neckline and I wore a lichen-green satin skirt and a

second-hand 1920s scarf. It's not that I remember our clothes –
I have a photograph taken later on that evening – so I am
supplementing memory every now and then. Still, I don't need
the photograph to remember how delighted we were with
each other. Anthony, too, drew Gina in immediately, asking
her about the play she was writing.

'How are you dealing with a central character who doesn't
move?' he asked, and I can remember thinking, that's a perfect
question.

Gina talked about screening videos on the back wall of
the theatre. The audience would see Dina's mindscape on
the theatre wall, her memories flickering. There would be
darkness, then small explosions of colour and amorphous
forms, and then distinct but brief scenes. Then darkness again.
A light on Dina's face.

'It's just an idea at the moment,' she said.

'But it's exactly right,' I said. 'It will be like looking inside
her damaged brain, parts of her past surfacing for a moment,
and subsiding.'

'Or she could get up with a mask on, and be her past self,'
Gina went on. 'Or perhaps I could use puppets for the past, for
her inner life?'

'So really, a one-woman play?' asked Anthony.

We sparked off each other, listened intently, the three of us
lost to the others in the restaurant, but conscious of the quick
glances of diners at other tables.

Towards the end of the meal, an American woman at the
next table leaned over and said without introduction, 'Excuse
me, but can I ask, what is your relationship to each other? I've
been sitting here watching and I can't work it out.'

I smiled. 'What do you suspect it is?'

'I think you – and you,' nodding towards me and then Gina, 'are old friends. But I'm not sure who you are?' indicating Anthony.

I smiled again, delighted that she had not got it right. 'No,' I said. 'Gina is a new friend and Anthony is my partner.'

'Ah,' she said. She chatted for a while longer while we gathered our things. I was happy to have been watched, but afterwards Gina exclaimed how nosy the woman was, how American.

'I didn't mind,' I said.

We emerged from the revolving door of the brasserie into the narrow street. The evening wasn't over yet.

'We have arranged fireworks at the Eiffel Tower for your birthday,' I suddenly said. I hadn't even thought of the Bastille Day fireworks until we walked out of the restaurant. It felt like I was making the evening up as I went, and everything sprang into being as I thought of it. Gina laughed happily.

'The limo didn't come,' I said, 'but no worries. Let's jump on the Métro – it will take us straight to Concorde – best place to see the fireworks.'

'There will be other people there,' Anthony said, going along with the game, 'but it's all been arranged for you. We let other people come if they want.'

Just as we came out of the Métro at Concorde the fireworks began, shooting up and down the Eiffel Tower and spraying out in fans of colour. Perfect timing. There's a flash-lit photograph of Anthony and me, me with a huge smile and glowing with happiness – it almost looks like a wedding photo. I think there was a photo of Gina and me taken there as well, but it seems to have disappeared. It was in the days of analogue photos, kept in boxes under beds, so that photo must have slipped out of sight and been lost in one of our moves.

But there is a surviving photo of us taken afterwards at the Ritz. Again, I had not planned on going to the Ritz, in fact I'd been much too daunted to have even gone inside it before, but when the fireworks finished we were still buzzing.

'Next is champagne at the Ritz,' I heard coming out of my mouth. 'A nightcap.'

'A nightcap at the Ritz then,' said Anthony.

We all laughed, impressed with our own audacity and nonchalance. I had only had a couple of glasses of wine – I'm not much of a drinker – but I was drunk with confidence, with the knowledge that the night was unfolding under my will. I had lost all my fear of someone seeing the uncomfortable country girl inside the shiny dress. I could swan into the Ritz and no-one would stop me.

And no-one did. We walked around the Place Vendôme and in through the discreet doors of the Ritz. We didn't know where to go, so we strolled down the wide lamp-lit hall – that's where the picture of the two of us was taken – Gina with her head tilted, smiling, and her arm out in a gesture of 'Well, here I am'. We ended up in the Hemingway Bar near the back entrance, the one that Princess Diana slipped out of minutes before she died, as if that was where we were heading all along. There's a photo of Anthony and me taken there with a poster of Ernest Hemingway on the cover of *Life* magazine in the background. We look happy and pleased with ourselves.

Three

Gina's playwriting questions were all deleted in the email clean-up, but I have a general idea of them. I have no notes, no diary record of our exchanges, but then diary theorist Philippe Lejeune argues, 'diary is the enemy of memory' because it doesn't allow the editing of memory, it doesn't allow the past to change.

It seems there is a constant war between the fixed nature of reality and the fluidity of memory. It's not just the differently observed and recorded 'realities' of each person, their opposing versions – that's the least of it – it's the differently perceived and recorded realities within each one of us. And then the regular, unnoticed changes each time a memory is taken out into the light, the slight or major changes made by the Memory Director who has a story in mind.

These are the questions Gina might have asked: What was Dina's birth family like? Did they visit her when she had the brain haemorrhage? How did Kit and Dina meet? How old were they? How old was Dina when Theo was born? Did she have a career before then? How did Kit explain to two-year-old Theo what had happened to his mother?

'Tell me,' said Gina, 'what about "Patti" – do you think she could have feelings for Kit?' She had her notebook open, but her eyes were on me. Ready to listen.

It was a work question, not a nosy one. 'Patti' was a character, so were 'Kit and Dina', Kris and Dolly in reality. It was disconcerting at first to discuss myself in the third person, but it was not too difficult to adjust because I've always known the *I* in writing wasn't the same *I* as the one sitting on the lounge or doing the washing. My feelings can still be hurt if someone criticises the *I* in a book, but I feel detached from her, the controlling *I* on the page.

As an actor, Gina knew this better than anyone. Later when I saw her perform on stage, I saw her embodying a character; her tongue and mouth moved, her eyes flashed, her cheeks flushed, her arms extended, her body convulsed, but it was not her. It was an intimate exposure of her body, but for the audience gazing at her face and torso and limbs she had disappeared and only a character existed. She performed a miraculous communion between an imaginary being and her own body.

But now she was the writer of the script and she could make 'Patti' and all of the other characters do as she wished.

Were we sitting in Chez Camille, just around the corner from the rue des Trois Frères, when she asked the question? It was a bar Anthony frequented during our first six-month sojourn in Paris. We only had a tiny studio then, so he needed to go out to work – we can't work in the same room, and he also wanted to smoke – so he worked and smoked in Chez Camille and felt at home. When our two sons arrived from their own travels for Christmas we took them there and played Scrabble in English, although someone had taken most of the 'e's from the box so it quickly became impossible.

Chez Camille was small and dim and local, ordinary looking, not the sort of place that attracted tourists. It could well have been here that Gina asked about 'Patti'. I was unsure the first time if she was asking about me, sitting there in front of her, or 'Patti', so I started with me, not yet used to the third person.

'I didn't, if that's what you mean. Not in the way you mean. Perhaps I could have if Anthony wasn't in the picture. Probably not, though. I don't think we fancied each other.'

I was trying to be honest. I am trying to be honest. Honesty takes a lot of effort for me. I'm not a natural. My first inclination is to be secretive. I suspect that for me, writing is about attempting to see the truth and then, against my nature, being honest about it. There is no point in saying truth is relative when, for the Storyteller, there is always an immutable truth if one can find it.

'There was a moment once. Nothing at all happened. But something did. We were working on a collection of stories that I was putting together for writing students at university. We were sitting at his computer; Dolly was behind us in the bed. It was before everyone knew how to format documents – well, I didn't know how – and Kris was showing me how to arrange the pages and headings. We were just working together, but I felt a sudden flow of warmth between us. It was only for a moment and that was it. It wasn't just that I was acutely aware of Dolly being there, it was as much that I didn't want anything else. It was a moment of human communion, that's all.'

I went on to tell her how the same thing happened with a French physiotherapist one day when we were chatting during a massage. It was the same silent knowledge that we had, for a brief unspoken moment, connected deeply. There was something frightening, exposing, in it, a vulnerability. I feel the urge to repeat now that nothing happened – but human communion is not nothing; I won't make it smaller by protesting my innocence.

'I've written about it already,' I said. It was as if to say it was all over and done with.

Gina looked intrigued, her dark brown eyes intent. 'I love those moments. But what I meant was, in my script, would you mind if Patti and Kit developed a relationship? I think it would make things more dramatically interesting.'

I laughed nervously. I had already told Gina that she could do whatever she liked in the script. It was hers after all. She was not reproducing my book; she was making her own work.

'I shouldn't really have any say in what you do. But I guess it could be a bit awkward. People tend to believe whatever is "based on real life".'

'I won't if you would rather I didn't.'

'I think it's okay. Yes, go ahead if you want to.'

Gina smiled. 'That's okay,' she said. 'I really don't have to. I might try it to see how it goes, but I don't have to. There's plenty of material already.'

We drank our kir and ate the peanuts the barman brought us now that it had reached that time of day between work and dinner that is so significant in France. More people came into the bar, looked at everyone, sat down, ordered drinks. It was getting noisier. Gina closed her notebook but kept talking intently, neither of us leaving our work behind now that the working day was over because everything we thought, felt, heard, saw, was our work. Everything mattered, everything still matters; the detail of ordinary life, the yellow door of Chez Camille, the occasional smell of marijuana, the fact that Anthony was coming to meet with us soon. The process of trying to put the ordinary details on the page also matters, the exact shade of yellow of the door – it was a sunny, buttery yellow, the same shade as my swimming costume when I was eight years old – and the shadow on faces in the bar, and the steady animated gaze of a friend who is listening. All of it stored in the light and shade of memory labyrinths. Mostly shade.

I've been trying to recall the places I met with Gina that first summer, but she came to Paris several years in a row during the times I returned to give writing classes, so it's difficult to know when and where with any precision. Researchers have shown that memories close to one another in time, a few hours apart, can overlap. For example, a tricky question from a friend that happens at three o'clock followed by a drink in a different café at five o'clock, could blend into one conversation, one location. But it seems evident – with scrappy anecdotal evidence at least – that events happening a year or more apart, but in the same unusual location, can also blend. I have a sequence of cafés in my head, some with distinct scenes in them – the Scrabble playing at Chez Camille, a homeless woman with a *South Park* backpack in a beautifully tiled art deco bar, which I possibly only remember because of the photograph Anthony took of her – but they are mostly not time linked.

Using fMRI, researchers have shown that when a single aspect of memory is activated, anything else linked to it will activate at exactly the same time via the hippocampus. This activation of a wave of memory is known as a pattern completion process. Apparently, remembering a single aspect can be traced to a single neurone, a fact I find astonishing. How extraordinary that there is one tiny nerve cell, amongst millions, containing the original sensory record from which all else springs. One nerve cell, one image, that can unlock everything else. All of which links in memory to a madeleine cake dipped in lime-flower tea by Marcel Proust early last century:

> ... so in that moment all the flowers in our garden and in M. Swann's park, and the water-lilies on the Vivonne and the good folk of the village and their little dwellings and the parish church and the whole of Combray and of its surroundings, taking their proper shapes and growing solid, sprang into being, town and gardens alike, from my cup of tea.

How well Proust understood the processes of memory a century before fMRI showed its beautiful electrochemistry; how its dancing miniature world encodes the large and obvious world around it.

I do remember a distinct scene from that summer, again influenced by a photograph. It was taken in another friend's apartment in the rue Labat – Vicky was away at her farmhouse in the Lot-et-Garonne and had let Anthony and me stay for a week or so in her place before we returned to Australia.

In the photograph I'm sitting between Gina and Trish – Trish was an Australian singer living in France whom I'd met at an exhibition at the Australian Embassy several months earlier. I hadn't been to an Embassy event in my life before and neither had Trish, but we both later admitted to going in the hope of making new friends. Harriet, the cultural attaché, had introduced us, saying: 'Trish is a singer, Patti has written a book about learning to sing.'

Now the three of us were in Vicky's apartment sitting around her Afghani coffee table – an exact copy of which I bought in Sydney several years later, not realising it was the same until I brought it home where the sensation of its pleasing familiarity coalesced into a memory of sitting at an identical table in her apartment. 'I think I just bought your table,' I emailed her afterwards, slightly embarrassed.

I remember it being unusually hot that summer, a memory triggered by the Balinese sarong I am wearing in the photo, tied halter-neck style. Gina is dressed in a strappy pink top and has her hair tied up, and Trish, smiling widely, is beautiful and sexy as always. The three of us have champagne glasses in our hands, making a toast. To what? Perhaps it was to the first draft of the novel I was working on at the time that never saw the light of day; perhaps to Gina's play script, which was read aloud in public, but never performed. It could have been simply we were toasting being together in Paris that summer.

~

I have had friendships that have lasted longer than the one with Gina, and some that have been as deep. Is a friendship that ends necessarily more significant than the ones that endure? Break-ups have more drama, like the sudden upheavals of earthquakes and volcanoes, but perhaps the slow changes of lasting friendships – the elegant carving of wind and water – alter us more deeply. It makes me wonder what matters about my connections to others. Some friends have disappeared, but others I have known for a lifetime. They have lived nearby, or in other countries, or have died. They have seen me, each one a different version, and I have seen them. They have been more than a cast of characters populating my life; they have told me who I am. What have I seen in them, and, by reflection, what have they seen in me? They have moulded me, polished me, chipped at me, reflected me, changed me.

And then, what of the friends that I've cast aside? The first was a long time ago when I was a teenager, which is not an excuse, nor a defence. But I do want to see what I did and why. The one who casts aside at least knows that much.

At the beginning of my second year at high school on a hot Australian day at the end of January, a new girl arrived. Mary was from Carinda, a town smaller and further west and even less sophisticated than Wellington. I was still anxiously free-floating; she was the new girl, another outsider; the pieces fell together.

She had blonde hair, blue eyes and an engaging smile in a wide-boned face, pretty in a raw way, and unsophisticated in the same way I was. She was a bush girl, open and outgoing and energetic and able to stick up for herself – in fact, very like the girl I had been at Suntop school before I lost, or had to hide, her. Even if we weren't both in need of a friend, we would have recognised each other.

To my relief, when I was asked on a sleepover, I discovered Mary lived in a house like mine. Drawers were missing from cupboards, broken hinges on wardrobes weren't fixed, the kitchen bench was crowded with open jars and tins and food scraps. I could safely ask her to my house.

Shortly after the first visit, one of the other girls sidled up and asked what Mary's house was like.

'It's fine,' I said. I wasn't going to offer any ammunition, but I had to give something. 'They haven't been there long, so there's still things to organise. They're just getting new wardrobes.'

Mary did come to stay at our farm and didn't seem to notice there was no running water in the bathroom and wasn't bothered by the broken fibro and tin toilet in the backyard. She fitted in as if she were made for my family, especially connecting to my mother. They developed a warm fondness for each other and even after I had left home and gone to Sydney and then to New Zealand, leaving her behind, she still visited my mother.

Mary was closely examined by everyone in the schoolyard, even the powerful girls, as possible friendship material – she was, after all, pretty – but was found wanting in a number of ways. The first problem was that she arrived at the school with chlorine-greened hair. The summer before leaving Carinda, the overly strong chlorine in the local swimming pool had dyed her Scandinavian blonde hair lemon-green.

The second problem was that she was one of those girls who, when they have their periods, have a fishy smell. I noticed it but didn't know at first that it was caused by her periods. It was usually a faint smell but was sometimes strong enough to make me embarrassed for her once I realised what it was. One of Julie-Anne's group advised me, *kindly*, that I should let her know. I could tell that I was being warned off Mary in the same way I had been warned off Cathy the year before, but this time I stood firm. I didn't want to be left without a friend again.

I have a faint memory of discussing period smell with Mary, wondering if we should use tampons instead. I am reasonably certain about this as I recall asking my mother if I could use tampons, to which, looking horrified, she replied, 'But you have to put them *inside* you!' That was the end of tampons until I went to boarding school in Year Eleven, where everyone was using them.

Mary's body was altogether more physically obvious than mine. Her breasts were well-developed, she sweated a lot and often had damp rings under her arms, she played basketball fiercely, she moved in an unselfconscious way – and boys liked her.

The third problem, an insurmountable one, which took several months to emerge, was Mary's mother. Not only did Mrs Dunn wear old-fashioned girlish dresses and a long red ponytail instead of the skirts and blouses and short-cropped hair everyone else's mother did, she also drank at pubs and, even worse and irredeemable, she became the town 'bike'.

'Everyone rides Ponytail Dunn,' one of the other girls explained when I looked blank.

Mary knew – someone had seen fit to tell her – and anyway, she had already seen her mother coming home drunk in her blowsy dresses night after night. Her worn father ran a small stock and station agency, which failed, and he gave Mary and her brothers dinner out of tins. He was kind and tired as his life went off the rails. Mary stuck up for him. 'Dad doesn't know what to do. Mum is just a bloody drunk. I hate her.'

I'd never heard anyone talk like that before. Not about their mother. 'Maybe there's something wrong. Maybe she's drowning her sorrows.' I'd heard that expression but had no idea what a grown woman's sorrows could be.

We talked endlessly – I knew how to talk now – and I watched and listened with a confused mix of love and hunger. It was my first contact with real emotional pain, and I soon found the role of confidante suited. I didn't want Mary's life, I was consciously glad it wasn't happening to me, but I wanted all the details of it. I listened, sympathised, offered explanations.

Sometimes, when we were down the street at lunchtime we bumped into Mary's mother in one of her out-of-date 50s dresses and her ponytail and beery breath. She had a plain reddish face and a thick body, she was not pretty like her daughter, and I wondered in my ignorance why men went after her. She wasn't always drunk but there was always an edge to her voice, as if she knew exactly how humiliated and furious Mary was and wasn't going to let her get away lightly.

One day she stopped to talk to us in the street. I fought the urge to keep walking. I didn't want to be seen talking to Ponytail. There was a kind of harsh, amused scorn in her eyes as she looked at me.

'What are you doin' down the street?' Her voice was slurry but weirdly bright and harsh.

'Nothing. Just walking with Pat – she has to get some shopping for her mother.' Mary's face was red and she couldn't look at her mother. She stared down at her school shoes.

'Nice to do some shoppin',' Mrs Dunn said, looking at me.

'Yes,' I said, far too brightly. 'Just some mince for dinner.'

'Righto, I'll bloody see you later on since you can't lift your bloody head,' she said to Mary's bent head.

We kept walking. I didn't say anything.

'Mum didn't used to be like this,' Mary said. 'In Carinda she was fine. It only started happening after we came here.'

I was curious about what had happened, what made things change enough for her mother not to care what other people thought of her. I have a very faint, nagging memory fragment of the death of a baby in Carinda, but that might have been a link from another neural pathway. A loss as enormous as that ought to have burned into my memory forever, but it would not have seemed as life-destroying to me as a fifteen year old as it does now. I was undeveloped emotionally, or at least inexperienced, and listening to Mary's life was my nourishment.

We talked all the time about her family, about boys – she liked my cousin, Neil – and about the world and what we wanted to do in it. We shared a strong sense of the inequalities between people and we both wanted to 'do good' – she wanted to be a nurse like my mother had been and I wanted to be a writer, although I worried that writing might not do enough, or any, good.

Soon after we had become a recognised twosome, Sue was dropped from her group and asked if she could join ours. Even though Mary didn't have the old association with her that I'd had, she generously said yes. She was kind and open-hearted, despite her damaged and damaging mother, and ought to have been treasured, but by the time I'd won a scholarship and left for boarding school in Year Eleven, I had decided to leave her behind.

In my twenties and a few times since, I had a dream in which I had done something seriously wrong, perhaps even committed a murder. I wasn't sure about the crime because the dream always started when I was hiding the evidence and continued while I was on the run. The dream sequence happened several times, each time over a few months, and pervaded my waking life as well. In the dreams there were a range of settings; I was fleeing over hills, or sometimes hurrying along streets or driving in a car, but the feeling was always the fear of being found out. I was definitely the bad guy.

I started to worry that I might have done something very wrong, not just banal wrong – such as leaving a good and kind friend behind because I had no further need of her – but something criminal that I had repressed. There was a pervasive feeling of guilt, but no memory of anything at all.

There's ongoing scientific debate about whether repressed memory or dissociative amnesia actually exists, that is, apart from normal forgetting and deliberately not remembering. Are retrieved memories real? It is apparently impossible to tell the difference between a pseudo-memory and a real one in electrochemical terms, which makes me shrug helplessly. Did something happen or not?

I began checking through various periods of my life to see if there were any incidents or gaps that could have been the lead-up or aftermath of evil-doing. I wondered if it could have been the fact that I decided to have an abortion once. Most people I know would not consider this a wrongdoing, but despite my feminism, part of me thinks and feels that it is; the part that understands that life, even nascent life, a bud, is an infinite mystery and ought not be destroyed. As it happened, I didn't have the abortion, I had a miscarriage, so the life left of its own accord.

The point is, I came up with no traces, no missing time that could justify the dreams. Perhaps there was simply an accumulation of smaller secret sins that reached a tipping point, an accumulation of guilt. But even that seems unlikely because, being brought up to examine my conscience at the end of each day, nothing is left secret. All my everyday failings are regularly hauled out and examined in annoying detail.

When I think about why I left Mary behind, the reasons blur. I want to say it's because it was too long ago, but the truth is that I have let it become blurred because I haven't wanted to look at it.

I told myself I had outgrown her. Without being aware of it, I was reconstructing myself as someone who could inhabit the world I found in books, a world far away from our country town. I had started to find her too obvious, too naive, which reminded me of the self I was trying to leave behind. It wasn't that my leaving for boarding school meant we grew apart, I already knew I wanted to leave our friendship. Boarding school was the opportunity to drop her without having to say or do anything. A way out.

~

In *The Epic of Gilgamesh* dreams are not a guilty mishmash of the fantastic and the obvious as in my dreams, but instead foretell the future. Dreams are the channels used by the gods to communicate with Gilgamesh and Enkidu.

The young men tell their dreams to each other as friends do now, or at least women do, and offer each other interpretations. The one who dreams mostly does not understand it, or misinterprets it, and needs the other to correct it.

One night the two of them slept on a mountain on their way to destroy the monster Humbaba, who was so sensitive to his kingdom he could hear a heifer stirring on the other side of the Cedar Forest. That night, Gilgamesh dreamed of a bull in the wilderness, which bellowed and beat up the dust until the sky was dark. Gilgamesh's arm was seized and his tongue was bitten. He thought the dream foretold his defeat at the hands of Humbaba, but Enkidu said the bull represented the god, Shamash, who, in the moment of peril, would take Gilgamesh's hand and help him win. He reassured and encouraged Gilgamesh, even in the face of fairly convincing dream imagery of doom.

Then, that same night on the mountain, Gilgamesh told of another dream where the two of them were small, 'like the smallest of swamp flies' and the mountain fell down and there came an intolerable light blazing out. In the light was a being whose grace and beauty were greater than the beauty of the world.

On hearing this, Enkidu, the child of the plains, said, 'Let us go down from the mountain and talk this thing over together.' I love his calm good sense – first, let's get off the mountain – and that he knows he needs to think about this from the ground of himself, back on the plains.

Sometimes Enkidu is afraid, sensibly afraid, his fear based not on dreams, although he has them too, but on experience.

'You do not know this monster and that is the reason you are not afraid. I who know him, I am terrified.'

Gilgamesh, filled with a sense of purpose, the desire to make an eternal name for himself, urges Enkidu on; 'He who leaves the fight unfinished is not at peace.'

I like the way strength and frailty, courage and fear, wisdom and impetuousness, is exchanged between them. And the way they discuss everything – their dreams, their fears, their feelings. When I read their story, it is clear the author understood the shifting energy of friendship, how it never remains static.

~

There was an air of excitement every time Gina and I met in Paris. I want to use the word thrilling, which might sound excessive, but it's the word I think of when I recall us together, the two of us, and then the three of us as Anthony started to join our rendezvous.

We talked about acting and writing, about the processes of creativity; how an unseen image, a connection, comes up out of the dark and finds its place so exactly it's as if it had always been there; how random pieces float together and form a shape that had been waiting to be made; how you sit down in the morning with nothing in your head, but by lunchtime, a room, a chair, a table exists, a painting hangs on a wall, a character has started to speak, someone is breathing.

'How do you write a play when one of the central characters is a small child?' I asked.

'I could use a puppet. Or voice over. Or shadow play,' Gina said.

We asked precise questions and found precise answers. We smiled with fire in our eyes. At times, there was such intensity that I felt afraid.

I remember one conversation, perhaps in the Jardin des Tuileries, as I have a note in an old diary about meeting there. I don't recall the words of the conversation, but I clearly see Gina's eyes and the pale oval of her face. There are no surroundings in the memory, only eyes in a face, but I can colour in the Tuileries from hundreds of other visits; white dust on my shoes, clipped rows of geometric chestnut trees, people sitting on green metal chairs around the ponds. It was just the two of us; Anthony was away in Amsterdam for work. We sat next to each other, our heads turned towards each other, deep in conversation. Her gaze was so intense and she spoke with such fiery passion and I listened with such absorption – what was she saying? – that I suddenly felt a light-filled self had been ignited inside me, the ordinary woman burned away. It created a falling sensation, a vertigo. I was falling into her, a kind of dissolution of self. It wasn't physical, or sexual, but it still frightened me. I felt myself draw back, a perhaps imperceptible drawing back from the edge of no return.

Why was I afraid? Does part of me fear being annihilated, being eaten alive. Why? Doesn't the whole universe long for oneness? Spiritual teachings say the individual soul despairs in duality, that it longs to merge with the Godhead in transcendental bliss; nature too, exists as Gaia, one unified ecosystem, each plant and creature needing other plants, microbes, soil, air. And sexual union is essentially the merging of two bodies, forgetting individual self in dissolving pleasure; psychologically too, each newborn baby drowns in her mother's eyes, having no sense, yet, of a separate self. Even at the level of physics, subatomic particles cling together, violently resisting attempts to split them apart.

If an element loses or gains one electron it becomes something else; but if I dissolve into another, I no longer exist. When Montaigne says, 'In the friendship I am talking about, souls are mingled and confounded in so universal a blending that it effaces the seam which joins them together,' part of me cries out vehemently, No!

No, I cannot lose my carefully made self in someone else. And yet, there is still the longing to be received completely.

One night in the Marais, the old quarter of the city, Anthony, Gina and I went to a Cole Porter tribute concert in one of the grand hotels. I had never been interested in Cole Porter, but Gina wanted to go and we had started doing most things together, so we all went. It was a hot evening in early August and the concert was held outdoors in a courtyard. I remember the feeling of warm air on bare skin in the dark and, to my surprise, enjoying the songs. 'You do Something To Me', 'Anything Goes', 'I Get a Kick Out of You' – I realised I knew them all. I had thought of Cole Porter as old-fashioned, of my parents' time, not the sort of thing a child of the 60s would listen to. But Gina loved Porter precisely because he was of her father's time.

She 'adored her father', one of those phrases I envy because it says something so appealing that I haven't experienced. I was fond of my father, a gentle, religious man, but when he died I was sad, not grief-stricken the way I was when my mother died. I was sad that he had been afraid most of his life despite believing in the safety of God; I was sad for my mother losing the love of her life, but I had no special relationship with him, he did not dote on me. There were eight of us, how could he?

Gina was the opposite. Her father had died when she was in her twenties, he had been central, her mother more problematic. Her father did dote on her and that often creates a problem for mothers. She shared her father's love of music; she told me she danced with him at family parties – I couldn't even imagine dancing with my father, neither of us could dance – she cared for him as he was dying, sitting with him as often as she could.

I told her that even though my mother was central in my life, she had said to me once that my younger sister was the prettiest of the three of us, and that my older sister was the best writer.

'Mothers!' Gina said, sighing.

These were the family stories we started to talk about that night after the show, creating a shift of energy away from the high frequency of creativity. It was a change of register in our friendship, or more exactly, it gave another dimension to it. The exhilarating life of art was still there, but it had the solid flesh-and-blood foundation of family.

Gina told me her father was of Syrian and Italian background, a mix originating in the goldrush days in southern New South Wales, and he had been a successful businessman, but at some point had lost money. It was a history with little overlap of mine – my family was Anglo–Irish with a dash of German, and unverified Asian and Wiradjuri ancestors had been recently included – except my grandmother had grown up on the goldfields near Bathurst. We shared a Catholic upbringing, the same incense and prayers, sins and hymns floating in childhood synapses. Neither of us believed anymore, but like Mary, like possibly every friend I've ever had, Gina wanted to do good in the world, to make the world more just. It's one of those legacies of a certain kind of upbringing that you cannot refuse, even if like me, you have little talent for it.

~

As I recall my friendships, it feels like a kaleidoscope, memories falling and shifting to make new patterns as I hold it up to the light. The story of Gina has exotic, brightly coloured fragments, scarlet, gold and blue, which makes it seem that she has been the most important of my friends. And certainly she has mattered a great deal. There was, I thought, a rare communion of thought and feeling between us, but I have had that communion with other friends at different times. I know I'm obsessively circling back over the friendship with her, twisting and re-twisting the kaleidoscope, but that's because it ended. A flow of warmth and connection was suddenly withheld, and I don't know why. I don't remember any unforgivable acts, any violent arguments, although there was one rift about halfway through our fifteen-year friendship, a ragged, stretching split that opened up between us. Perhaps that serrated the edges of the kaleidoscope pieces or created a flaw in the glass. I have to continue to let them fall to see where the flaw was.

In the beginning, I was trying to understand what had happened to the broken friendship. I was hurt and bewildered, and bewilderment is a strong engine. But since I've begun writing the hurt has faded. Now there is a pure desire to try to recreate what was, to see how we know anyone and how anyone knows us, how others live in our minds at the cellular level of memory, to see how all the knowledge we have of each other and of existence, all we have ever had, is a selective electrochemical story in our brains about the things we have seen, smelled, touched, tasted, heard. Right back to the first story ever written.

Four

'I don't know what I'm doing here,' I said. I meant existentially, as well as back in Sydney.

'Neither do I,' said Gina

We were walking along Darlinghurst Road in front of St Vincent's Hospital, our first meeting in Sydney after the Paris sojourn. It was a flat, grey day and we were hunched against a light drizzle, both of us having forgotten umbrellas. We were walking towards Kings Cross, which suggests we were coming back from seeing a film at Verona cinema, but I recall with snapshot clarity only the two of us walking, the weather, our mood, and fragments of the conversation.

I felt disconnected being back in Sydney. I hadn't lived there for more than twenty-five years, not since I was a university student. The intervening years of child-raising and rich community had been spent in the Blue Mountains, but now that our sons had grown and I'd had my eighteen months away, I didn't know what to do. I hadn't wanted to go back to the old life in the Mountains, the all-surrounding gum trees, the quiet days.

Anthony and I had been decisive when we arrived back in Australia. We sold our house with a creek at the bottom of its yard and bought a small apartment in Kings Cross. It was lively and distracting here in the middle of the city, but I was restless, couldn't see the point of being here, didn't know what to do with myself.

I looked up at the rainy street, the grey footpath and wet buildings, and suddenly saw our two hunched selves from the outside; how small and self-indulgent we were.

'The two women trudged miserably along the dull street in the rain, missing their old life in the city of light,' I said in a solemn voice.

Gina burst out laughing.

'They knew that life was over, their brilliant youth, but they couldn't give it up,' I continued.

'They were lost,' said Gina, picking up the story. 'But they would always have the city of light, nestling in their hearts forever.'

'Would they ever return?' I said. 'The uncaring world didn't answer as it slipped by them in the gloom.'

We continued laughing at ourselves, elaborating the story until we parted at the corner near the hospital. She headed down Liverpool Street to her recently rented bedsitter and I went onwards to our apartment in Victoria Street. At that time, we lived only a fifteen-minute walk away from each other.

A couple of weeks later, we bumped into each other at the traffic lights at the top of William Street. We had already arranged to meet later at Bar Coluzzi on the other side of the street, but we were both presently out and about on other tasks. Gina was carrying a shopping bag.

'What did you buy?' I asked

'I found a few tops at this place in town. I've never been there before but it looked interesting and I needed some summer clothes.'

'Show me,' I said.

Gina pulled out three pastel-coloured tops, a pair of bone cotton trousers and, I think, a straight short skirt. Everything was fresh and unfussy.

I remember thinking, 'Oh, the clothes are ordinary. I wouldn't have bought any of those things.' Gina must have read my thoughts because she said, 'They're just a couple of things to wear around the place,' and quickly put them back in her bag. When the lights changed, we parted ways, reminding each other about meeting at Bar Coluzzi later.

At first I couldn't see why I remembered this insignificant meeting when I've forgotten so many others, but now I wonder if it was because I first registered something different about us. It was only a choice of clothes, but it revealed that I drew attention to myself and Gina preferred camouflage. A friend from university days, Michael, used 'camouflage' to describe his own ordinary jeans and shirts, and ever since I've noted who likes to attract attention and who prefers to remain unnoticed. 'I can go anywhere and no-one will know what I think,' said Michael. 'I will see and hear everything in my camouflage, and no-one will suspect.'

Gina used clothes to signal only when she was in character on stage or in front of a camera. Or for an audition. One day we were exchanging origin stories from childhood, the stories that our selective memory vaults had chosen and polished to indicate that we would, one day, become a writer, an actor. We were offering evidence of the longevity, even the preordained nature of the paths we had chosen.

Gina's story was about dressing for an audition when she was eleven or twelve. She had seen an audition notice in the newspaper – it was in the city – and she set off on her own on the train from the southern suburbs where she lived.

I expressed astonishment at her going into the city alone at that age, but she was impatient with my reaction. That was not the point of her story. It was about how she took care to dress for the part. She chose a particular cardigan with, I think, glass buttons. They might not have been glass, but there was something significant about the buttons, about the way she did them up, or left them undone, her child-mind fully aware that she was presenting herself in a role. Perhaps she added a brooch. The right shoes. She thought about being another character, about how they would think, how they would dress themselves, the minutiae of daily life that show what a person is like. Since childhood, she had been dedicated to the details of her craft.

My story was about the poem I had written when I was eight or nine, inspired by the acres of dewdrops on the young wheat in the paddock I walked through to get to school. 'They sparkled, like a distant star / And the sight stretched for miles afar.' It was a story I had told before, a memory of writing what I thought was a poem, evidence of a childhood impulse to communicate what I saw.

The scene with the clothes at the traffic lights was a small moment, seemingly irrelevant, but the fact that I remember it, makes it matter. When neuroscientists talk about recalling episodic or autobiographical memory, they use the concept of salience. It's the ordinary idea that we remember an aspect of an experience because it matters to us, and someone else involved in the same experience forgets it, or remembers it differently, because the experience was not salient to them. Gina remembers the exact details of the cardigan, I don't. The concept of salience will matter considerably as the story about my friendship with her unfolds. I will remember the long wooden table where we had a conversation one evening, she will remember the dismissive comment I made.

The first time I saw Gina perform she played a Syrian Muslim, a modern well-educated woman with a degree in medicine. She was a woman of faith, but she had decided not to wear the hijab because, for her, it was a symbol of control and limitation, the life she had escaped to come to Australia. The story revolved around her daughter deciding to go back to Syria as an act of commitment to her faith and cultural heritage.

I was nervous before the play. We had talked many times about the creative process; the mystery of how something comes from nothing, about how an actor physically breathes life, god-like, into a being who had only been made of words. And we talked about this particular play, about playing someone from a different religious culture, about Gina's Middle-Eastern inheritance, about what she would wear, how her hair would be done – dyed black. I loved these conversations. I could talk about process endlessly, and listen endlessly; I wanted to know how actors do it, how musicians do it, how painters do it.

But I had not seen her perform yet. What if I could only see her on the stage and not the character? What if all I could see was Gina acting?

I already had friends who were actors, but I had seen them on the stage before I met them, so I was not influenced by seeing them in my kitchen as Connie, as Michele. When I first met Michele off the stage, especially, there was the opposite effect. I had already seen her in many productions – she was a brilliant Chekhovian actor – so at first she had an aura, not so much of a particular character, but of having a performing body, a kind of glowing surface that prevented me from seeing her. This was, of course (as is everything we think we know about others) entirely in my own mind, not anything she was doing. Proust talks about how his friend, Robert Saint-Loup first sees his mistress on the stage and thereby falls for the illusion of her, the glossy facade, rather than the actual woman. Perhaps it's only a heightening of the way we see others, whether on a real stage or not, as strangers performing their lives outside of us when we first meet them.

Anthony and I sat a few rows up from the stage at The Wharf, both of us slightly tense. There was no need to worry. Within a couple of minutes – it always takes a couple of minutes – Gina was replaced by a Syrian woman, Aisha. There was the same fierce dark eyes, the creamy face, her glorious mane of now black hair, but Gina had withdrawn into her centre, animating her character, but unseen.

Her manner was held back, simple, not overdone. I want to use the word natural, but I understand what skill, what work it takes to appear natural. The story of the warm and tender relationship between mother and daughter unfolded, becoming more tense as the reasons for the mother's flight from Syria were revealed in a frightening scene. When she was a young woman, her best friend had fallen in love with a Christian and was 'honour' killed by her father and brother.

Aisha had arrived just after it happened. The brother had grabbed her arms, hauled her away from the gruesome scene. It was all in her memory, there was no actual blood, but the audience relived it with her. It was intense, highly coloured, I could hear her gasping breaths. I felt my heart thumping.

Afterwards, we waited for Gina in the foyer. When she came out, she looked fresh, as if cleansed of something. I had expected her to be exhausted after all she had been through. I hugged her excitedly and so did Anthony.

'You were brilliant!' I cried.

It seemed Gina didn't have to stretch or strain as the Muslim woman. She came to the role as if finding herself, her equal, 'stormy heart for stormy heart' amongst the plain-coloured Australian crowd. I thought the passionate and intellectual role suited her perfectly, as if it were made for her. But the next production I saw her in she played a dry, detached detective in a suit, as different from the Syrian woman as imaginable, and again, Gina disappeared. She strode about the stage or stood with authority, her daily self so subsumed into the detective I would not have recognised her if she had passed me on the street. The rhythm of her words, the erect way she held her body, the angle of her head, her breathing, was not her own but the detective's. It made me aware that she must know others more intimately than the rest of us, from right inside her muscles and organs and sweat and tears. She had a secret entry into the body and could look out through others' eyes, not even a gleam of herself showing through.

I can only watch from the outside. Even those I have called my friends, I have only watched. How do I know my friends? What do I see? What memory engrams are waiting to be activated? I've been thinking and dreaming about the friends

I've had over the years, especially the friends I had when I was young, and most especially Jane whom I met at school and who changed my life.

~

Although it was decades ago, I was sixteen at the time, I can remember the first time I saw Jane; what she looked like, what she wore. It was the day we all arrived at Perthville, a small convent boarding school near Bathurst several hours west of Sydney. It was solid but not comfortable with large cold dormitories and bathrooms – the religious order which ran it had been founded to educate the children of the poor. I was the first person in my family to go to boarding school – the scholarship paid for it – and I was nervous and excited, absurdly primed by Enid Blyton's *In the Fifth at Malory Towers*, for midnight feasts and jolly adventures, but I was trying for grown-up nonchalance. It was the beginning of my life away from the farm.

I saw a girl about my age walk across the gravel towards the steps of the boarding house. She had light brown curly hair and light brown skin and wore a brown leopard-print dress that both fitted and floated around her slim body. She carried a leather satchel. So elegant! I had never seen anyone like her before. A pang of fear. Did everyone here look like that?

The dress makes Jane sound glamorous, but that's not what she was. I try *bohemian* in my mind, but that's not it either. Then I realise that that day and always, she looked so exceptionally herself that it's inaccurate to describe her as pretty, or elegant, or glamorous, or any other complimentary term. She looked always and only like herself. What did I see when I looked at her then? She had a smooth oval face, unusual almond-shaped eyes, perfectly unmarked skin, soft brown curls. But there was something else distinctive, ungraspable about her that I, and probably, everyone, felt immediately. I didn't know it in that first moment, but she was the person I was hoping to meet.

I said hello when I saw her in the dormitory upstairs, nervous of her striking appearance, but making an effort to overcome my shyness. We unpacked our things and put them in our lockers and narrow wardrobes along the wall. She had a guitar – two of my brothers had guitars but I'd never met a girl who played guitar before – which had to be left downstairs in the Year Eleven study, so I went down with her. When we came back up, two girls who had been friends from before asked to swap beds so they could have their beds next to each other. Jane said she would have the bed next to me and I thought with surprise, she likes me. On very little evidence, I felt chosen.

That evening we were placed at the same table in the dining room, and we talked again. At first, the usual things, where we came from, our families. She had grown up on a property, Wongalea, outside of Coonamble on the western plains, with her older sister, Annabel, and brother, Jamie – whom I later had a crush on – and younger sister, Meghan. I noticed the posh names, well aware of country town class distinctions, and understood her family must be graziers, not scratching-a-living 'cockies' like mine. I imagined her house was a homestead, large and made of stone. As it turned out, her father had not been able to make a living on the property and although they still owned it, they had moved into town where he ran the local airport.

I told her about my five brothers and two sisters, but what I remember distinctly, what was salient, was Jane's reaction to one of my memories. It was about lying on the lawn in the dark all summer long with my brothers and sisters, talking about the stars and satellites and murmuring about our lives. She was thrilled by this story.

'Your family is amazing!' she exclaimed.

I felt nonplussed. We only did it because it was so horribly hot in the dingy house that we couldn't sleep, and because we had no television to keep us inside. We dragged blankets outside and put them on the scratchy dry lawn and marshmallow grass and lay on them and looked up at the sky. We pointed out constellations and shooting stars, or just lay quietly looking up. We also said the rosary, a long repetitive group prayer, but I didn't mention that.

Then, in a moment of insight, I suddenly saw my brothers and sisters lying in the dark looking at stars as poetic, as Jane did, and I realised this was the kind of thing she noticed and valued. She was just like Emily in the LM Montgomery books I used to read, sensitive to beauty, creative, thoughtful. Our currency of friendship would be what was poetic, beautiful, remarkable. These things would become what I valued most, what I looked for, what I pointed out and talked about. Jane changed the direction of my life, or at the very least, shifted the angle of trajectory to the one that it has taken ever since.

We became a twosome very quickly. We spent our days at school in Bathurst together, took most of the same classes, and back at Perthville at the convent, sat next to each other in the study to do our homework. We walked next to each other when we were allowed to go on walks outside the school, at night we whispered quietly after lights-out. We were in the same English class and read Yeats, TS Eliot, GM Hopkins aloud and discussed *Hamlet*, *The Tree of Man*, *Tess of the d'Urbervilles*. Jane especially loved poetry and writing songs. She liked fantastical books and introduced me to Ursula Le Guin's *Earthsea* trilogy and JRR Tolkien, which I read, but secretly thought were for children. With Jane's encouragement – and for her admiration – I embroidered a stanza of Yeats' *The Stolen Child* on a red velvet skirt I'd found in a second-hand shop:

Come away, O human child!
To the waters and the wild
With a faery, hand in hand,
For the world's more full of weeping than you can understand.

It took weeks to embroider and gave me some small status as word went around that I was sewing a whole verse on a skirt. Jane sat with me playing her guitar and singing as I stitched, both of us feeling arty and industrious.

I recall other girls sidling up to me. 'What is Jane like? Isn't she a snob?' Word had got around that Jane had been at Rose Bay Convent, an expensive boarding school in Sydney, before coming to Perthville. And then there was the way she dressed. 'She thinks she's better than the rest of us.'

'No, not at all.' I was used to defending my friends by now and I could see why the others judged her, her leopard-print dress and her silky clothes. 'She's not like you think. She's nice.'

The nuns, too, kept an eye on Jane. I'm not sure what they knew, maybe there was a report from the nuns at Rose Bay where Jane told me she had suffered from anorexia and ended up in hospital, but it seemed more that she was suspect because of her guitar, because she wrote songs, because she wasn't one of the gang. I could see them watching her, and by association, me.

We found quiet spots away from everyone so Jane could practise the guitar and sing without worrying about mistakes. We often used the drying room under the dormitories, which had thick cement walls and was only frequented by the other girls in wet weather. I sat and listened or sometimes read a book as Jane sang in a sweet, clear voice. She taught herself using songbooks; I remember a Fairport Convention folk song, 'Little Matty Groves', and songs by Cat Stevens, Joan Baez and Bob Dylan, although I can't remember which ones.

I could check which songs by asking Jane – she lives in Florida and we email and send messages on social media and see each other in person every few years – but I'm trying to record the patchy, torn, sometimes faded, sometimes brilliantly coloured fragments of memory, not a fact-checked record. It's whatever still exists of the sixteen-year-old girl in the electrochemical pathways of a woman at the end of middle age. Whatever I can retrieve, I cannot help but feel tender towards the teenage girl, her insecurities and inadequacies, her passions for the world of ideas and creativity, her love for her new friend.

Jane introduced me to Carole King, Joni Mitchell, Frank Zappa and Janis Joplin – oh, *Pearl*, I cannot hear any of the songs without Jane appearing. And *Woodstock*? Did I see the film with Jane? No! It was Clare Bowers! I suddenly remember my friendship with Clare and I must backtrack to include her.

In the vision of hindsight, which selects and deletes according to its preferred version, it's clear that Clare was the beginning of the shift that changed my life, a precursor to Jane. She slipped from my mind because of the memory frame I've been using to recall friends – 'which school I was at'. I didn't go to school with Clare – she lived in Orange, about a hundred kilometres away from Wellington – but met her at an interschool tennis match. Only a few girls played tennis, the ones who had grown up on farms and a few others who didn't like team sports – Clare was one of those.

We probably started talking because I had developed the pose of taking a book with me to the sporting events we were forced to attend. At one stage I was carrying Joyce's *Ulysses* because I'd heard it had been banned, which worked well for starting conversations even though I'd only read a few pages.

I didn't see Clare very often because we lived so far apart, but we developed an intense friendship. When we met we didn't talk about clothes or boys but about whether God was real or not, about the rules of life, how you were supposed to marry and have children, how we were going to do something else with our lives. I stayed at her place several times and met her parents, who also liked to discuss ideas. I have a distinct memory of talking to them in the hallway in their house – I was leaning on a doorframe and I recall the feeling of surprise at their interest and respect.

Clare was also wild and troubled. She soon told me she was adopted, the first adopted person I'd ever met. She had an intense dark gaze and a rebellious angry attitude that I found fascinating.

After I left school I think I only saw her once. In my thirties, a mother of two boys by then, I learnt that Clare had killed herself. I was devastated and remembered her wildness, her anger. I found out her parents' address and wrote to them telling them how much Clare had meant to me. How she had changed the direction of my life. They wrote a gentle letter back and told me that Clare had struggled bravely with mental health difficulties for a long time. I had not framed her wildness in that way and felt shocked. I saw then that I had romanticised her pain, made it into something I needed. It makes me wonder now how much I have constructed my friends for my own nourishment.

Chronologically, Clare belongs in the schoolgirl years in Wellington, but that's not how memory works. The hippocampus does its best to splice moments together, to make sense, but moments of the past fire into conscious life when you least expect them to. It was Woodstock that brought me back to Clare. And Janis Joplin singing 'Piece of My Heart' and 'Bobby McGee', the music tearing at my heart, the bleeding, bloody power of it vibrating through my body, and then Joplin's raw-throated voice slipped time forward to Jane and I walking along the street in the middle of the night in Sydney, belting out Mercaaaaydeez Benz.

It was the Anzac Day long weekend in 1971. Jane and I had been friends for just over two months and were already inseparable; we made plans to go to Sydney for the weekend. I had never been to Sydney without my family, had only been there a handful of times in my life, and to my parents, it was a den of iniquity and danger, so I was astonished that they let me go. I think I presented it as a fait accompli, my first use of a tactic I've often since found useful. That, and the fact that I said we would stay with my sister Kathy, who was eight years older than I was, a trained nurse, and considered sensible by my parents.

In reality, we spent most of our time in town and in Balmain at Reynolds Street, where Jane's sister, Annabel, lived.

'My sister is incredible, beautiful,' said Jane.

Annabel was small and rounded with long golden Botticelli hair and the same glowing, unmarked skin as Jane. She wore floating dresses, patchouli scent wafted around her, she looked perfect, but seemed wounded in some way. She worked as a psychiatric nurse, although I don't think she had any training, and so did her boyfriend, Patrick, and another friend, Tom, who shared Reynolds Street.

It seems odd that I remember so many decades later the name of a teenage friend's sister's boyfriend and her housemate, but through Jane's stories they had attained mythological status in my mind. They were emblems of all that was waiting for me, a life of my own choosing, a life outside the 'straight' world as I learnt to call it that weekend. They were 'bent' and that's what I wanted to be.

Of the Reynolds Street house, I remember a dark hallway, jars of chickpeas and lentils in the kitchen, embroidered and mirrored cushions and the smell of incense and marijuana. I don't recall smoking any dope that time, but Annabel gave Jane two joints, which she brought back to boarding school. She gave them to me to hide in my locker, thinking the nuns would be much more likely to check her things than mine. I hid them well under my underwear on the top shelf, but to our horror, they disappeared a few days later. We were sure the nuns had found them, and we lived in terror for a couple of weeks, but nothing was said. Perhaps they thought it more effective to leave us in suspended anxiety.

The other contraband we brought back from Sydney was two Moratorium badges. I remember going to an anti–Vietnam

War concert in Victoria Park near Sydney University that Anzac Day, but I've checked the date – despite wanting to represent my fragmented memory, it's not a good idea to get the verifiable facts wrong – and found the Moratorium march that year was in June, not the Anzac Day weekend. I did go to many other concerts and marches – including one with Jamie, Jane's brother – so it's likely I've layered in memories from later.

We pinned our badges to our uniforms and proudly wore them to school and gained some notoriety for our stance, and even more, for our weekend away without parents. I kept my badge for years. When I saw one in a museum display recently, it created a complex set of emotions: longing for the youthful past, sorrow for a world that appears to be in a much worse state than it was then, a sentimental sympathy for the girl who was making herself a new identity, and a desire to see Jane who now lives on the other side of the world.

We did sleep at my sister's flat, which was attached to the hospital she worked at in Burwood. I remember sitting on the floor in her narrow kitchen one night with two boys we had brought back with us. Who were they? Where did we find them? And I remember the next night walking back from the railway station along a suburban street to the flat; it was late, hardly anyone about, when Jane and I sang 'Mercedes Benz' at the tops of our voices all the way up the street. *Oh Lord!* I will remember the feel of the dark air all my life, and the clinging of the silky dress I'd bought at Paddy's Market that day – it was actually a dyed maroon nightie and I'd bought knee-high leather boots, too – and I will not forget the feeling of wild freedom, joy and friendship.

When we arrived back at boarding school, both of us in our second-hand dyed nightie-dresses and boots, Mother Marie, who was in charge of the boarders, spoke to me about Jane, carefully. 'She's a troubled girl. You ought not spend so much time with her alone. Mix with the other girls, won't you.'

The other girls looked critically at my maroon nightie but didn't say anything. It was the first time I wore clothes that made people look at me, a small notoriety, and I enjoyed it. One day when the dyed nightie-dress was in the wash and I had to wear my plain skirt and top, Mother Marie remarked approvingly, 'You look much better in that skirt.'

I reported it all to Jane and we both laughed. Jane and everything about her – her face, her thinking, her singing, her family – was transforming. I wanted to be like her.

I've always honoured Jane as the friend who changed my life. I've thought of her as the one who showed me there was another way to be outside of pursuing a career, getting married, having children. It felt like she opened the door to a parallel world where consciousness of being – and the expression of it – mattered. Where lying in the dark looking at stars mattered. It sounds absurdly romantic, but that's not the point; the point is that at a certain time, a friend can alter the trajectory of a life.

~

In The Epic, Gilgamesh and Enkidu changed each other, but the first and most dramatic transformation is wrought by Shamhat, the temple prostitute. She is sent by the gods precisely to change wild Enkidu into a civilised man during seven days and nights of sacred love-making. She transforms his inclinations and his mind so that he gives up his life with the animals and becomes part of human society, taking on the responsibility of caring for it. It could be read as a woman bending a man to her will via sex, but I prefer to think she revealed Enkidu's potential to himself. I think of Shamhat as a friend to Enkidu; she teaches him about food and wine and conversation, she advises him, she encourages him, and most of all, she reveals to him his destiny. He must go to the city, meet Gilgamesh and change him for the good of his people. Certainly, when she tells him about Gilgamesh, he is pleased because he had 'longed for a comrade who understood his heart'.

When Enkidu and Gilgamesh first meet, people in the street do remark on their likeness, but the crucial element, the thing the two of them are delighted by, is that they recognise each other's restless hearts. Gilgamesh is transformed from his exploitative ways by finding his equal, by the recognition and exchange of friendship, but overall Enkidu loses out in the friendship. He advises Gilgamesh, loves him, takes his insults, goes on adventures with him, stands up to him – and in the end is cursed and killed because of him. I wonder if there is always a power imbalance in friendships, sometimes huge with one serving the other, sometimes slight, only flashing out as an occasional impatience.

Five

It was coming up to Christmas of the year we arrived back from Paris and Anthony and I were planning to go out west, as we usually did, to have Christmas with my family. As I visualise that summer, it connects to enough neural pathways to make me remember that when we first arrived back we had rented an apartment in Glebe on the other side of town and didn't move to Victoria Street in Kings Cross until after Christmas. And then I remember Gina lived in St Peters for a while, south of town, which means Gina and I didn't live close at first, but that we both moved closer to each other. I'm not trying to make a correct and legally binding record, but I do want time sequences and places to be in order, and also to note that we moved towards each other.

Later on we met at local cafés and bars, the Coluzzi, Dov, the Fountain, the Old Fitz, but that first Christmas back we had drinks at our place in Glebe. I think it was the time that Dolly's son – I called him Theo in the book, and that was the name he later adopted – was staying. I need to mention him because Gina developed a friendship with him over the next few years. She connected to him first, felt protective of him, through meeting him in the book, and when they met in real life, it was as if they always had known each other. He was only sixteen, but they had the same passionate interest in films, a shared creativity, and a wicked sense of humour. After the first meeting in Glebe, they met up independently for a film or a coffee whenever Theo came from Melbourne to stay with me. From the beginning I liked the way Gina opened herself to the people I loved, giving them the same attention she gave me. I wanted everyone to see what I saw, my beautiful friend.

That pre-Christmas gathering, Gina arrived early so there was just the two of us. We sat drinking wine on the balcony over which a huge Moreton Bay fig hovered. It created a moist tropical microclimate in summer and a damp chilliness when autumn arrived. I had never lived closely with a fig before and was very aware of its immoveable spirit and the way it hunched its skirts around the balcony every time I went outside.

Gina told me that she wasn't looking forward to Christmas with her family. As well as her mother, she had a younger brother and an older sister, and they always had to meet at her sister's place.

'We always have to go there, to her place. It's always her world, her family. Why can't they come to me for once?' There was a flash of anger behind her tone.

'I know,' I said. 'We never have Christmas at our place either. We always go out to my brother's place near Bathurst, but that's because it's too far for my mother to come to Sydney. We used to all go up to her house in Wellington, but then my brother and his wife thought it was easier for Mum if we didn't all stay there, so now we meet up at his place. It's okay though.'

'I don't like it at all. They treat me as if I don't have the right sort of life. They don't come and see any of the plays I'm in, not one, and talk as if acting is some silly indulgence of mine.'

'Really? You'd think they'd be proud of you being an actor.'

'Maybe, but no. If I had a husband and children it would be different, but without that, and no proper job, I'm a joke.'

'Who is "they"? Not your mother.'

'No, not Mum, nor my younger brother, he has enough troubles of his own. Just my sister. She has no respect for the way I live. For who I am.' I could see the hurt and anger in her eyes. 'It's as if I can't be taken seriously. Or because I'm not the way she thinks I should be, I don't count.'

'I know what you mean. I think in my family, it's like "Oh Patti" when I say something a bit intense. As if I'm having myself on. Not my younger sister, she is the same as me in a way, but Mum and my older sister are more practical.' It was the first time I had admitted that to anyone except Anthony. At times I did feel uncomfortable in my family, ill-at-ease, as if I didn't quite fit, but I hadn't wanted to say it aloud. They were my good and loving family, if I didn't fit, it meant something was wrong with me.

Gina looked at me with understanding. There was such warmth and acceptance in her gaze that I again felt that vertigo, the sensation that I was falling into her. It was the intensity of her openness, no sense of separateness, which again made me afraid. Not of her, but of my own capacity to fall, to lose my own definition. I could dissolve, disappear into her dark eyes and never emerge.

I wonder now if that's why she was such a good actor. She allowed characters to fall inside her, to inhabit her, move their limbs through her, breathe through her. I am a separate person, folded in, watching; I will never allow that. It's not that I don't long for spiritual communion but I also need to be distinct. Perhaps that is the tension of friendship; to long for oneness and for distinction at the same time, to know someone sees us fully, and yet to remain separate, the edges of self distinct and strong.

I went to see a play at the Opera House with Gina. She knew some of the actors who were in it and had been given two free tickets for the opening night.

'You can dress up a bit if you want,' she said, smiling.

'Any excuse for a frock,' I said.

I did dress up a bit, a narrow black dress with lots of Goth zippers I found in an op-shop, and showy beads and earrings. We met in the foyer of the Drama Theatre – Gina was also dressed in black, the same dress she wore on her birthday at Bofinger – and she was already talking to another actor I recognised. She introduced me to him and we said a few words, but I could tell he wasn't interested in me. Gina talked animatedly with him for a few minutes, both of them laughing and exclaiming, and then he excused himself and went to the bar. Other actors walked past, stopped, nodded, said hello, hugged and kissed, stopped for a chat. The same excited cries and embraces swirled around her at interval. They were all people whose faces I knew from television or the stage, so they felt familiar, but I didn't want to appear starstruck, which made me more awkward than I needed to be.

Gina was always lively, warm, engaged, but in this crowd she was also quick and funny, utterly at home in her tribe. When others told a story, she laughed delightedly and with full complicity, her eyes focused on the teller. It gave her an effervescent, rose-gold glow and it made her beautiful. I noticed each person's face light up as they spoke and listened to her, and I thought, yes, other people feel it, the warm light shining on them.

Another evening when it was just the two of us – I have no location for this memory – Gina was talking about a successful Sydney theatre director.

'When he pays you attention it is like the sun is shining on you, and you alone. You feel like you matter, you feel like you are blossoming, you can do anything. You feel so believed in. And then he turns his attention to someone else and you feel like the sun has been switched off and you are cast out into the cold dark. He doesn't imply you have done anything wrong, it's not your fault, he just switches his gaze.' She pulled a wry face, mocking her own dependence on his attention.

The words stuck in my brain, caught in the synapses, but it was much later, a decade later, before I really knew what they meant.

It's not your fault but you are cast out.

Gina and I always walked between each other's apartments, back and forth for years, and even now when I occasionally turn down Liverpool Street and towards the footbridge near where she used to live, the locations are still stamped in my neural pathways with an expectation of a warm greeting, even though I know it will not happen.

She often walked around to our place in Victoria Street for dinner. I poured drinks and Anthony cooked. He was, is, a much more elaborate cook than I am with an idiosyncratic cordon-rouge style of his own, not fastidiously presented, but always very good to eat. After he stopped writing and took a full-time job, he gradually took over nearly all the cooking.

'It's my only creative outlet these days,' he explained, whenever I admitted to guilt at not doing my share. I have had enough time and space to write only because he worked full-time. He would have liked to be writing. He'd had one book published early on in our life together, but with his job at university, he had little time for expressing his own thoughts on the page. He was still a passionate reader though, one of those readers who immerse themselves in a writer, reading every book they have written. Gina was the same. Both of them took up a writer, often at the same time, and disappeared into his or her books for weeks, drowning themselves in one writer's world, one writer's being.

There are runs of books by the same author on our bookshelves, evidence of Anthony's obsessions, but they are not arranged chronologically so I am not sure what he was reading, and by inference, what Gina was reading in those early years of our friendship. Elena Ferrante and Karl Ove Knausgård came later, each devoured in their turn by Anthony and Gina, one book after another. There was always Patrick White though, Gina was as devoted to him as we both were.

I remember how thrilled Gina was one evening at our place when I told her our younger son's name was Patrick Manoly. She smiled in recognition. I ran to the hall closet to find the postcard that Patrick White had sent us after we had boldly posted a note to him saying we had named our baby son for him and Manoly, his lifelong partner. The card had a delicate botanical drawing of a bush violet on it. And then the plain white card that Manoly Lascaris had sent us when we wrote to him after White died. How I sobbed in the shower when Anthony came in to tell me.

We didn't know White personally. Anthony had been a part-time taxi driver all those years ago when our Patrick was born, and one day he had picked up the painter Brett Whiteley, then a friend of White's. Anthony had told him, as he drove him around Sydney, about his new son and his honourable name, and Whitely said, 'You must write and tell Patrick, he will be so proud,' then gave him White's address.

Gina's eyes shone as Anthony told this story.

'We don't have anyone else like Patrick White,' Anthony said. 'He's in his own category in Australia. Head and shoulders.'

'Yes. And so many people don't even read him anymore. What is that? People say he is difficult, but I've never thought so,' Gina said.

'Probably because he's not about narrative. He creates the light and shade, the texture of consciousness,' Anthony said. 'We are each one of us alone in ourselves and the pleasure of reading him is in feeling the incredible hum of another human consciousness out there. We are lucky to have had him. We don't deserve him.' He was leaning forward and there was an intensity to his words, a forgetting of the rest of the world and ordinary concerns.

It was a usual conversation for him to have with me – from the beginning we talked books, not in a dry dissecting fashion, always passionately – but I rarely saw him express this level of his experience with others. With his friends and our sons he mostly talks politics. He is well informed about issues, keeps up to date with the evil machinations of politicians and enjoys elaborating with whomever will listen. I listen, but politics is more an amorphous wave of feeling for me, for or against, not particularly nuanced, so he can't get a detailed response from me. I feel inadequate because I know it matters, but I just can't experience the same level of intensity as I do when books are on the table.

Gina, though, loved talking politics, and was as well informed as he was. When the conversation turned to the depressing realities, I made a few general comments but quickly found myself unable to contribute any detail. I stepped back then, and if we were at home as we were on this night, I'd become something of a handmaiden, filling glasses and getting more olives and cheese from the fridge. I didn't feel left out, or at least not in a way that bothered me. I liked that Anthony was open to Gina in the same way I was, and I wondered a few times if he had felt the same vertigo.

It crossed my mind that if I wasn't around he could possibly fall for her. It wasn't a sharp thought, almost a lazy, confident one; I would have to be out of the picture first. And then I thought, it would not be reciprocated even if he did, he was not Gina's type. I had seen who she was attracted to several times, often enough to have a fair idea. Despite their intense openness to each other, and even despite sometimes feeling left out, I felt safe. Not everything in my friendship with Gina is clear, but I don't want to hint at betrayal in trying to observe the shifting slideshow, the light and shadow of friendship, the infinite patterns in the air.

~

I listened to a podcast recently about 'the incredible hum of human consciousness'. It was a scientist talking and he didn't call it that, in fact, he argued that there was no such thing as consciousness, no such thing as mind. That's a controversial claim, because we all know there is consciousness, we all experience it. There it is, humming away, the endless being behind our perceiving, our knowing, our thinking, our friendships, our loving.

But, he said, what we call consciousness is all physical, is all brain function. There is no inner world, only synapses firing, re-presenting experience. Even for people who can 'see' in clear juicy detail an apple in their minds, or a castle, or a diagram of artificial intelligence, there is no actual inner double of the world. No double even of ourselves, no homunculus in the brain. The world is there, outside of us, and what we call consciousness is our experience of the world, or, as the scientist said, 'our interface with the world'.

He argued that perception, thought, memory, dream and emotion are all the same, that is, they are all brain function, all electrochemical. It means the physical nature of the long-ago past is exactly the same as the present in our brains. Then he went on to argue that there is no present, no now, that we are milliseconds behind physical reality in the case of seeing our friend's face, or thousands of years behind in the case of seeing stars in the night sky. We are never in now.

I enjoy the way all this makes my synapses light up and blow a fuse, but I wonder how much it matters. And then, because I'm thinking of my friend Jane again, the history of our friendship extending over time, I realise that the scientist is right, and it does matter. As I write, she lives in me as if in the non-existent present.

~

Jane's parents and younger sister moved from Coonamble to Leura in the Blue Mountains, much closer to our boarding school. I'm not sure why they moved, but it may have been because her father had a heart attack and had to leave his job. It meant that Jane's home was now only a couple of hours from school and so I was invited to visit.

I remember the feeling of sleeping in another family's home, the arrangement of rooms, the different – better – furniture, the different smell of soaps, shampoos, food, but more than anything, different parents. I hadn't slept over at friends' houses very often – my father didn't allow it – which made me conscious of inhabiting a new space in close proximity to adults I hardly knew. Jane's younger sister was also there, a plumpish, soft, imaginative girl whom Jane loved dearly, but who was shy and didn't say much to me.

Her mother was conversational and arty – she painted and made pots – and liked to have a glass of wine with her meal, a refinement that impressed me. I tried to talk about art and ideas with her, I wanted her to like me, but I felt as if I wasn't quite up to the mark. It wasn't that she was a standard middle-class housewife, in fact the house was in general artistic disarray, but she did have a cultivated accent and a disregard for the rules that belonging to a privileged class can give you. I think she could see I was trying to hide my background and reasonably enough, mistrusted me.

I didn't speak to Jane's father much at all but was aware of her parents having a relationship with each other that was separate from their family. I think it was the first time that I realised parents could have something between them that was nothing to do with their children. A few years later, Jane told me that the night before her father died unexpectedly, he had said to her mother out of the blue, 'Peggy, you have made it all worthwhile,' and I felt again everything I had sensed between them.

I can't remember the details of the first visit – I visited several times after leaving school as well – only the atmosphere of being in a different family, but I want to include it because being woven into the edges of another family is part of many of my friendships.

Jane talked about her mother and father, about Jamie and Annabel and Meghan, and I talked about my family, and in all the years since, we always ask after each other's families. The visit to Jane's house was also significant because it came just after a time when I felt painfully insecure in our friendship.

It was because of Johanna, a daygirl at the school as most of the students were. Johanna was beautiful, with astonishing blue, black-lashed eyes, dark hair, and a 'well-developed' body. You would assume this made her popular with boys, but they were afraid of her cleverness and her sexuality and watched her with suspicion and hunger. She was also a gifted science and mathematics student, although not the sort of schoolgirl the nuns took to their hearts. She mercilessly mocked the science teacher, a small nun with thick legs whom we called Effel (FL= Fat Legs), who had a poor grasp of the subject she was trying to teach. Effel got her explanations of diodes and cathodes mixed up, Johanna relentlessly pointed out and corrected her errors in a sarcastic voice, then smiled as the nun spluttered in enraged humiliation. The maths teacher was a far too clever and eccentric nun to mock, but Johanna's sexy, insolent beauty stood as a challenge to consecrated virginity even when she was being respectful.

She and Jane took modern history together, the only class that I wasn't also in, and the two of them started hanging out at school. They shared the class just before lunch break and when they came out, found a place away from the other girls to sit and talk. I wasn't forbidden to join them, but it was awkward to find them on their own and then to have to walk towards them and break into their intense conversation. We were all clever girls together, but Johanna was more forceful, more edgy. She was funny and lively, and liked to break the rules and stare down the consequences. Some days I couldn't find either of them anywhere and it seemed evident they were hiding, so I had to face the stomach-churning anxiety of finding a group kind enough to let me sit, humiliated, on the edge of it. School breaks, morning tea and lunch became a time to dread, the first year of high school all over again.

Back at the boarding college though, it was the same as it had always been between Jane and me, our intense, intimate conversations about ourselves and the nature of life continuing every afternoon. We talked about Buddhism – I did a presentation on it for religious knowledge class, which wasn't what the nuns expected – and about how physics had shown the true nature of things was light, just as eastern spirituality had said for thousands of years. We talked of the beauty of nature and a natural way of life, and about how we didn't want boring jobs and marriage, we wanted freedom and adventure. At those times, my mind and body buzzed with delight, but what was happening at school began to impinge. Why was I good enough at the boarding college, but not at school?

Each day at that age lasts a lifetime and my lifetimes were taken up with feeling abandoned each day and picked up again each evening. I started falling into a spiral of self-pity and began imagining what Jane would do if I harmed myself. I didn't have any serious intention of self-harm, but I took a maudlin pleasure in imagining what Jane would do if I were found bleeding somewhere. Maybe in the nuns' graveyard out the back – we were allowed to go and sit there in a meditative fashion. It was melodramatic, but I was in a churning adolescent misery and could think of nothing else.

Then there was a school religious retreat in Katoomba in the Blue Mountains, and we all stayed for several days at the California guesthouse. We had to do group exercises, 70s 'get to know yourself and each other' games. We were allowed to choose our roommate and Jane chose Johanna. I walked away from the guesthouse early the first morning with the intention of not coming back. They would all wonder where I was and feel guilty when I didn't return. I walked several kilometres down the highway towards Sydney, my thoughts circling obsessively, until I realised I had better get back before I was in real trouble. When I walked in I told the nuns that I hadn't been feeling well and had gone out for a walk and got lost. No-one had noticed I was gone.

Then Johanna had a party at her house and Jane and I were invited. I think it was her parents' party because lots of young students from the tertiary college where her father worked were there. I don't know why the nuns allowed us to go – outings were limited and strictly controlled – but I suppose we must have had notes from our parents saying we could. Johanna's place was a large colonial house, solid old brick, and Johanna had two rooms to herself in the renovated stables out the back. All the rooms were furnished with art objects and books and there was a piano, and quirky features such as the front door being a window that you had to lift from the bottom. Like Jane's mother's house, it was bohemian, messy.

I remember we drank wine although we were still all underage, and I chatted to one of the college students.

'Want some?' he said, holding out a couple of pills.

'Sure,' I said, and popped one in my mouth. And then I asked, 'What is it?'

'You swallow it first then you ask what is it!' he said.

I felt a glow of pleasure in his admiration of my boldness. I could break the rules if I wanted to. I didn't find out what the drug was and as it happened I didn't suffer any ill effects. I didn't notice much in the haze of drinks. I had negotiated a grown-up party and had even enjoyed talking to people I'd never met before. I started to think perhaps I could be just as bold as Johanna.

Johanna was, in fact, having a hard time at home and around town. She had gone driving with a couple of day-boys from St Stanislaus' College, who afterwards spread stories about her. In those days in a country town, it was easy to trash a girl's life simply by suggesting she was sexually available. It meant she could be treated as rubbish by anyone. And there were also problems with her parents. She told Jane and me that her father was having an affair with another lecturer at the college, that her mother was distraught, and they were always coldly fighting.

Shortly after the party, Johanna ran away from home. I didn't know what had happened at first, but the next day Jane told me the whole story. Johanna had fled to Sydney and was staying with one of Annabel's friends. I remember the pang of being left out of the conspiracy; they must have arranged it all without me, but also a sudden surge of relief. Good, she's gone, I hope she stays away.

Several weeks of intrigues, secret phone calls and lengthy inquisitions by the nuns followed. I enjoyed being the holder of secret knowledge, being the one who did not take risks but avidly listened to the tales of those who did. There was an atmosphere of high drama every day, for me underpinned by the anxiety that Johanna would return from it all in a few weeks with even more power. As it happened, she didn't ever come back to the school, although I saw her once in Sydney and then once at a school reunion decades later. Even all those years later, I realised I was glad Jane wasn't there so I didn't have to compete for attention.

Jane and I returned to the rhythm of our days at school, although by now boys from St Stanislaus were woven in whenever we had the chance. We were allowed to go to town on a Saturday morning, so Jane met up with Adrian, who liked to talk about the meaning of life and listened to Bob Dylan. We had coffee together at the Acropole Café and sometimes went to his place and listened to music. I had a crush on him, too, but it was clear that he was fascinated by Jane.

I don't recall, if I ever knew, how much their relationship was sexual – there was little chance of even kissing and cuddling in our brief releases from boarding school – but at the end of the year Jane suddenly took up with another boy, handsome in a young Johnny Depp way – and left Adrian to me. Straight after finishing the final exams, she moved into a small flat in Bathurst with her handsome boyfriend, but all I can remember of the flat is her sitting cross-legged on the satin sheets of the unmade double bed. I thought how free she was and how she had started her adult life already.

Jane also rebelled against school tradition by refusing to

go to the Formal after the exams, which at our school also included a white-dress presentation and curtsey to the Bishop. It was the event of our school lives, a final release after all our studies, and a goodbye to most of our friends. Because we were country girls from all over the region, it was unlikely we would see each other again.

But Jane said, 'I'm not going to be offered up like a bride to some Bishop.'

I admired her cool and her resolve, but I resented it as well. I thought, she's just trying to make herself stand out; I didn't like being made to feel like one of the herd just because I wanted to go.

'I know, that's silly. I'm not going to curtsey or whatever, but that's only two minutes of it. I want to celebrate with everyone. It will be the last time we are all together,' I said.

But she wouldn't budge.

'You can go with Adrian if you like though.'

I did go with Adrian. I sketched a dress and had it made in a heavy clinging jersey that fitted and flowed around my body. I've only just realised that it was an almost exact copy, in white, of the leopard-print dress that Jane was wearing the first time I saw her.

After school finished, Adrian and I went on a trip to Melbourne together and we had a few kisses, but nothing else. All I can clearly remember is lying in a field when we hitchhiked to Bacchus Marsh – we were heading there because we liked the name – and he was gazing into my face.

'I can't help myself,' I said, and kissed him. Then I said, 'That wasn't really true.'

'I know,' he said, laconically.

And then we gathered up our things and kept hitching. I

knew Adrian was still in love with Jane and that I could never match her.

If I asked them, I am sure Jane and Johanna, and Adrian too, would have other and possibly truer stories about what occurred when we were teenagers. Even recorded history is a set of stories shaped by individual perception and memory. There can be many versions of the same stories, many fragments stored in different memories, or recorded in different accounts. When I first came across *The Epic of Gilgamesh*, for example, I was confused by the number of different stories about its origins, and even about who really found it.

Even putting aside for the time being the fragments of earlier versions found at ancient Nippur in present-day southern Iraq, and various other fragments found throughout the Middle East, the discovery of the twelve tablets at Nineveh, the most complete version of The Epic, has a number of different 'discoverers'. The Englishman, Layard, is given most of the credit because he was the one who began excavating at Nineveh in 1839. He subsequently brought back to the British Museum 25,000 tablets inscribed with cuneiform script. He was also given the credit, I suppose, because he was English. In fact, it was his collaborator and successor in the excavation, Hormuzd Rassam, who uncovered the actual tablets containing The Epic. An aside: Rassam also identified the location of The Hanging Gardens of Babylon, a discovery that makes him even more of a hero in my eyes.

Then there was another Englishman, Henry Rawlinson, who began the work of deciphering the tablets. Rawlinson was a political agent in Baghdad, but earlier, when he was employed by the East India Company, he had discovered the 'Record of Darius' on a rock in Persia, which, like the Rosetta Stone, had three languages inscribed on it, in this case, in cuneiform script. He was able to use this discovery to start deciphering The Epic. Back at the British Museum, he was joined by George Smith, who, in 1872 translated the Deluge tablet and the story of Noah and the significance of *The Epic of Gilgamesh*, at least for students of the Bible, was finally realised. Perhaps the unknown writers who recorded the Old Testament were simply borrowing their stories from other, older, cultures.

There was also the American expedition in 1888–89, led by Paul Punnet Peters, to Nippur. Peters found 40,000 tablets, a small number of which contained older versions of The Epic in the Sumerian language of southern Mesopotamia. Researchers had known there must be earlier texts than the ones discovered at Nineveh because the tablets written in Akkadian noted, 'Written down according to the original and collated in the palace of Assurbanipal, King of the World, King of Assyria'.

It's not that all these names matter much anymore, and nor does the nineteenth-century controversy about the existence of a text older than the Bible matter, but what does matter is that a culture lost for thousands of years, since the sacking of Nineveh in 600 BC, was brought back into human minds *because someone wrote the stories down*. Gilgamesh and Enkidu, and the heifer stirring in the Cedar Forest, and the people in the House of Dust, and what they thought at that time about friendship and immortality, are firing across synapses in my head on a sunny day in Sydney just as they did five thousand years ago in Uruk in Sumer, because an unknown writer pressed cuneiform letters into clay, letter after letter, adjusting the angle and direction of his stylus for each letter, until the tale was recorded. Millennia later, I breathe those words in and the ancient world and its inhabitants, taking their proper shapes and growing solid, spring into being inside me.

Six

Gina was still working on the play script of my book when she came to Wamberal, a large old holiday house north of Sydney that Anthony and I had been going to with a group of friends each summer for nearly twenty years. For most of that time, before Gina, everyone in that group had lived in the Blue Mountains and all had kids at the same alternative school, so the gatherings had been an elastic but homogenous mass, shifting a little each year. The cream stucco house expanded to fit in countless children and their friends, mostly boys, and their parents who had become friends, into the five bedrooms, lounge room and two verandas, with sometimes a few tents on the lawn. As the boys grew and had their own lives, the now child-free group loosened as new friends were added and old friends who, it turned out, were really only the parents of sons' friends, were left behind.

I try to picture Gina there with her manuscript, but the image eludes me. No stack of pages being rifled through, no discussion. I know she read Anthony and I drafts of the play, but possibly not at Wamberal.

Instead, I see the old kitchen, the heart of the house where we all took turns, in pairs, to cook for the other eight or thirteen or seventeen people. There was a kitschy seashell curtain hiding the hot-water tank and a window looking out into a courtyard. Friends who were not cooking hung about outside the window or wandered in and out, drinking wine and talking.

One day, Gina was being assisted in the kitchen by Anthony, who was slicing eggplant under her instruction. She washed large bunches of parsley for making tabouli and spread it carefully, stalk by stalk, to dry on the table and bench near the window and on the windowsill itself. The kitchen looked like a kind of greenhouse or perhaps a harvest barn. I had never seen anyone do that with parsley before. I just washed it under the tap then dabbed it with a tea towel.

'How thorough!' I exclaimed.

'It's the way my father taught me to do it,' Gina said. 'Spread it and let it dry. Don't bruise the parsley.'

It struck me then that everything Gina did, she did with fine attention. There was nothing slapdash about her, not even the way she made tabouli. As someone for whom near enough was often good enough, I found it impressive and fascinating. I also noted that it was her father, not her mother, who taught her how to treat parsley.

That's the only exact fragment of conversation I remember from that week at Wamberal. It was about ten years ago now, but in line with the controlling vagaries of memory, every time I have since washed and then dried parsley with a tea towel, I feel I am not doing it properly. Don't bruise the parsley. I recently mentioned the memory to Anthony, and he too admitted he thinks of Gina whenever he makes tabouli.

While I don't remember any other conversations, I remember

Gina walking from her room and through the house in her contained way. I remember her sitting on the long side veranda reading, and at the beach in her black cossie, and sitting at the big table playing Dictionary and laughing. I remember too, that my younger brother Kevin was there – he was a Buddhist and liked to joke around – and I noticed the natural way they discussed philosophy and laughed together. I was happy she liked my family and they liked her. These are isolated and imprecise memories, without narrative.

It's the same with most of the years of coffees, plays, films, drinks and make-do dinners we shared in Sydney. There is a scattering of small, detailed scenes, falling through the kaleidoscope in a rush of colour, the details clear sometimes for only a few seconds.

Once we went to see a show – it was a drumming performance, energetic and physically thrilling – with another friend, Connie, also an actor. The few seconds I remember are of the three of us sitting at a high table on stools during the interval and Gina starting to make a critical remark about a play she had seen, that it was shallow – she had strong views about the serious purpose of theatre – but halfway through the remark, she remembered Connie had been in the play. I had looked at her warningly, seeing where the sentence was going, and nearly laughed out loud as she skilfully changed the direction of her sentence. But it was too late, Connie had seen where it was going and questioned her on what she had been going to say. It was uncomfortable, but not too bad because it was the play and the playwright she was critiquing, not anyone's performance.

And other moments emerge briefly: meeting at the Darlo Bar in Darlinghurst Road and both of us finding the music too loud; seeing her in a play at the Stables Theatre; visiting her at her bedsit in Darlinghurst and noticing how pretty and feminine her single bed was; a gathering at our place in Victoria Street when my older son was there, the one Gina had directed in a play, and seeing them talking animatedly and realising that they too had a friendship.

Memories of our rendezvous each year in Paris are the same, fragmented but creating a warm continuity of feeling. After that first visit, when we were back in Sydney, I told Gina I had another writing course to teach there in October. My flights and accommodation were paid, it wouldn't cost me anything.

'I'm coming too,' she said.

'Really!? You can do that?' I was thrilled that she wanted to, but wondered how she could do it on an actor's income.

'I've decided that if I can't live in Paris, then I'm going to get myself there each year. It's what I'm going to do for myself. I've decided, I'll find the money.'

The writing course turned into an annual event, so for several years Gina kept her promise to herself and turned up around the same time as my course. Because it happened for several years, time has concertinaed so there are fragments of memories without chronology. It seems liked a blessed time, no doubt given a golden shine as I look back, but even so, I know it was the heyday of our friendship. All that remains are small, glowing, seemingly insignificant moments.

I remember, for instance, walking up the rue Marcadet in the 18th arrondissement and stopping outside a small gallery to look at the sculptures of monsters made of wire coathangers. They were whimsical but fierce-looking beasts.

'I love them!' she exclaimed, laughing. 'They are so exactly right. Wire coathangers are just like that, they do turn into monsters in my wardrobe. And they turn me into a monster trying to untangle the bloody things.'

'Oh yes,' I said, pleased with the aptness of her remark. Again, the firing mechanisms of memory ensure that whenever I am wrangling wire coathangers, I think both of the sculptures in the rue Marcadet and of Gina.

I remember, too, Gina staying with me once for a couple of nights in my apartment in the rue de Birague, which runs off the Place des Vosges. It was a small one-bedroom apartment with two single beds; I recall the slight awkwardness of sharing an intimate physical space with someone with whom I wasn't physically intimate. I remember the same discomfort when I shared the same space for a few nights with my younger son, who was also working in Paris. In both cases, we undressed in the bathroom, stepped around each other in the bedroom, lay facing away from each other. Every relationship has a clear, probably measurable, delineation of physical space, even with those who are dear.

And then there was the man, a handsome French playwright, whom Gina had been seeing. I went out with them to dinner once and afterwards Gina confessed she was very interested in him. We had many conversations about it at the time, but despite my constant rifling through every aspect of our friendship, I've decided not to use them or any of our conversations about men. Even when a friendship is over it requires keeping confidences, that is, concealment, whereas writing demands revelation, a conflict I can't reconcile and yet, despite my hunger to examine every detail it strikes me as wrong – a simple word, wrong – to reveal her heart in that way.

A friendship between a single woman and, if you like, a coupled one, carries not so much a power imbalance as a safety imbalance – I have always had someone there for me, a champion and a haven; she had only herself. I ought not speak from my heart-harbour about anyone braving the high seas. I only mention the playwright at all because that kind of 'girl talk' about relationships was also part of our friendship. It's a dismissive phrase for that deep sharing, but in a way I like it. It really isn't for the boys to hear. I offered some of the endless shifts in my long connection to Anthony; she offered the intricate uncertainties at the beginnings of love.

We met almost daily at cafés around the Marais, one of the older parts of the central city. I worked each day until four in the afternoon; a class in the morning and individual consultations afterwards, and by evening felt as if I were full to overflowing with other people's stories. I rang Gina, or she rang me, and we arranged to meet each other at the café on the corner in the rue de Birague, or Café Français in the Place de la Bastille, or, once or twice, in Bar de l'Entracte a few minutes' walk from La Comèdie Française. Some evenings I thought I shouldn't ring as we had met only the evening before, but the memory of how much I had enjoyed it pushed aside convention and I'd ring for a rendezvous anyway. Each time Gina would exclaim, 'Oh yes! Let's have a *verre du vin rouge.*'

We smiled when we met, ordered wine, and began. I talked about my class, hashing over the day. We both talked about writing and theatre and family. Sometimes we met with Trish, the singer, who had connected immediately with Gina. They were both performers so had intermittent, uncertain work in common, and a shared sense of the absurdity of life. I can hear Trish's earthy laugh and Gina's delighted one, making heads turn in the café. I liked that they were friends and felt some pleasure in having put them together, despite feeling like an awkward country girl in their company at times. The overall glow of that time though, is warm and rosy and tends to dissolve any anxieties. I can't remember how many years they went on for, our meetings in Paris, but it was enough for me to think it would go on forever.

Nothing does last forever, not the experience, nor the memory of it. I used to think – because of haphazardly gathered faulty knowledge – that memories were lost because of *pruning*, the process of the brain that eliminates unused or unnecessary synaptic links. I've since learnt that pruning happens only during periods of great physiological change from birth to the mid-twenties. It does not happen at all after that.

To put the pruning in context; humans, even babies, have something like 85 billion neurons. Each one of the neurons may be connected to 10,000 other neurons, resulting in something like 1000 trillion synaptic connections. Apparently, the storage capacity of the brain's memory neurons is estimated in computer terms to be as much as 1000 terabytes – for comparison, the data in the 19 million volumes of the US Library of Congress represents 10 terabytes.

These absurd numbers – who can say trillions seriously? – are context for the fact that the brain works better when some of the original, unused synaptic connections are pruned. It's a kind of brain self-correction for its own excesses. It's not done by killing cells, brain cells in general don't divide or die off, but synaptic connections are severed by degeneration and retraction of the axon. It's necessary for efficient function of the brain, just as it's necessary for a gardener to prune a tree to improve its yield of fruit, or to make its shape more beautiful.

Even though it's a cut, a reduction, it is seen as an improvement. The dead wood and tangled branches are cut and thrown to the ground and later burned, and no-one thinks about them again. The brain self-prunes and the tangled bright chaos of a child is turned into a brilliant focused young woman. Pruning is a positive, necessary cut for the good. What is removed and abandoned is not mourned in the flourishing and fruitfulness that follows.

When I received the text from Gina that, in hindsight, I realise had ended our friendship, the word that came into my mind was 'pruned'.

'I've been pruned,' I thought.

The thought caused pain. And bewilderment.

It is difficult to know what to do with bewilderment. It is disturbing not to understand why things happen. A reason why, a cause, is needed. The magnificent edifice of religion provides an elaborate tracery of unseen original cause and the elegant structures of science provide a narrative of logical cause – isn't the impulse of all narrative the uncovering of a reason, who did what to whom and why? If you don't know why lightning strikes, why a child dies, why a friend leaves, then it feels like life could – and will – give you a random smack in the teeth whenever it wants to. Show me how one event, one action, causes the next one. Step by step. Maybe that way I can keep myself safe. There has to be reasons. Let me look at all the pieces, all the connecting stories, histories, explanations. Lay them out in front of me.

~

In *The Epic of Gilgamesh*, when the two friends set out on their journey together, each had different reasons. Enkidu was weighed down with a loss of purpose, the discontent of having nothing useful to do. He had grown up in nature with animals for companions, spending his days hunting to survive, and missed the fierce strength and energy of necessity.

'I am oppressed by idleness and the cry of sorrow sticks in my throat.' He had lost joyful immersion in the moment, when purpose is not even a question. He was depressed; he needed something to happen.

Gilgamesh had a definite aim; he wanted to make a name for himself and so he suggested the journey and the battle against Humbaba. He thought it might save his friend from depression and it would give him the chance to 'set his name in the place where the names of famous men are written'. He wanted people to talk about him, tell stories about him.

Enkidu was not so keen on this plan. He knew what Humbaba was like. 'When he roars it is like the torrent of a storm, his breath is like fire, and his jaws are death itself.'

But Gilgamesh was on fire with enthusiasm. Even if Humbaba killed them both, stories would be told about them forever – that was the whole point. The two friends set off together, keeping up the same dynamic – Gilgamesh full of blind determination and Enkidu cautioning and advising firmly.

In the final battle though, it was Enkidu who saved the day. When Humbaba tried to trick Gilgamesh, saying he should spare him because he would become his servant and build him a palace, Enkidu said, 'Don't believe him, he's not to be trusted.'

This was when Gilgamesh became insulting, disdainful, saying that Enkidu was acting like a 'hireling', but Enkidu remained firm, insisting that he must get rid of Humbaba, or all would be lost. Finally, Gilgamesh listened to his friend who knew the ways of the wild, and united they succeeded in destroying their enemy. Without Gilgamesh, there would have been no adventure, no story told down through the ages, but without Enkidu, the journey would have ended in disaster with no-one left to tell the story. Without a story, there are no reasons for anything.

I don't think the dynamic was so obvious with Jane and me. We each had elements of Gilgamesh and Enkidu; both of us restless, longing for adventure, searching for purpose, but I think I was the one marked by the desire, if not to do it all for a story, then at least to make sure I took notes. And that has probably made all the difference to the paths we each took.

Ever since Gilgamesh and Enkidu headed off, journeys have been a metaphor for transformation, but I don't know whether Jane and I were conscious yet of wanting to transform. I simply wanted to be elsewhere, to devour the whole world, to pierce through the skin of my ordinary life into the largeness of everything. I was with my friend and together we could face dangers, we could go anywhere and do anything.

It's easy to slide back to those intense few years after leaving school when time stood almost still, when each day was forever and there was no mortality at all. In those mythologised years, Jane and I, like Gilgamesh and Enkidu, were ready for adventures, ready to set out on journeys. When I remember that time, it seems that the clay of our lives was still damp, ready to be imprinted with any kind of story.

We each decided to take a year off before going to university. Jane, in fact, said she wouldn't go to university, which, like

Sue Bestwick's decision to not finish high school, I didn't understand. No-one else in my family had been to university – my parents had not finished primary school – and none of my brothers and sisters had yet studied for a degree, but I was sure it was what clever girls did. I won a tertiary scholarship, and the new Prime Minister was soon to abolish fees, which meant, for the first time, disadvantaged students could easily go to university. Still, I wanted to see what the world was like first. I was innocent and arrogant enough to think I would see what needed doing before I decided what to do.

It was mid-May the year after finishing school. Jane was still in Bathurst, working at a pub and living with her boyfriend, and I was in Sydney working as a live-in mother's help, cleaning the house and looking after four little rich girls for their bored, intelligent mother. We were both ready to move on.

'Let's go to the Snowy Mountains and work there for the ski season. We can save enough money to go travelling,' Jane suggested.

I jumped at the chance, handed in my notice and stuffed my clothes in a backpack. We hitchhiked out of Sydney together one morning in early June, heading for the Snowy Mountains with no plan except to hope we would find jobs when we got there.

We got as far as Jindabyne by eight o'clock that night. It was a small town on a lake, and it was chilly by the time we arrived. We didn't have enough money for a motel room or caravan, so we curled up with our packs in the porch of a little church. It was uncomfortable and very cold, and too late to buy any food, but neither of us cared. No-one could tell us what to do; we had each other for company and we were in charge of our own lives.

Next morning we hitched the last thirty kilometres to Perisher Valley and began to ask for work. As we trudged from lodge to chalet to motel it soon became obvious that we should have looked into the job situation a bit more carefully. Most staff had already been engaged by an agency several months earlier and they had all just arrived in the Snowy Mountains for the beginning of the season. I was scolded in a fatherly way by the manager of The Valley Inn for hitchhiking, for not having a job arranged, and for having no money.

'Your parents would not be very happy with you. But you're in luck,' he said. 'One of the housemaids hasn't arrived and I need someone to make thirty beds and clean thirty bathrooms tomorrow.'

The job came with a shared room and meals as well, so I had landed on my feet. Jane stayed with me that night and she found a job the next day in a takeaway shop in Smiggin Holes, a scraggly settlement a kilometre or so down the mountain.

I had most of the afternoon off each day and had time to learn to ski and to go out with other staff, including the handsome boys, mostly New Zealanders, who operated the ski lifts and worked in the ski-hire shop. The Valley Inn was basic, as ski motels tended to be in those days, but everyone gathered there in the evenings because it had a bar and, on the weekends, a band and lots of marijuana. Jane walked or caught a lift up the mountain every evening and we had a Bacardi and Coke in the bar and talked and danced with the boys. Sometimes we were invited back to lodges and had dinner there and smoked dope and learnt to drink red wine.

I was eighteen, and unlike Jane, still a virgin. I was desperate for that to change, not because I had an overpowering libido, but because I wanted every experience. One night I stayed over in one of the lodges with Peter, a handsome blue-eyed, blond twenty-year-old, who was a follower of Krishnamurti. We had awkward, uncomfortable sex on a mattress in a spare room. I had sex with him a few more times but it was never great and he implied its inadequacy was my fault. I was attracted to him, although I soon became wary of his tendency to judge my behaviour and appearance. I don't remember who Jane was seeing, but Adrian came to visit one weekend.

We all took acid on the Saturday night, Jane and I and Adrian and a few others. I remember standing in the snow under a light outside The Valley Inn and Adrian and I being enchanted by the millions of glittering diamonds spread out all around us. The fiery jewels held us in thrall until we drifted off in different directions. Later on, I found him in my room sunk down on my bed listening to Leonard Cohen. 'Where's Jane?' he asked.

After the season finished, Jane and I decided to go to New Zealand on the first leg of our trip to see the rest of the world. I hitchhiked up to Sydney with Peter who had broken his leg skiing – I can't remember where Jane was – and we stayed the night in Sydney with Johanna who had her own flat by then. She was even more beautiful than she had been, her dark blue eyes glittering with cleverness and humour, and Peter was mesmerised. The three of us had dinner and then smoked dope in her lounge room but I was manoeuvred to the edge of the conversation. It soon became clear what was happening. I slept in the sunroom off Johanna's bedroom and tried not to listen to them having sex in the next room.

Peter went to Queensland and Jane and I caught a trans-Tasman ship, the SS *Ocean Monarch*, to New Zealand.

We landed in Wellington and stayed a few nights at the YHA where, again, the manager scolded us for our lack of preparation.

We had no job lined up and no idea of where we would go. For no reason other than not wanting to stop yet, we hitched out of Wellington northwards up the west coast towards Auckland. I remember the brilliant emerald green of steep hillsides, the whiteness of sheep trotting along narrow tracks on the slopes, the ferns and trees that I learnt were called ponga, rimu, totara and kauri, and I remember the symmetrical shape of the mountain then called Mount Egmont and now Mount Taranaki.

Most of the time hitching was easy; we were two eighteen-year-old girls so older drivers, fearful for our safety, regularly stopped for us, and Kombi vans always picked us up no matter how many people were already crammed into them. On the afternoon of the second day we were standing outside of Ngāruawāhia, only a couple of hours from Auckland, but no-one was stopping. We had been there for nearly two hours, when a car slid to a halt. There was a lone middle-aged man driving, not our favourite kind of ride. We looked at each other, it was Jane's turn to sit in the front. I took the back seat to myself with our two packs and relaxed. Music was playing on the car radio, Jane answered the usual questions about where we were going and what we were doing. I didn't have to say much. We would soon be there.

We had only been going about fifteen minutes, if that, when Jane suddenly said, 'We are getting out here. Stop the car.'

I sat up and looked around. We were driving through another flyspot town. What the hell was she doing? Jane was overreacting to something again. Sometimes she didn't like the look of a driver and wouldn't get in. She sensed things.

'Where are we?' I asked.

'We're here. Stop the car.' Her voice was calm but had a strange edge to it. The car swerved and came to a sudden halt.

I grabbed hold of our packs, annoyed, and hauled them out onto the verge as Jane jumped out of the front passenger seat. The car sped away and we were left standing in the middle of nowhere.

'What was that for?' I demanded.

Jane looked at me. 'You couldn't see from the back seat. He had his cock out. He was pulling himself off while he was driving.'

'Shit. I'm sorry. I couldn't see. Fuck, when did it start?'

'A couple of minutes ago. I was trying to figure out what to do. How to get us out of there. I was trying to let you know but you didn't see me.'

Jane started to tremble and I felt ashamed of being angry with her.

'I thought there was something wrong with him before we got in,' she said.

We were both rattled but we had to keep going so we decided on a signal in case anything went wrong again. We stood for a while, and then put our thumbs out because there was nothing else we could do. Two young boys stopped for us – Jane looked at them carefully – and we arrived safely in Auckland at dusk.

We spent the first three nights at the YHA in Mount Eden where all the newly arrived backpackers stayed. We searched in the newspapers for jobs and went to the university noticeboards to find somewhere to live, looking only at places that had two spare bedrooms because we wanted to live together. There wasn't much available, but we did find a place in Bellevue Road with two spare rooms listed.

We walked down the street and found a two-storey wooden house behind a hedge. It was large and rambling, five bedrooms, a large living room with stained-glass windows and wood panelling, a big shabby kitchen and a couple of dank bathrooms. It had once been a fine home and was now a rundown ever-expanding house with a shifting population of travellers, musicians, hippies and the homeless, all apart from the people who actually lived there. It was the house that sent my life off along one of the paths it has taken right up to now, because it was there that I met Anthony.

Seven

In the story of my friendship with Gina, there was an incident at the Old Fitz, the theatre pub down the road from our place, in Woolloomooloo. It was a small incident, so small only the French Boy and I saw it, but it did have an effect.

The French Boy was staying with Anthony and me for a couple of weeks. We hadn't met him before he came to stay – it was one of those situations where a friend of a niece's friend had met him in Vietnam and suggested we might give him a roof over his head when he came to Sydney. He was only seventeen and travelling alone, so we gave him a bed in the study. He settled in and made himself at home in our apartment, although I did kick him out of the study each morning so I could write. He was no trouble, open and direct – and proudly French. He scolded me for grabbing lunch on the run when he saw me take a sandwich into my study, and when I explained that I didn't have time he gave me the French Lunch Lecture on the personal and social benefits of sitting down to lunch with others. I came back from the study twenty minutes later

and saw him sitting at a properly set table and felt my lack
of civilisation. He also gave a lecture on the importance of
one's family name. His name, he said, had its roots in a long
connection to the soil of Normandy; it was his connection
to his ancestors, what he was made of. I stood there in my
own lounge room listening to the sweet-faced teenage boy
who sounded like an elderly conservative, feeling that I was
uprooted, disconnected.

One Friday night, the French Boy, Anthony and I met up
with Gina at the Old Fitz – we often went there to see a show.
We were drinking red wine and talking together, at first about
France. I laughingly retold the story of the Boy giving me the
Lunch Lecture and we all enjoyed the affirmation of French
culture. Then, gradually, Anthony and Gina became involved
in a passionate conversation that left the Boy and me to one
side. I don't remember what they were talking about – probably
politics – but I do remember the intensity and the fact that the
Boy and I had disappeared from their world. I took a sip of
wine and tried to pretend I was part of what was happening.
The Boy looked at them, and then directly at me. The look was
unmistakable – don't you see what is going on here? Then his
look shifted subtly to sympathy. I smiled and took another sip
of wine as if I hadn't seen anything, but the Boy knew I had.

Later that evening at home, when it was just the two of us,
I brought it up with Anthony.

'I know it's just your passion for whatever you are talking
about, but I felt humiliated,' I said

'Why? I don't see why. You were right there, part of it.'

'No, I wasn't part of it. A seventeen-year-old boy could see
that. He could see I was being ignored. And that you were
absorbed in Gina.'

We to and fro'd about it for a while. I trusted that both of them loved me, I said, and I didn't feel as if I were in any danger.

'So what was your problem?' he said.

I realised then that what I minded was the appearance of being the neglected wife. It was what it looked like that I minded, not what it was. That, and attracting the sympathy of a teenage boy.

Around this time I also met Gina's mother. We had talked about our families a lot – I love talking families. I find the shifts and complications in family relationships intriguing; the way we never let them go, no matter how troubling. Even if we cut from them, they are still with us. Gina talked about her adored father who had died, her mother whom she often found difficult, her younger brother, Angus, who was troubled, and her older sister, Marcella, who had everything sorted.

I met Angus only once, but I felt like I knew him. Gina did her utmost to look after him; rang services for him, gave him money, listened to him, fiercely defended him. Her sister didn't need looking after – she was successful. Marcella had a husband who loved her, two healthy children, a senior managerial income, a nice house, but, Gina said, Marcella still disregarded her. It's a strong word when you think about it. Disregard. She had told me about it before, the ongoing burr of Marcella's unwillingness to 'see' her life.

'I'm still mucking about being an actor, being a leftie, I don't have a bloke or kids. I should be over that by now.'

Then Gina said she had decided not to see her sister anymore. Literally not see her, not invite her to anything, not attend family events she was invited to, not even for Christmas.

Although I found such steely resolve unsettling, it was a decision I thought fair enough at the time. I empathised with her.

'She doesn't respect your life. She thinks it has less value than hers,' I said.

'That's it,' she said, looking right at me, and I could see the hurt and anger in her eyes. I was sure she knew I understood.

One day, Gina asked me to meet her for lunch in Darlinghurst near where she lived and when I arrived, her mother was also there. I sat down opposite her, happy to be included. It felt like an honour to be invited this far into her family, to be one of a small set of friends who knew her mother. As with Jane's mother, I was struck with the difference in appearance from my own. Decades older now, used to meeting people from every background, an old memory schema still expected mothers to be like my own shabby and quintessentially kind mother. Gina's mother was smartly dressed and well-groomed, hair pulled back from a narrow well made-up face, a cultivated and intelligent woman. Again, as with Jane's mother, I wanted her to like me.

My memory is that I tried too hard and that she wasn't interested in me. We chatted, rather than had a conversation, but it looked as if we were getting on well.

Then her mother had to leave. She had another appointment, with a friend. I said goodbye, Gina stood up and had a few words with her mother, then when she had gone, sat down next to me again.

'Your mother is lovely, so elegant,' I said.

'Yes, people always like my mother,' she said drily. 'All my friends always liked her when I was at school.'

~

There's an aspect of memory known as the peak-end rule. All it means is that humans have a cognitive bias for remembering intense moments, and in particular, intense endings. After a film, after an argument, after a relationship, what you will most easily remember are the peaks, and the peaks will also change your perception of earlier events. Small changes in any experience can significantly alter the way you remember the overall experience. It's not just positive peaks that are remembered most easily, in fact negative peaks are stronger and are more likely to be remembered and to change your memory of the whole. One hurtful remark can change all the kindness that went before it. If you had asked me about Gina in those years, say on the day I met her mother, I would have said that of any of my friends she read me in the way that I want to be read. I would have said, or at least thought, a friend can interpret the secret story written in hieroglyphs inside you and get it right. But now I question her interpretation of my story – and mine of hers. I wonder if we each created a story that suited us for the time being.

It was different with Jane, I suppose, because we were both unformed, the clay still damp. We were sixteen when we met and, in a sense, because we have lived most of our lives since then apart, we probably still are in relation to each other. I don't mean we act like teenagers, but that we see each other as a work in progress so we allow each other to be unsure.

In 1973 we were school friends on an adventure when we moved into Bellevue Road in Auckland with our backpacks and nothing else. I had the front room just off the entrance hall to the left and Jane was down the hall on the other side of the living room on the right. She made her room interesting with a few dainty objects she had collected, a piece of lace, a small soapstone cat and incense burning in a sequined Indian holder. I bought a couple of posters – one was a scene of fields and mountains and one was the Desiderata – and draped a few scarves around the room. There were several other people already living there, but it was the people who arrived soon after who came to matter.

We had not been in the house more than a few weeks when a truckload of hippies arrived from the Hokianga, an isolated forest area in Northland. They had been kicked off their commune and one of the household who knew them said they could park in our driveway. They all tumbled into our house and took over every available space, including the attic and the cellar. Three of them – Barbara, her small daughter, Michelle, and her boyfriend, Keith – stayed in the covered truck that had a stained-glass window fitted in the wall. It looked like Aladdin's cave inside, crowded with Indian embroidery and cushions, incense holders, cane baskets and a large mattress. It was Barbara's creation, an exotic small world she had gathered from second-hand shops and Cook Street market, all on her single-mother's pension.

I was drawn to Barbara the moment I saw her. She was only three years older than me but seemed more grown up and much more at ease in her skin than I was. And she was beautiful. I often say that about my friends, but it is truest of Barbara. She was a classic English beauty, fine golden hair, full lips, dark blue eyes, but she also had an elusive sparkle of naughtiness that I didn't notice for a while. I think I was in awe of her beauty at first, and for a long time, maybe right up until I realised she had lost it.

The way Barbara looked matters, because I think it shaped most of what she did and what happened to her. I didn't think about it then, but I realise now she was conscious of her beauty and its effect. She wore her fair hair pinned loosely up, looking as if it might fall down at any moment. She used no make-up except kohl under her eyes and dressed in flowing clothes that both revealed and concealed her figure. Men were always attracted to her, nearly every man who met her desired her, but she didn't hang around; she had not stayed with the father of Michelle, born when she was seventeen, nor with the father of another baby a couple of years later whom she had adopted out.

For now she lived with spiky, nonconformist Keith – and, I learnt once we started exchanging confidences – was having a passionate affair with Dave, an upcoming rock'n'roll star who was as handsome as she was beautiful. Dave and Barbara were a perfect looking pair, sexy mirror images of each other, and it was evident that Keith – who would always love her, just as Barbara would always helplessly love Dave – wouldn't stand a chance in the long run.

At Bellevue Road though, Keith and Barbara were still a couple, and it was because of Keith that Anthony arrived there. Anthony, not-so-spiky but still nonconformist, was Keith's closest friend from school days and one of the Hokianga hippies. He was the one who moved into the cellar. He put a red-patterned carpet square on its dirt floor, painted the foundation posts red and yellow and installed a double mattress, a flute and a basket of clothes.

What a gypsy, I thought.

He wore colourful clothes and a silver Buddha around his neck, and I could tell he was good-looking under his beard. When he first arrived, he entangled himself with Karen, another Australian girl who lived at Bellevue Road, who looked a lot like me and played the flute. But this is not the story of meeting Anthony, it's about Barbara who became one of my dear friends.

Barbara was mythologised by everyone who met her, not just men. I remember at one point thinking of her as the White Goddess from the Robert Graves book. We were all reading it in Queen Street, the household we congregated in a couple of years later after the Sunburst Ohu commune we'd established in the country had collapsed. I was astonished by how well Grave's description fitted Barbara; 'The Goddess is a lovely, slender woman with a hooked nose, deathly pale face, lips red as rowan-berries, startlingly blue eyes and long fair hair.' I wouldn't have said Barbara was 'deathly' pale, perhaps delicately pale, and the slight hook of her nose was aquiline, refined, like an English aristocrat, but she *was* the White Goddess.

I suppose it needs to be said that, even then, I was aware that I didn't have the kind of looks that anyone mythologised. I had thick wavy red hair, my best feature, which I wore Botticelli fashion flowing down my back, smallish blue eyes, a friendly smile, freckles, a few pimples, and had not yet lost my teenaged round face and plumpness. I had never longed for fair beauty, although I did desperately want to be one of those pale, dark-haired girls that poetic men desired, not yet knowing that women easily mythologised very often become trapped in other people's stories.

~

I've been wondering if my friends are imaginary, especially the ones I mythologise. I didn't think I had a strong tendency to mythologise – I have always scorned the male mythologising of women – but I see now that I did it not just to Barbara, but also to Jane, and to Gina.

They each, from the first moment I met them, became an idealised figure, a perfect friend. It's not as if they had similar personalities – they are quite different from each other – but in each case it was as if I had a pre-existing model or schema in my brain, and when I saw them, I fitted them into my schema. The Imagined Friend became real, and I loved each one immediately, not realising that I had made the frame which allowed me to see a certain picture of them and obscured the rest. They were each entirely beautiful, shining and true; all else outside my frame was invisible to me.

The schema must have been made from all my connections to family and childhood friends, and the friends I'd read about in books, and my own sense of who I was. But, like everyone else, I'm also biologically programmed for friendship – the evolutionary model argues it is necessary for our survival that we are valued by more than just our family. We need a larger community of allies to get through the jungle alive. Even animals need to be part of a group. So how do we select who will be on our side?

The neuroscience of friendships – a new area of research – suggests that the central connection between friends is that they share a similar schema of themselves, and of others. It means I am friends with people who value the same things in another person as I do. If I value insight in a friend, it means she also values it in me, and we also see and value the same qualities in others. There is something doubling in this idea – together we are more than what we are alone. The singularity of our existence, the aloneness of it, each consciousness wrapped up in skin and bone like a weird jangling puppet show, is transformed into a warm human reality as you and I recognise each other.

Friends also share similar versions of the world. When the neuroscientists scan the brains of friends, the same areas light up more often than people who are not friends, even if the non-friends are talking about the same topics. If I am talking about books or politics or my children with a friend, our brains light up together, two electrochemical lamps shining golden luminescence for each other, more than when I discuss the same topics with a colleague. Together, you and I not only acknowledge the reality of each other, but of our world. It is really there, that stand of gum trees, that mad leader, that childhood we told each other about, it all exists, *because we agree that it does.*

It is strengthened by the way friends affect each other's bodies – we all affect each other's bodies – but according to the research, friends can more strongly affect heart rate, blood pressure, sleep. Friends get inside your body, no matter how imaginary they have been. It appears to be due to the *mirror* effect; the same neurones light up in our brains when we watch someone act as when we do it ourselves. When my friend breathes in, moves her body languidly, when she lifts an eyebrow, mirror neurones light up in my brain as if my body too, were breathing in, stretching, lifting a quizzical eyebrow. She lives in a mirror inside my body, and I live in her. That is how we both know we are here.

~

When I think of Barbara now, several decades later, there are so many conflicting images. The earliest images are of her sitting on the floor with her books of herbal lore and the I Ching and Tarot cards spread out around her. Her mother had been a herbalist and psychic, so Barbara was already steeped in an alternative culture that I had only recently stumbled into with Jane. Barbara knew about the healing properties of chamomile, comfrey, sage, slippery elm, golden seal, ginseng, and all kinds of herbs I'd never heard of. She had jars of dried leaves and barks on a plank shelf, and tiny glass phials of homeopathic and Bach Flower remedies which she dispensed to anyone who had colds or stomach aches, or was pregnant. She was a vegetarian and knew how to cook dried beans, lentils, tofu and miso, how to add brewer's yeast for Vitamin B, and how to gather dandelion greens or grow silverbeet and beetroot for iron.

Barbara taught me to use the I Ching, both with coins and with yarrow sticks, and I used it for years, right up until both my sons were grown. In fact, I gained something of a small reputation myself for interpreting the strange poetry of the Chinese method of divination, but then I became scornful of irrationality and let it all go. Once my children had left, I suppose I didn't have such a deep need for knowing the underground forces that could damage my family. Barbara also used the Tarot at times, but that didn't interest me, I thought it was just a game. I preferred the mysterious words of the I Ching, the way meaning was revealed as I contemplated its poetic images.

While we were at Bellevue Road, Barbara started doing tai chi before anyone else had heard of it. I remember walking up the street and Barbara explaining it to me. 'It restores the natural balance of the body. It helps you flow with the forces of nature, be in tune with everything around you,' she said. With that memory is a slight flicker of resentment. How did she always know things before anyone else did?

Barbara also talked about Dave. She said the affair was over, but she kept slipping away to see him. She told me with a kind of delicious naughtiness, how she couldn't help herself. I felt sorry for Keith, but I listened to all her stories, enjoying being the confidante, just as I had with Mary Dunn and her stories of her mother, and with Jane and her secrets about Johanna. I wasn't exactly the handmaiden, I think there was more equality than that, but especially with Barbara, the exchange between us was not quite reciprocal. I didn't see it at the time, but I felt some sense of imbalance and attributed it to Barbara's beauty.

At that time, the men, mainly Keith and Anthony, were organising a move to the country, to Coromandel Peninsula southeast of Auckland. It was crown land, the first granted on lease by the New Zealand government at the beginning of the Ohu scheme, a plan to enable communal living in the country. Anthony named it the Sunburst Ohu – but everyone simply called it The Land. Before the move, I returned to Australia intending to work and save from the higher wages paid back home so I could travel and see the rest of the world, and Jane stayed at Bellevue Road with the hippies.

But once back in Australia, I realised I had lost touch with my other school friends, and I didn't have anywhere to live except back on the farm with my parents. After a month of indecision, I returned to New Zealand to find that Bellevue Road was breaking up. Jane had moved out to her own flat and Barbara and all the Hokianga hippies were getting ready to move. Anthony was not entangled with Karen anymore and quickly became entangled with me. It meant that I became part of the group that piled into the green truck and finally drove down to the Coromandel and along Gentle Annie Road to The Land.

We parked on one side of the Rangihau Stream, then clambered over the rocks and waded through the thigh-deep water to the other side. There it was, all regrowth ti-tree and ponga, with no electricity, no shelter, not even a clearing in the forest. We stood there in our colourful clothes, ten or twelve of us that first day, smoking joints and laughing excitedly, overwhelmed by what we had done. Then the men cut and dug in ti-tree stakes and threw up a stolen railway tarpaulin to sleep under the first night. The women lit a fire and we cooked rice in an iron pot and stir-fried vegetables in a wok. We were back at the beginning of time, all in our early twenties or younger.

There were other women on the land: Maori Lily – as distinct from Lily Bean on another commune – Kirsty and Lynne, each of whom had small children, and dainty Marguerite who visited a few times but didn't stay. But Barbara and I were a little apart from the others. Over the next few months we sat together and talked while the men dashed around with land-clearing machinery; we cooked over the open fire together, Barbara showed me how to make bread in a cast-iron camp oven that we buried in the ash and coals; we planted herbs and vegetables when the soil was dug over; we threw the I Ching and interpreted its meaning; we embroidered clothes with rainbows and suns; we had an acid trip together. She told me each time she went to Auckland she slipped away to see Dave. I played with her daughter, Michelle, and read her stories, and noticed I was the only one without a child.

After a few months we each had our own huts made of canvas and ti-tree. Anthony and I built ours down a narrow track on the bank of the Rangihau, and I filled our tent-house with Indian scarves, cushions, a small ceramic Buddha, incense, and baskets for our clothes. Lily told me she always peeped in even when we weren't there because she loved to see our cave shimmering golden under the orangey stolen tarp. There, naturally, I became pregnant, and Barbara made me raspberry-leaf tea with honey and dark herbal mixtures full of iron.

One day, five-year-old Michelle said to me anxiously, 'Don't give your baby away, will you?'

I told Barbara and a look of anguish went across her face. 'She remembers I gave my baby away. I couldn't do anything else.' Her eyes glistened with tears.

'I know. I said I will keep my baby for sure. And I told her another nice woman wanted your baby so much you let her look after him, but you still loved him. And I told her you will keep her forever and ever.'

One weekend, Dave came down to the land and the Dave–Barbara–Keith triangle came flinging out into the open like a jagged three-cornered weapon. Dave slept with Barbara in the perfect tiny house Keith had made for her. It was a one-person A-frame high on the hill, looking down over the river to the forested mountain on the other side of the valley. It was already filled with Barbara's embroidered scarlet and emerald Indian cushions and smelled of sandalwood incense. A love nest.

Keith slept in the truck by himself.

After that, Barbara went back to Auckland with Dave. The group began to come and go from The Land. There was no money – we had often relied on Barbara's single-parent pension to buy food – and eventually we all ended up back in Auckland, ostensibly to earn money to return to The Land. Anthony and I moved into a large terrace house at the top of Queen Street, the main street of Auckland, just a few houses down from Karangahape Road. Marguerite and Harry and Barbara and Dave were there already – and Keith.

Barbara and Dave had the large front room with gold curtained bay windows looking over the street; Keith had a poky room upstairs. Whenever I walked past him on the stairs, the pain vibrated off him so powerfully I could feel it entering me like a serrated shadow. I couldn't fathom why he was living in the same house as Barbara, why he was doing it to himself, the constant stab of watching her glow with extraordinary beauty in the light of her new love. Perhaps he loved her so intensely that the exquisite pain of seeing her with another man was better than not seeing her at all.

Anthony and I were married when I was six months pregnant. We didn't believe in marriage, but I didn't want my parents to be upset about me 'living in sin' and Anthony didn't mind going through the ceremony to reassure them. One day, after I came home from my job as a housemaid, and Anthony came home from his job with the council rubbish collection department, we had a bath together, and then I dressed in a second-hand dress I borrowed from Barbara. It was dusty pink, soft and flowing, loose enough to fit over my neatly rounded belly. Michelle was a dainty, shabby flower girl in a second-hand pink velvet dress with a heart-shaped patch on it where it was torn, and Barbara and Keith were our witnesses. All the people from The Land and Jane and my mother and older sister came to the party afterwards at Anthony's parents' place and his brother took photos on his instamatic camera. One of Anthony's aunts gave us nappies for a wedding present.

Around this time most of the group from The Land, including Anthony, began following a young Indian guru, and attended meetings, Satsang, in the ashram in Parnell. I piled into the back of the green truck with everyone else and went to Satsang because I wanted to do what everyone else was doing. My intellect rebelled against most of it, but that was just my 'monkey-mind' I was told, and so along with everyone else I had the meditation techniques revealed to me. I sat in Barbara's room and practised meditation with her in the evenings.

I often hung about in her room because Dave and his friends had taken over the lounge room as the rehearsal space for Hello Sailor, the band that would make them nationally famous. The lounge was crammed with speakers, amplifiers, electric guitars and leads, and there was nowhere to sit unless under a microphone, so Barbara and I sat on cushions on the floor in her room and talked. Sometimes we went out together, usually to Cook Street markets on a Saturday morning. One day we each bought an Indian wall-hanging, embroidered and sewn with tiny mirrors – I still have mine – and I noticed she chose the more delicately beautiful one.

Another day we went to see a naturopath, one of the very few at that time, who had a practice in an arcade at the bottom of Queen Street. He also ran a small college, teaching herbal and homeopathic medicine and massage, and we thought we might learn massage from him. We went up the stairs and into his reception room together and the naturopath greeted us both, but after that, I may as well have not been there. He was an older man, to us ancient, possibly around fifty, greying, fit and slim. He looked only at Barbara and talked only to her except when I asked him a direct question. We had a short practice massage each, using each other as a body to learn on. Barbara practised on me under his instruction, but when it was Barbara's turn to be the 'body', he demonstrated the strokes on her while I watched. We laughed about it as we went back down the stairs. He was so obvious.

I wasn't going back there. Beside the fact that I didn't like being ignored, I realised I didn't want to be a healer of any sort. I already knew I didn't really like looking after other people and wondered how I would manage with the baby who was starting to kick inside me. I thought Barbara would not go back either, and was surprised when she said she was going to enrol in the course.

'But he's a creep,' I protested

'That's all right. I can deal with him,' and she smiled a knowing, naughty smile that had become more frequent since she had been with Dave. She had the same smile when she told me that Dave had written a song called 'Gutter Black' that became a hit for Hello Sailor. The second stanza began, *Barbara O'Reilly / She come into my house / Trouble, trouble, trouble.*

'It's me,' she said, unnecessarily. She smiled the smile, and I thought with a pang of certainty, no-one will ever write a song about me.

And then there was another conversation that I can't geographically pinpoint. Sometimes I see it happening in the front room at Queen Street, both of us sitting on Barbara's cushions in front of the long gold curtains, but other times it's in the bare, desolate lounge room in Ponsonby where Barbara lived after everything had fallen apart. It makes a difference where it happened. If it was beforehand at Queen Street, it was Barbara making a deliberate choice for destruction, if it was in Ponsonby, she was merely defending what had already happened.

What is certain is the look on Barbara's face as she spoke, defiant and rebellious, and something else I find difficult to name. A kind of delicious pleasure – in what?

'I don't want to be good. Everyone has thought I am good. I don't want to be what people think I am. I want to be bad,' she said.

Anthony and I went back to the Coromandel in July when I was seven months pregnant. The one-room hand-built house had been more or less finished before we all left for Auckland a few months earlier and was ready to live in. There was still no running water or electricity, so we chopped wood and carried water and lay in front of the open fire and made love around my growing belly. We gardened, we took turns cooking our dinner on the fire, and in the evenings, read by the light of a Coleman lantern. After two months of cool fresh air and simple days, we hitchhiked to Auckland and I gave birth to a golden-haired son a month before my twenty-first birthday. We stayed in Auckland but moved to a smaller house next to Lily and her boyfriend, Bruce. They too had a new baby and sometimes Lily and I looked after each other's babies. One day I came home from a trip to the shops to see my golden baby sucking on Lily's long brown breasts and thought it was the most perfect thing I'd seen.

'He was hungry,' she said.

I didn't see Barbara as much by now. She was being drawn into an edgier rock'n'roll world, going out several nights a week and staying in bed half the day. She took Michelle to school each day, but even she knew what her mother did. 'After you take me to school, you go home and get back into bed with Dave, don't you?' she said one day.

Luckily for my baby, I took to mothering and enjoyed that year of intense symbiosis between my body and his; the throb of breast milk flowing, the tenderness of his soft limbs, the feel of his hard head on my shoulder, his body asleep on mine, breathing infinity into my being. It didn't feel like a disruption of my identity, only an extension.

I did see more of Jane though, now that I was back in Auckland. We met at my house or hers – it was before people started meeting at cafés all the time – and I brought my baby with me. We talked like we always had, but things were changing. She worked for a computer company and had become fascinated with them. I knew nothing of computers – this was 1975 – and was dedicated to all that was natural. I felt disappointed in Jane. I wanted her to sing and play guitar and draw and write songs like she used to when we were at school. She was the one who had shown me the alternative life of art; she couldn't leave me alone in it. I hadn't started yet, but I knew I would.

'We will all have one of these computers in our own home one day,' she told me.

How out of touch with the times, I thought. That won't happen. We are turning to nature, not to machines.

She told me about the people in her office and we both caught the giggles when she told me about a woman she worked with who had said she felt 'all unnecessary' when she meant sexually aroused. I told Anthony and we adopted it. Even now I sometimes say, 'I feel all unnecessary' when I am aroused, and whenever I say it I think of Jane. It's a private joke that connects me to Anthony and to her.

Jane had also joined a small esoteric sect called Eckankar, based on Eastern mysticism. I read the books on it because she gave them to me, but it seemed both too ordered and too far out to me. It elaborated the world of the spirit almost as if it were another solid geography, and I couldn't accept that that sort of detail could be known. Jane became more involved with the group and its members became her friends. She started meeting them on the weekends at their homes, not just at their spiritual gatherings. I met her, went for walks, went to the beach with her, but it felt as if I were losing her and I felt a little bereft each time I saw her.

Still, one day when we were having a lemongrass tea together – Anthony and I had moved by then to Devonport on the other side of Auckland Harbour where we lived in an old house with Keith – she said, 'I am so glad you still see me, that we are still friends. Most people when they have a man, they forget about their friends. You've not done that.'

I was moved by her confirmation of our connection and by her letting me know that I meant as much to her as she did to me.

I said, we will always be friends, and meant it with my whole heart.

I keep trying to rein in this period of time as it threatens to take over the whole story like a wild vine climbing over forgotten fences – I lived in New Zealand for only four years after all – but each time I go to the fragments of memory, the details of friendships expand like the little crumbs of paper that Proust described being dropped in a porcelain bowl of water, 'which until then are without character or form, but the moment they become wet, stretch themselves and bend, take on colour and distinctive shape, become flowers or houses or people.' His image exactly conveys what it feels like to me, the way a memory that has become reduced, small and folded can, if the right 'moisture' is applied, unfurl itself into ever-expanding scenes of the utmost intricacy.

Time, too, concertinas outwards. It was a period of my life when so much happened it felt like eons – I met Anthony, I had a baby, I started at university, I had a part-time job as a nude model for a group of artists, I lived in a commune and at least five different other houses – it felt eternal, we were eternal, but then I look back and find with astonishment that it was only a few years. I keep thinking of *The Autobiography of Alice B Toklas* where Gertrude Stein says she and Picasso were chatting about the various things that had happened, 'and one of them said, but all that could not have happened in one year, oh said the other, my dear, you forget we were young then and we did a great deal in a year.' We did a great deal in a year, too. Some of it was dangerous and even though we were immortal, not everyone survived unscathed.

Everyone, or at least everyone I knew, took drugs of various kinds in those days. Out of curiosity and a desire not to miss out on anything, I tried everything that came my way. There were always large amounts of marijuana, which I smoked most days, some hallucinogenic mushrooms, hash cookies often, coke once or twice, half a dozen acid trips, and a couple of times, heroin. After the two hard-drug experiences, both of them pleasurable, I knew not to have any more. I had no desire for annihilation, but it wasn't the same for Barbara. Or maybe that's unfair, Barbara probably didn't desire destruction either, but she did like living nearer the edge.

Hello Sailor were starting to make a name for themselves in Auckland and there was a buzz of excitement at their pub gigs. Barbara was sharing in the excitement, and in the heroin that swirled in a kind of dark glamour around them. It was beginning to take hold of her; she wasn't just dabbling anymore. We still visited each other – I went to her house mostly – and we talked about our men and about our other friends from The Land, but we were slipping into different worlds. I started at university when my baby was eighteen months old, enrolling in sixteenth-century and twentieth-century literature, as well as developmental psychology and educational philosophy. I had essays to write on Milton and Thomas Pynchon and Plato's approach to education; Barbara was going to gigs and scoring drugs and avoiding arrest – and working in a massage parlour. She had finished the massage course and got a job at the parlour, which was in a back street in Ponsonby, still a poor inner-city area at that time. I wanted to believe Barbara was just giving therapeutic massages, but one day she told me about the men she massaged having hard-ons.

'I give them a hand-job,' she said in a confiding and oddly pleased voice. 'Just to finish. I feel sorry for them.'

I was disconcerted but tried to hide it, just as I had when Peta had naughtily said she liked *La Dolce Vita* when I was twelve.

'There's nothing wrong with that, is there?' Barbara asked in a slightly defensive tone, and I realised she did want my approval.

'No, there's nothing wrong with it,' I said. But I couldn't get rid of the image of Barbara's hand slipping up and down some sweaty middle-aged businessman's dick. It didn't fit with the image of the White Goddess surrounded by her books of herbal lore, her thoughtful gaze as she threw the I Ching, her vegie garden on The Land, her bread-baking in the ashes.

One day when I visited, she showed me a short iron bar – where the hell had she got it? – that she kept in her Indian patchwork shoulder bag. She laughed as she showed me, but with a disturbing hard look in her eyes. She was doing some low-level dealing, just to keep herself in drug money, but even at that level there were dangerous people.

I went home to Anthony. 'I don't think I know how to be friends with someone who keeps an iron bar in her bag,' I said.

We were leaving anyway. I still wanted to be a writer and had found a university in Sydney where I could study. Anthony and I had talked about it for months and decided to move to Australia. I said goodbye to all the people from The Land, to Barbara whom I now knew to be an addict, and to Jane. With Anthony and our two year old, I left for Sydney.

I hoped Jane was coming back to Australia too, but soon after I left she fell in love with an American and moved to California. She was still working in computers – it wasn't yet called IT – and made quite a lot of money while I subsisted on a student income and scraps of part-time work. She and her husband lived on a boat in Los Angeles for a while and sailed around the Pacific. She visited her mother and the rest of her family every few years and she always caught up with me in Sydney, and then at my place in the Blue Mountains where we moved after I finished my degree. I had started writing books and had one published, but still lived on nothing much. We talked about life, the universe and everything like we did in the old days, and it always felt real, but the visits were too fleeting to knit our lives into each other's.

Jane divorced her first American husband – he had turned out to be controlling and manipulative – married again and moved to Florida. They set up a trucking business and Jane drove a huge, articulated semi-trailer back and forth across the States.

'I love the feeling of being high up, driving this giant creature across the vastness,' she said, and sent me a photograph of herself wearing boots and little shorts, standing next to her rig, looking both dainty and sexy. Jane was a truckie! I felt as if I couldn't fathom her anymore. I was doing what we had both expected I would when we were teenagers; she had become an unexpected and original mix of things. I think my life could have been predicted from what was observable when we were together as teenage girls, hers could not.

She still followed Eckankar and had made Eck friends in the States. Then she told me she had started writing and sent me a manuscript, an historical romance, which I felt ill-equipped to critique. It was nerve-wracking to write notes on, at first because I didn't know the genre very well, but more because she was my friend. I knew exactly what it felt like to be told, 'It's not there yet', and that's what I had to say to her.

Jane started a local newspaper in her town in Florida. She said she had always wanted to run a newspaper, which I hadn't known. It was a good local paper – she sent me several copies – and she loved doing it. I sent her copies of my books when they were published. Sometimes I talked about going to New York and meeting up with her there. She encouraged me and we both said it would be brilliant to meet up there for a week or so, but secretly I wondered if we had a week's worth of things to talk about. I didn't go to New York.

Jane's mother died a few years ago and she has not returned to Australia since. I still love her and I believe she loves me, but the truth is that after those intense seven years between sixteen and twenty-three, our lives diverged. I wonder if I saw her the way she was, or the way I wanted her to be; the friend who shifted my life to the tangent it has taken ever since.

Anthony and I went back to Auckland when we could afford to, not often, to see his family and visit our friends. I always visited Barbara. At first, she was still a junkie – she had long broken up with Dave – and when I visited there was usually not even tea to drink. She seemed to live on chocolate, and, unusually for an addict, put on weight. She came to stay with us once in Sydney, probably because Hello Sailor was there at the time, and we went to see them play at the Coogee Bay Hotel. She told me years later that Dave was the love of her life, even after he had married someone else and had children.

Then – I don't know the exact date – after she returned to Auckland, Barbara was arrested for dealing and went to jail for a year. One of her other friends looked after Michelle until Barbara was released. I saw her after her jail sentence and she was not 'using' anymore, but she wasn't repentant, at least not for herself and her life. She did admit that she regretted not being there for Michelle when she needed her. There was an edge to her voice and in her eyes, and I knew she'd had experiences that set her apart from me, that made me look naive and sheltered to her. I think that had always been the case, but now the gap was too wide.

After that I didn't see her for many years. I had written more books and had another child and when the youngest was fifteen, we took him on a holiday to New Zealand to show him some of the places of our youth, which of course did not interest him. After driving to the Coromandel Peninsula and walking across the Rangihau Stream we drove to Auckland and

I went to see Barbara on my own. She was in her mid-forties, overweight, and her face had aged more than mine. I have never been beautiful, but from my late twenties to early forties I had a sparkle that could draw a gaze. At that time I was slender, had a short cap of golden-red hair, blue eyes, good cheekbones, and an idiosyncratic arty way of dressing. I looked at Barbara and thought, here and now, I am better looking than you. I felt ashamed thinking it, even at that moment, but also felt a shifting of the balance, a relieving schadenfreude.

It didn't last long. A few days later, Anthony and I visited Keith who lived on a section of land north of Auckland where he was building a house. By then he lived with another woman whose name I don't remember. The topic of Barbara came up as we had our lunch at his place.

'She was so beautiful, Barbara was,' I said. I knew I sounded saccharine, false.

Keith looked at me with his piercing, scornful eyes. 'Barbara *is* so beautiful,' he said. 'She is always the most beautiful woman in the room, wherever she is. She always will be. Anywhere. Any time. No contest.'

I reddened. He had seen what I was thinking and put me brutally in my place. I would never be anything to look at compared to her.

~

Scientists studying the neuroscience of beauty have found the same areas of the brain, the anterior insular and the medial orbitofrontal cortex, light up when we see a beautiful face, look at a beautiful painting, hear a beautiful piece of music, feel the beauty of nature, even when we appreciate a beautiful mathematical formulae. It supports the idea that beauty, as we perceive it, exists as a reaction in the brain. It was also measurable; the more beautiful we think something is, the more neural activity in those areas.

I know only the barest outlines of the neuroscience of beauty, but I've often noticed my reaction to beauty and wondered why it means so much to me. The effect of the beauty of nature is obvious, the way it bathes all the cells of my body in light, but human beauty?

I've noticed that when I see another woman, I subliminally assess whether she is more, or less, or the same as myself in terms of beauty. I don't mean to do it – I don't like it – but it happens. The results of the assessment? Truthfully, I'd say I have been in the vast middle that no-one points or laughs at, but no-one writes poems or songs about either. Why it matters is that it influences my friendships, who I am drawn to. The fact that I like to gaze, to admire, means I am attracted to beauty.

I once said to Peter, a writing colleague in the Blue Mountains for many years who became a dear friend, 'All my friends have a degree of beauty. They all have faces I like to gaze at. I don't have any plain friends.'

'Hmmm?' he said, with an unconvinced look. Peter is an extraordinarily gentle man and could hardly look disapproving if he tried, but I saw the faint shadow in his eyes.

I was embarrassed. I wanted to mutter, perhaps I did, 'Well, I think they are beautiful.' But I wasn't trying to say that beauty was in the eye of the beholder, I was trying to confess that I valued beauty, that I loved looking at my friends.

I know I'm not alone in valuing physical appearance. There is emphasis on beauty of all kinds in The Epic; the beauty of

Gilgamesh himself, the beauty of jewellery and clothes and hair and objects. 'When the gods created Gilgamesh, they gave him a perfect body. Shamash the glorious sun endowed him with beauty ... the great gods made his beauty perfect.'

After his battle with Humbaba, Gilgamesh washed his long locks and 'flung his hair back on his shoulders', put on his royal robes and his crown. The goddess, Ishtar, saw him and fell for him immediately. She said she would give him a 'chariot of lapis lazuli and gold, with wheels of gold and horns of copper'. His beauty drew love and desire and beautiful objects towards him.

Later on, as he searched in despair to overcome mortality, he became tired and worn out, his body and face were thin, his cheeks drawn and he wore dirty animal skins. Before he returned home to the city of Uruk, there is a detailed passage where his body is washed, his long hair is 'made as clean as snow in the water', new clothes are given to him and a ribbon is tied on his forehead.

Long ago, in the oldest written story, before glossy magazines and social media, before the constant flow of perfect images into our ordinary lives, physical beauty – and clothes – mattered. I'm not saying it's fair, but I don't mind. Beauty will be given love and the job and riches and friendship and pretty things, and will be the heroine of almost every story. I doubt the medial orbitofrontal cortex will stop influencing perceptions any time soon.

It's clear physical beauty is more important to me than wisdom says it should be. The fact is, I've always secretly thought wisdom was wrong. It seems to me there is something essential in beauty of any kind; that it is necessary. Human beauty is falsely mythologised, it makes the rest of us bridle at its unfair power, it is used to sell everything and anything, but still, we are drawn to it and can only resist it in bitterness. I have never thought it worth resisting. Barbara was granted the random gift of beauty, a gift that has been honoured since the beginning of storytelling, and I don't want to make less of it. She was my beautiful friend.

Eight

Some of my friends are imaginary. Well, they have existed, but I have never met them in the flesh, and they are no longer alive. Michel de Montaigne, for example. He lived nearly five hundred years ago in his chateau near Bergerac in southwest France, and yet, whenever I read his *Essays*, especially when I read him day after day, the feeling grows in me that I know him, personally. It's a living connection, not intellectual, not rarefied, but in the heart. I feel that I really do know him in person – and that I love him as a dear friend.

That is, probably, normal enough. I imagine others feel that they *know*, are friends with, long-dead authors, but what is strange is that I feel, equally, that *he* knows *me*. He understands me, he cares about me, he shrugs at my flaws, he delights in my insights, he enjoys my company.

It comes, I think, from the intimacy of his writing. He confides in me, he is honest and open and direct. He knows that I will get what he is saying, and he gets what I am saying. He values my opinions and understands my experiences. He is occasionally irritated by me, but tries not to let it show. He knows that I don't agree with everything he says – about women for example – and that I am as aware of his mistakes and foolishness as he is of mine. He knows I wear a bra not because I need one but to make my small breasts seem larger; I know he wears a little velvet hat all the time because he is hiding the fact that he's prematurely bald.

We are friends. Perhaps of any of my friends he sees who I am, admires what is worthy and let's go what is not. He doesn't even mind if I am sometimes ridiculous.

~

One year, instead of meeting up with Gina while I was in Paris for the writing course, we met in Lacapelle-Biron, a small village in the southwest of France. I had tried to arrange a group from the days when we had all gone to the Wamberal holiday house in the summer, but as it turned out, only four could make it to France: Anthony, Gina, Cathy, who was a photographer, and me.

We stayed in an old farmhouse owned by Vicky, the friend I'd met during the year I lived in France. Vicky had lived there as a single parent, bringing up her two children, working on the fish farm next door – now an adventure park – and trying to make ends meet. She had let me use the farmhouse to get away and write several times in the quiet of the Lot-et-Garonne. That was the idea this time as well – each of us would work on our projects – writing or photography – in the mornings, and in the afternoons we would hang out together, walking, exploring, reading, cooking.

It was a two-storey stone house on a few hectares of meadows, a kilometre or so outside the village. There was a stream, the Lède, at the bottom of the unruly garden, woods with deer beyond the stream and out the front a road leading down the Gavaudun valley to a ruined chateau. The farmhouse had four bedrooms, if you counted the attic room with mattresses, so there was plenty of room for everyone to work separately. It was a sociable, vaguely shabby house, crammed with books – Vicky was a great reader – and an old dining table that had fitted more than a dozen people around it many times in its life.

It was an unbalanced foursome I see now. Anthony and I, the couple, were a slightly separate unit; Cathy was an old Blue Mountains friend of mine, she was friendly towards but not particular friends with Anthony; Gina was friends with Anthony and me, but had only met Cathy once. I was the lynchpin, but wasn't aware of it, and didn't register that my closeness to each person didn't mean they were close to each other.

That might have been why we started playing at being the Mitfords. We didn't use their actual names, just the idea of a wilful, arty, entitled bunch of people swanning about the south of France. Gina arrived with the game after spending a couple of weeks with an actor friend whose Italian family owned a house in Tuscany.

'And now, dearest, here I am in the south of France having a house party with another delightful set of writers and artists.'

Her Mitford name was Winter-Monet, mine was Clarissa, Cathy was Bobbie St Clair, and Anthony, our chauffeur, was Boydie. Winter-Monet was the younger sister who did whatever she pleased; Bobbie was rather boyish and took pictures; Clarissa presented herself as correct and keeping up appearances, but in fact, she was having an affair with the chauffeur. We elaborated on it, laughing, whenever we were all together, and especially when what we were doing looked like a golden idyll; sitting in a medieval village square with a glass of wine, lying on the thick grass reading by the stream, riding bikes through the wheat fields; it was perfectly acceptable for the Mitfords to be living this life.

We settled in to work though, all of us. Anthony had not written much for years because he had a full-time job but was now working on a collection of short stories, I was writing a book, Cathy was selecting and arranging photographs – she was preparing an exhibition – and Gina, I think, was working on a performance about the French actress, Simone Signoret. We went to work in our rooms each morning, came together around eleven for coffee on the back step, then went back to work. Just before lunch, one of us rode to the village on Vicky's old bike to buy two baguettes and then I prepared lunch – cheeses, saucisson, fruit – and brought it out on a tray to the outside table under the pergola with grape vines curling over it. In the afternoons we often went for a long walk together through the woods and fields or explored one of the medieval towns and chateaux scattered around the countryside. In the evenings, Anthony, Gina and Cathy took turns to cook dinners in the large kitchen; magret de canard, tian de lapin, green beans, potatoes roasted in duck fat, fig tart. Afterwards, we sat around and took turns sharing our work – Anthony, Gina and I reading passages aloud, Cathy showing us photographic images on her screen. It was idyllic, privileged, of course it was, but there was a ridiculous little worm in the kingdom.

It didn't manifest itself right away. Early on, all four of us had a perfect day visiting Biron Castle, built on a hill a few kilometres from Vicky's farmhouse. It could be seen from every direction, a romantic watercolour with towers and turrets and parapets, becoming more magnificent as you drove towards it. Anthony and I had been there several times on other visits and were proprietorial as we revealed our very own castle. I was pleased when Gina was excited by the spaces inside, the courtyard flanked on one side by a chapel and a colonnaded belvedere looking out over the valley on the other – she said it would make an ideal site for a play.

'The actors on the belvedere, with the valley behind as a backdrop. The audience would be seated in the courtyard.'

'What would you present?'

'Shakespeare, maybe *Hamlet*.'

And then she started planning it in detail as if it were going to happen and we all listened. These spaces would be the wings, here the ghost of Hamlet's father would appear, and here is where the travelling players would arrive. While she talked, I really believed it would happen.

Another afternoon, it was mine and Anthony's anniversary. We drove to see the prehistoric drawings in the Les Éyzies caves north of the Dordogne River. All of us went into the Grotte des Combarelles with a French guide who pointed out an ochre painting of a male deer gently licking the forehead of a female deer. 'You see,' he said in French, 'we think the tribesmen of fifteen thousand years ago who made these paintings were very different from us, but they have the same feelings of tenderness as we do.'

I was thrilled with this, it's just the sort of evidence of a continuity of human feeling that reassures me, and I talked about it excitedly when we came out. Back down the hill at the small shop and museum, Cathy and Gina seemed to be plotting something, but I didn't see what. Afterwards, they gave Anthony and me an anniversary present, wrapped up with a greeting card – it was a reproduction of the ancient deer painting, a sensitive copy in the same ochre tones. I had it framed, and it is still above our bed. Whenever I look at it, and despite what has happened since, memory re-presents the pleasure of that day.

On another day there was a conversation at the big table in the farmhouse, which at the time seemed to be of no great significance. In fact, I forgot it entirely until Gina brought it up several months later.

What did Gina say? A remark about her mother letting her down in some way?

What did I say? Something like, 'It will be all right.' Whatever it was, it suggested that the issue with her mother was no big deal. I didn't notice I had said something wrong at the time.

But I did know something was awry. I noticed it when we all went walking together in the afternoons that followed. There were several narrow paths near the farmhouse; one that led past the back of the village into the woods and up as far as the castle, then across the road back into the woods; another went through the village and across several farms before heading into a dappled wood of oak, chestnut, birch. Each time, because there were four of us on a narrow path, we fell into pairs that shifted a little and then became a pattern, Anthony and Gina ahead, Cathy and me behind. Anthony and Gina were often having intense conversations. Sometimes Cathy glanced at me and I remembered the French Boy's eyes glancing at me. I wanted to explain that I didn't mind, that I didn't feel threatened, but saying anything would have made it sound as if I did. I tried to act as if I was utterly unconscious of their conversation and Cathy's glances. Of course, it produced an atmosphere, a strange disjunction. The more relaxed and cool I tried to look, the weirder it became, but I told myself the atmosphere was all in my own head, that no-one else noticed.

Then, towards the end of our stay, Gina needed to buy a train ticket to return to Paris. Anthony, being the chauffeur – the rest of us were unwilling to drive on the 'wrong' side of the road – offered to drive her to the nearest town with a railway office. I had some shopping to do in nearby Monpazier, so they dropped me off on the way. It was going to take half an hour to collect the tickets. Over an hour later I was still standing in the medieval square, fuming. I had bought the fruit, vegetables, cheeses and bread, sat on a bench for a while, stood up and wandered around, sat on the bench again. Where the hell were they?

It was another forty minutes before I saw them walking towards me across the square.

'What the fuck took so long?' I didn't try to be polite. Clarissa had disappeared.

'We couldn't get tickets there, it was closed. We had to go on to Fumel, to the station. It was a hassle for me as well.' Anthony's tone was irritated but placating. Gina stood back a little. I snapped back at him, then I suddenly realised I should behave better and shrugged.

'Okay. It was a bloody long time to wait. Sorry.'

We got in the car and drove back to the farmhouse. I made up for being rude by being extra sweet to Anthony.

The next day, Anthony and I drove Gina to catch the train at Fumel. I acted lighthearted, but the atmosphere that had been seeping through most of the stay was thick in the car.

When we arrived at the station and got out, Anthony hauled Gina's bag from the boot. He gave her a hug and got back in the car. I hugged her and then said, 'See you back home.'

Gina muttered something as she walked away. Her head was facing away from me, so I wasn't quite sure but it was something like, 'We'll see about that.' I felt a nasty thud in my heart as I got back in the car, but I didn't say anything to Anthony until later.

'What was that about?' he asked, after I told him.

'I don't know,' I said.

Anthony is my truest friend, the one who delights in my strengths and who accepts my absurd flaws and limitations, but he is excluded from my inventory of friends because he is, at the same time, other than a friend. He is disqualified under Montaigne's 'no other traffic' rules. With Anthony there is plenty of other traffic: intimacy, sexual passion, the bringing up of children, the running of a household.

Montaigne does allow that it could be possible to combine sex and friendship but, he says he has not met a woman who is capable of the intense knot of true friendship. It's the opposite of the current belief that women are much better able to maintain friendships, at least between themselves, although I suppose it depends on what one thinks friendship is. Montaigne, being uncharacteristically ruthless, reckons most of what we call friendships 'are no more than acquaintances and familiar relationships bound by some chance or suitability'. Friendship, to him, is the one he had with Étienne de la Boétie, the only one in his life where souls are mingled and confounded, where they are one.

If you press me to say why I loved him, I feel that it cannot be expressed except by replying: Because it was him: because it was me. Meditating this union there was, beyond all my reasoning, beyond all that I can say specifically about it, some inexplicable force of destiny.

It makes me wonder if any of my dear friendships qualify under his beautiful criteria. My friends have inspired me, have poured energy into my being, awakened ideas, uncovered feelings, led me into new geographies of the self, forced me to act, extended who I am. Without them I would be less, but I have not experienced inexpressible union with them. I wonder if the fact that de la Boétie died young, early in their friendship, cast a warm, honeyed light of memory over the short time they knew each other, obliterating the shadows and separations in their souls, making it all glow with unnatural beauty. Memory can do that.

~

When I left Auckland and moved to Sydney, I was twenty-three years old and already felt I had left one life behind to start again. Time and place appear to be shuffling, even though I am trying for a chronological unfolding of the friendships that have come into my life. Most of them slip forward into other times and places and in trying to trace each friendship the threads overlap and tangle. Some threads fall away, new ones are added, but more than that, from my perspective in the powerful autocratic present, the past and future blend, become part of the same sequence.

Anthony and I moved into a large old house in Spofforth

Street, on the north side of Sydney Harbour in mid-1978. In the six months since moving from New Zealand we had already lived in a garage flat, followed by a small share house with mould growing on the kitchen wall, in Waters Road, Neutral Bay. One day while I was at lectures, Anthony had set out with Chris – who later married one of my brothers – to find another, drier, house.

They found Spofforth Street; a shabby, sprawling place that had been divided into six poky bedsitters but then abandoned for years. It was bordering on derelict; electrical wiring hung out of sockets, it was filthy from long neglect. It was evident from the piles of bottles and dirty blankets in some rooms that it was an occasional refuge for the homeless. It was also extraordinarily cheap. Anthony and Chris took the house on, first assuring the real-estate agent we would fix everything ourselves. We moved in with other friends from university and art school, had it re-wired, painted the whole inside of the house ourselves and knocked down the flimsy dividing walls of the flats into one house. One of the former flats became the lounge room and kitchen and the rest were bedrooms. Spofforth Street was born.

Anthony and I had a room out the back with a small room leading off it for little Matthew, and there was another room on the veranda with a spare mattress for anyone who needed it and a bookcase and two makeshift writing desks. Spofforth Street was where I started to become a writer; we were all becoming something.

Chris in the front room was holed up with her history books, although she later became a scientist; Beth, whom I'd met in Auckland when I was the drawing model for a group of art students, was painting and drawing; her shy fellow-student,

Miriam, made hand-built coil pots; Alan, who stayed for a while, wrote beautiful poetry; Murray, who was recovering from a suicide attempt, was working on a novel; my brother Tim was painting – he lived in the cleared-out shed until he was found in Chris's bed one morning; Michael, a friend of mine from university who became a friend of Anthony's, was studying journalism. At one point Barbara stayed for a couple of weeks; Kirsty came and fell in love with Anthony and left; two Krishna devotees stayed for a couple of weeks; my sister Mary came back from Perth after a bad relationship and stayed for a couple of months; Lesley from university stayed for a while, reading in the hammock on the back veranda; Jane came to visit twice. It's just a confusing list of names on the page, but in memory it's a vast three-dimensional Escher drawing with stairs and ladders and walkways in all directions, everyone connected and bumping bodies as they saunter up and down. We took turns cooking vegetarian dinners, went out to films or to see bands, smoked dope and read all the same books – *The Alexandria Quartet*, *Anais Nin's Diaries*, *A Room of One's Own*, *The Vivisector*, *Monkey Grip*. And we argued accusingly about who had cleaned the bathroom last.

I met Elizabeth at university. When I first knew her, her name was Mary, and she was heterosexual. We had just started to develop a friendship when she took six months off from university and went to Berlin, then came back as Elizabeth and gay. It felt strange at first, but soon 'Mary' faded and I only thought of her as Elizabeth.

Elizabeth was the person everyone noticed in the room, not just because of her striking looks, her long dark hair, pale skin and brown eyes, but her air of knowing she was attractive was an attraction in itself. She wore worker's overalls but didn't adopt the short spiky hair that the other lesbian feminists at university did. She once said to me with a degree of satisfaction that her new girlfriend had told her that while all her girlfriends were beautiful, she was the most beautiful of any girlfriend she had ever had.

She had the confidence that I had already recognised as formed by a privileged, well-off background, taking up whatever space she needed, but her politics fiercely opposed her privilege. I was in awe of the way she was so sure in her view of the world. She was outspoken and passionate; expounding her views with a determined set to her face, a sideways slant to her mouth.

We took writing classes together – she wrote experimental poetry and I wrote stories based on my life. Along with our desire to be writers we shared our left-wing politics, which was really a shared desire, again, to do good. Writing and politics were not the same thing, but there was little distinction between them. We went on Women Reclaim the Night and peace marches, critiqued each other's writing and worked on an anthology together. I visited her at the Birrell Street wimmin-only household, which was now lesbian-only, except that I was allowed to visit and bring three-year-old Matthew with me. Elizabeth invited the two of us, but not Anthony, to her family's beach house at Mackerel Beach with several other women, including her latest girlfriend. We went to see experimental theatre at the new Performance Space and to parties together – I remember Elizabeth wearing a plastic garbage bag, torn and painted, while I wore a 50s blue velvet cocktail dress she had given me, to a wimmin-only party.

At that time, Elizabeth was also part of a wimmin's collective that looked after a baby, born to one of the other women at university. Each of the women looked after the little girl for a day or two, and no mother, including her biological mother, was considered more important than any other. It was meant to break down the idea of 'possessing a child' and to relieve everyone of the weight of twenty-four-hour childcare, to return children to the care of the tribe. I liked the ideology but was unconvinced by it in practice – what about the intense give-your-life-for–the-child love of a mother – but didn't say anything. I remember Elizabeth one day confiding that she wanted more than anything to have a child of her own, but feared that she might not. I was surprised, women in those revolutionary days rarely said they wanted to have babies – I had never said it – and it made me see a yearning in her that I hadn't suspected.

One night, I went out with her and a couple of others to a nightclub in Oxford Street where there were nearly all women dancing and drinking. One of the women flirted with me, sat on my knee, kissed me and asked me to go home with her, but I pretended Elizabeth was my girlfriend and that I had to stay with her. It felt easier to say than admitting I was *het*, which I always thought was a wavy line in the sand anyway. In all of this, it was always clear that there was never any feeling other than friendship between the two of us. I don't think we talked about it, but it always felt uncomplicated. Our friendship frayed for other reasons after I finished university, and after I had moved to the Blue Mountains.

After three years in Spofforth Street, Anthony and I found another, smaller share house, a cold weatherboard place on the side of a hill in Katoomba in the Blue Mountains. I began writing a book, tucked up under a rug on the bed, and found a part-time job at the local Women's Centre. I went to Sydney and visited Elizabeth at Birrell Street and joined her in more street marches, but I wanted her to come and see my new life. She promised to come twice, but both times rang and cancelled; she had a dentist appointment, her girlfriend needed her. We arranged a third date, this time it was definite. She said she would come up on the train on Saturday and stay for the weekend – we would have lunch, go for a bushwalk then have dinner and talk half the night. On Friday she rang.

'I'm sorry, but I have to go to this amazing thing. It's called Aeroplane. It's just incredible. Everyone puts in money and gives it to the next woman, then you find other women to join, and they give money to you. You end up with $15,000. It's women helping other women.'

It sounded like a pyramid con scheme to me, but I didn't say so. She sounded too enthusiastic to criticise her involvement.

'Can't you go another time?'

'No. I have to be there tomorrow night. It's really very cool. I will come and see you another time.'

I responded stiffly and put down the phone. I sat down and wrote Elizabeth a letter. I couldn't believe she would fall for a scam and felt it was the poorest excuse for not seeing me. I wrote what I felt and posted the letter. She didn't answer and we didn't see each other again for years.

When I remembered the incident, I looked up the Aeroplane on the internet, wondering if I had misremembered or imagined the name, and found that it had particularly targeted feminist women with the idea that it was 'women helping women', exactly as she had said. I had only recognised it as a scam because my mother had told me about a similar scheme that had taken many people's money in the 30s when she was young.

I bumped into Elizabeth ten years later in a street in Glebe. We spoke briefly in a friendly way – she was a drama teacher at a private school and was out with her students, so it was necessarily brief. She did tell me that she was with a man now and that at work they didn't know she had been with women before – her voice was lowered as she told me.

I didn't see her for another two decades and then one morning not long ago I was reading the names out in a writing class. 'Elizabeth,' I said. As usual I looked up as I read the name and the woman's eyes locked with mine. She had a direct gaze and a forthright manner.

'I know you!' I exclaimed in front of the whole class. As I said the words, she turned into my old friend Elizabeth. She had morphed from a stranger to a precise and particular friend in a split-second melting of time. The same dark hair, shorter now, the same thoughtful brown eyes.

'Yes,' she smiled. 'You do.'

We talked during the break but not in any depth. I was excited to see her, but I couldn't show it without making the rest of the class feel side-lined.

'Do come and see me,' she said quietly. She lived in the Blue Mountains with her girlfriend – she was back with women after several years of marriage to a man – and she had a daughter, now a young woman herself. I had moved back to Sydney after twenty years in the Mountains, but I had a writing course to teach there soon, so I arranged to visit on my way home one afternoon.

I arrived at her house, not quite knowing where I stood. We had made no attempt to see each other in decades, did either of us care? And yet here I was. Perhaps it was simply curiosity, a desire to know how her life had played out since the bright days of our youth.

She came out the door of her house as I got out of the car. She must want to see me. In the front garden there were flowering rhododendrons that matched the house, pink and purple.

'I like the way your trees match your house,' I said, by way of greeting.

'I knew you'd notice that!' Elizabeth said, delighted. 'It wasn't us though, it was the gay guys we bought it from.'

We went into her house as she told me how they had renovated the inside, knocking down walls to make it more spacious. It was open and arty with books and paintings and collections of objects, a familiar space. The living room had broad windows looking out on a glorious mountain garden, azaleas, more rhododendrons, eucalypts, dappled with sunlight. While Elizabeth made tea I sat on a sofa bed piled with cushions, but it was a bit too wide, and I felt that I was lounging awkwardly.

Elizabeth came in with the tea and cake on a plate with a magpie painted on it. 'Are you okay, do you want to move to another chair?'

'No, I'm fine,' I said. I tucked my knees up onto the sofa. 'I like the plate,' I said, pointing at the magpie plate. 'One of my books had a magpie on the cover.'

'Ah, yes, it did,' she said.

She had noticed what I'd been doing.

We caught up on the facts of our lives; I was still with Anthony after all these years, I'd had another son; she had married and had a beautiful daughter who had just headed off to Mongolia to work as a volunteer.

'You said way back then that you wanted to have a baby,' I said, smiling.

'Did I?' She looked and sounded surprised, and doubtful. 'I don't remember that.'

'Yes, you said you were afraid you might not be able to.'

She had left her husband but they were friends. Elizabeth and her girlfriend had bought the pink and purple house together, her girlfriend was a psychologist; they had been a couple for ten years, but her girlfriend had been unwell lately, with depression. She wondered aloud, with tears in her eyes, how she could help her, and I suddenly thought, I have forgotten how loving and compassionate she was. It was central to her being, where her politics and art came from.

'She's quite a bit younger than me,' she said, and I saw a small smile of pleasure.

We talked for several hours, covering decades, but particularly about the now of our lives, like old friends do. We talked about relationships, children, the state of the world, our work; I thought that both our lives had gone along the track that could have been predicted from our university days. She had started writing poetry again after years of teaching drama; my new book was about to come out. I felt pleased I had something substantial to show for the intervening years, aware that I was holding on to the life-raft of my books as if I'd be nothing without them.

Then Elizabeth leaned forward. 'I had been wondering what our friendship was about then. We are such different people. But now I see ...' And then whatever she said was not recorded in my memory because I suddenly felt defensive. What did she think I was like then, to say that we were so different?

'I don't think we are so different. Different temperaments, yes, but our characters are similar. We have the same values, we've both lived a life in the arts without much money.'

'Yes,' she said, but didn't sound convinced.

She didn't elaborate any further and I didn't ask her what she meant. Whatever this was about still dangles like a vaguely irritating thread from a garment.

Just before I left when we were standing in the kitchen, Elizabeth washed the magpie plate and gave it to me.

'Keep it. It's yours,' she said. She stopped for a moment, and then said, 'Look, I know something happened, but I don't remember what it was. Why did we break up? I think it was something I did.' She looked a little uncomfortable for the first time.

'I remember what it was. And it was me. You had not come to visit after promising to, and I was pissed off and wrote you an angry letter. And that was it. You didn't answer.' I didn't mention the Aeroplane because at that point I had not remembered it. It was only recently that it came back into my mind.

Well, I am sorry,' she said. 'I want to say that. It has been bothering me. I really am sorry.'

'Me too,' I said. 'I'm sorry, too. It's okay. We should have sorted it out, but we didn't.'

I have thought about it many times since then. How we both missed out on a lifetime friendship because of – what? My hurt and pride? Her carelessness? We have apologised, but there is still a thread or two to weave. It is a relief to know that even friendships that seem to be long over can sometimes be picked up when old hurts have faded.

~

I don't think Gilgamesh and Enkidu ever apologised to each other. Gilgamesh was insulting and hurtful when he told his friend he was acting like a mere hireling. He accused Enkidu of speaking out of envy and fear of a rival. But Enkidu didn't appear to take offence, he just kept on with the point he had been making. Perhaps men don't take offence in the same way, or don't feel the need to apologise. They argue, they fight physically, and then it's finished, one way or another, but for women it is not so simple. I know that I have held on to hurt, stewed over it, when it would have been better to let it go. Or at least to try to sort it out face-to-face, rather than put it in writing where it stands, terse and unbending, on the page. Elizabeth would have come to see me another time if I had not sent the angry letter.

~

It was the same with the terse email I sent to Merril, whom I met the same year as Elizabeth. It would have been better to wait a day or two and word it differently. I met Merril at Waters Road when she lived in the back half of the mouldy house where our children, Matthew and Gria, were friends, but it was only after I moved to Spofforth Street that we ourselves became friends.

At Waters Road our children played in the shared overgrown yard. Gria was five, an extraordinarily sweet and gentle child who treated Matthew as an adored little brother. She played with him every afternoon, and, not wanting their time together to end, Matthew would take his dinner plate around the back to her house to eat with her. I carried it for him at times and collected him afterwards, so I was on a nodding acquaintance with Merril. She had a thick mane of dark hair, amused grey eyes and a curious way of bending her head a little as she smiled, as if to hide the humour she found in the world.

I occasionally saw a tall lanky man walk down the side of the house and assumed, correctly, he was Gria's father, an artist it turned out. He didn't live there, and I found out later that Merril had left him because he was becoming too interested in one of his artist models. That was as much as I ever learnt about Merril's relationships with men.

Gria and Matt's friendship matters in the story of my friendship with Merril – it was because I wanted to make sure they could keep seeing each other that I kept contact with her after we both moved house. They had a tender and creative connection that was beautiful to see – I have pictures of them both in painted masks that they made, and others of them playing together on the beach and in the bush. Years later, on our Big Overseas trip – Matthew was seventeen and Gria in her early twenties – they met up in London and when I saw them walking towards me in Bayswater one afternoon, I felt as if I were bursting with joy to see the two little children now stepping into the world. All these years later, Matt is a filmmaker and Gria is an artist, and while they rarely see each other, they take a brotherly and sisterly interest in each other's work. It was for them that I made the effort, because at first, Merril daunted me.

She was a few years older than me, in her early thirties, and her mind seemed cultivated compared to my unguided country girl and hippie mind-wanderings. She knew all about art and music, philosophy and literature – or so it felt to me. She would mention a Greek playwright or a French novelist and I couldn't pretend to know who or what she was talking about, although in my absurd refusal to let my ignorance show, I often tried.

Merril was an editor by trade, and literature and philosophy were her life. Apart from Anthony, she was the first friend I ever had who centred her life, her thinking, her feeling, around books. I've had many since, it's almost a criterion, but she was the first one who showed me it was a way of being and a way of relating.

Gradually, via picking up and dropping off our kids, we started to make a connection. I felt for a long time that I must not let my ignorance show and talked about what I was studying at university, the latest up-to-the-minute post-structuralist and postmodernist thought about literature and culture. Merril simply gave me books to read. If I look through what is left of my books from the late 70s and early 80s, they reveal a mix of university-introduced novels, and books from her; the intense and passionate Violette Leduc's *La Batarde*, Simone de Beauvoir's *Memoirs of a Dutiful Daughter*, Colette, Doris Lessing, Marguerite Duras. They were nearly all women writers and mostly European.

She became a literary mentor, filling in the vast gaps left in my postmodern studies. We had rarefied conversations about philosophy, literature and, later, history. There was little that was ordinary or everyday. We didn't talk about household concerns, relationships or men, and rarely talked about our children, although she was devoted to Gria. She had an extraordinarily meticulous and wide-ranging mind, which made her an excellent editor, but which later made my relatively loose and messy mind impatient.

I gave Merril a new story of mine to read, which was to be published in a literary magazine. It was called 'Discontinuous

Narrative' – that was a cool title then – and it was about my father who was having another nervous breakdown at the time. He was treated with electric shock therapy and afterwards, for a while, his sentences didn't make any narrative sense. 'Like frogs with holes in them and worms coming out the holes,' he said one day, setting my heart thumping in fear for him. I visited him at Royal Prince Alfred hospital after my classes and sat with my mother at his bedside. She said one day that if he didn't come good then that was all right, she would look after him because he had been 'a bloody good man'. Merril gave me the story back covered in corrections and with whole sentences re-written in her tiny, neat script.

I retreated, shocked and confused. I had given it to her to read and to respond to, not to have my words replaced with hers. I didn't give her any more of my stories to read.

After I finished university and went to live in the Mountains, Merril came to stay, usually at Easter. We both loved the blue autumn air and the swirling mists and the mysteries of the Australian bush, and our children still loved playing together. There was a much easier exchange between us now, but I still felt she knew more, and knew it more precisely than I did. I still had to hide my lack. I remember one day sitting down at Minnehaha Falls near Katoomba with her and a woman who shared our house, and Merril referred to *Aristophanes*. I knew from the sound of the word it was Greek but had no idea whether it was the name of a person or a play or a place. My housemate asked what *Aristophanes* was and I felt a sudden shock as I realised, oh, so it's okay to reveal ignorance.

Merril moved to Canberra for a public service editing job, and I regularly visited her. I had another child by now and there had been a couple of years of broken nights and days, a couple of years of tiredness and trying to snatch time to write. Then one weekend when Patrick was two and I was thinking I had emerged from that difficult period unscathed, I drove with my sons to Canberra to visit her and promptly fell apart in the middle of the first night. I was on a mattress on her lounge-room floor and woke up with a start, knowing that the world had seriously veered off course. It looked the same, but everything had lost its sense of reality. I stayed awake the rest of the night, thinking things would assume their normal solidity in the morning, but they didn't. I have written about this before in detail, the way it went on for weeks and months, but what I want to convey is how Merril looked after me.

I told her what had happened in the night and she understood exactly. She took me out for a walk in the bush. 'The trees will look after you,' she said. When we got back to the house, she tucked me into her own bed, put Mozart in the cassette player by the bed and brought me chamomile tea. More than all of that, she was calm and still, not at all puzzled or bothered. She did not tell me to get myself together nor tell me I was perfectly all right. She simply looked after me with such a quiet and centred sense of being it was as if she already knew what to do when a friend arrived and fell to pieces on her doorstep. She picked up the broken bits and held them together. She had talked to me before of her belief in 'lovingkindness' as a central value in her life and now she practised it naturally and with no sense of having to extend herself. I will always owe her a debt of gratitude for that time. She is the friend who saved me.

Still, it didn't mean that our friendship sailed smoothly on ever afterwards.

Later, Merril lost her public service job and left her home in Canberra. For a while she rented a farmhouse near Hartley below the western escarpment of the Blue Mountains – it was owned by a woman I had introduced her to. But while she was there an escaped prisoner from the nearby jail hid under the house and she ended up in the middle of a siege. Police surrounded the house and she had to flee on foot then fling herself on the ground to escape gunfire. She stayed with me afterwards and retold the dangerous events without the slightest trace of excess, and I listened with horrified fascination and some story-envy.

It could have been then, or later, time sequences are blurring, that Merril was diagnosed with breast cancer and stayed at our place in the Mountains when she was recovering. It was after Matt had left home, which meant there was a spare bedroom for her, but we were away for the first few weeks she stayed there so she had the house to herself. When we returned she had moved desks and chairs to other positions and re-organised the kitchen and bathroom. She was a more orderly and precise person than I was, and her order was more logical than mine, but I silently moved everything back the way it was.

She stayed with us while she worked out where to go and what to do next. Over cups of tea and coffee and over lunch and dinner, she talked. She had developed a Proustian narrative style of conversation, branching and qualifying each additional element so that it multiplied in all directions before reaching its destination. It was as if she needed to chase and pin down every stray element of reality so that not a strand of it flapped in the wind, the construction being so tightly made it was almost impossible to chip in with any stray remark. It was like watching one of those geometric progression graphs, expanding infinitely outwards and then inwards until it finally reaches where it began. The words were always insightful, well-observed, but being an essentially impatient person, I found myself fidgeting and sighing inwardly.

One evening when Matt was at dinner with us, Merril began one of her stories, which then continued in the usual expanding fashion throughout the meal and afterwards as we had tea and coffee around the table. When the story ended a few hours later she stood up and excused herself for bed. As soon as she left the room, Matt looked at me in astonishment. 'Is it always like this?' he burst out. 'I can't believe it!'

I felt let off the hook – it wasn't just me being impatient – and then immediately felt ashamed. Merril had helped me when I was falling apart and had done exactly what was needed with infinite lovingkindness. Her current endless pinning down of the details was a reaction to the world becoming random, out of control – she had lost her job and her home, she had survived cancer and had been involved in a terrifying siege. Why couldn't I be as generous as she had been with me? I controlled my impatience as best I could, which truthfully was not so well.

It was around this time that my first book was published. There had been a writing text, but I didn't count that as it was a practical book and hadn't required hauling out my heart and guts. This was the first real book, a melange of memoir, fiction and personal essay, which I had poured myself into. I had been struggling with it for most of the years I'd been in the Mountains, over a decade, in between bringing up two kids and working, and Merril had seen a lot of that struggle. I don't know that I could have kept on going if I had known it would take me so long.

I proudly posted her a copy. By then she had found a house in the village of Golspie in the southern tablelands and her life was settling down. I didn't hear anything from her about my book. The next time I saw her, which was many months later, she remarked, 'There were a lot of proof errors in your book.'

I was devastated. Writers are absurdly delicate creatures for the most part – some are tough, I suppose, but I haven't met them – and are dismantled by the slightest remarks. And then I was angry. She knew how many years I had put into this book, how much it meant to me, how, apart from my family, it was the centre of my being. Surely there were a few other things to see in the book apart from some jumbled or missed letters in words? I stewed silently, too hurt to say anything.

Half a lifetime later, another dear and precise friend remarked about proof errors in another book, but this time I was able to say that it was not her job to point out errors in an already published book, and this time it was a mere hiccup in our friendship. But with Merril I started to think I didn't need a friend who saw only proof errors in my many years of work. I still saw her, but not nearly as often, and then lost touch with her for several years. Every now and then I would think of how she cared for me in Canberra when I lost all sense of self, and at those times I felt ashamed of my egocentric wounds.

By the time I finally left the Mountains and moved to Kings Cross in the heart of Sydney, I had not seen Merril for some years. I occasionally heard from her. According to her last letter she was still living in Golspie, writing a local history. Then, one day when I was walking up Orwell Street in Kings Cross, there she was coming towards me. Her wonderful mane of hair was still as long and thick, but grey now, and her shoulders a little rounded. We both stopped, stunned, and delighted. We hugged and began talking and laughing over the top of each other. Neither of us could stop smiling.

It turned out that she now lived in the same area. After that we saw each other several times, often by chance. She still had that smile, almost a chuckle at times, that she bent her head over as if to hide. We always exchanged news of Gria, who had a daughter herself now and who had become a well-known painter like her father, and about Matt who was working on another film. One day I bumped into her in the garden in front of Elizabeth Bay House when she was looking after her small granddaughter. I could see how she glowed with love for her. I suddenly realised that the sweetness of nature I had always seen in Gria had come from her, that under her precise mind was great purity of heart.

She had also become interested in her Jewish heritage. In the early years she had never mentioned it – I don't think it was part of her upbringing – but now she had read histories and studied its teachings and practices. She touched on these ideas in an intellectual way, and I could see their rigour and elaborate precision appealed to her.

One day, she asked if I had any editing work for her. I had been doing manuscript development – structural editing – for years, mostly for former memoir students, and had begun to find it overwhelming. I had already passed most of the manuscripts to another young editor, but there were still enough to offer Merril some work. I remembered the way she had re-written sentences and paragraphs of mine all those decades ago and felt uncertain. I met with her to talk about my looser approach, and the kind of thing my students expected. Knowing her lifetime of working as an editor, I felt like the servant telling the master what to do, but I persisted, carefully.

I gave her a manuscript I knew she would enjoy, a memoir by a Jewish-Hungarian woman who had lit up my classes with

her warmth and intelligence. The details of the conflict that
followed look foolish from this distance; perhaps it's enough to
say Merril's editing report seemed to me to be the opposite of
my careful guidelines. I was tired. I wrote a brief, correcting
email to her. She wrote a long one in return, challenging my
corrections, referring to them as the beginning of a dialectic.
I wrote another, sticking to my point. She wrote another.
I defended. She referred to my controlling behaviour. You
see how it went. A long hand-written letter in Merril's tiny
script, with accompanying photocopied pages, arrived in
the post. I skimmed the letter and saw that it would send
me into turmoil to read, so I folded it and put it away. The
photocopied pages were about dictatorial managers who tell
others how to do their work. Perhaps it was accurate.

For several weeks, defensive chants circled through my
head in their soggy, obsessive fashion. It was exhausting,
but then I remembered again how she had taken care of me
when I needed it. How gentle and insightful she was. I felt sad
and sorry, but it seemed that the break in our friendship was
definitive. I didn't see her on the street even though she lived
nearby and, after several months, started to worry she might
be ill. I contacted Gria, explaining that we didn't see each
other anymore, but I wanted to know how her mother was.
Gria reassured me that all was well. A few more years passed.
Sometimes we act as if we have forever, as if we can leave hurts
untreated and they will resolve themselves in time.

Then one day last year, I bumped into her in the street again.
We stopped and greeted each other with delight. We were both
on our way somewhere else, but we talked excitedly for some
minutes. The fine shadow of our split — it had been a fight over
editing, for heaven's sake — was there in the background, it felt

like a scrunched greyish veil hanging behind us, but in the foreground was our pleasure in seeing each other again.

A few months later, I emailed her to say that Ann, the Jewish-Hungarian memoirist, had died. She sent me a warm note in reply saying she had just been thinking of Ann during the week. It was as near a reference to the split that either of us made until the year when the world closed down during a pandemic. It became impossible to see any friends and it gave me time to examine what other people meant to me. I wrote an email to Merril, apologising for my past bad behaviour and thanked her again for helping me when I needed it all those years ago. She wrote back and said I too had helped her when she was needy, when she stayed at our place after having breast cancer, and I felt embarrassed, remembering my impatience.

She finished the email by saying, 'a fortnight ago – when the first snow fell at 1000 metres – I longed for a few days back in the remarkable Golspie district, as humblingly metaphysical as a soul could desire', and I felt delight at the fineness of her sensibility and fortunate that I had a friend who could forgive me.

Nine

In the broken and re-patched friendships with Elizabeth and with Merril – who have never met – I have been overly reactive, too impatient. When I bumped into both again, each time by chance, I knew that I still cared about them. But I realise now with a sudden sense of shock that they too must have still cared about me. All this time, in all my friendships, I have been thinking about what I see in each of them, not what they see in me. But even the briefest consideration reveals it's not something I can know, nor want to know. I can only examine my experience of each of them.

I am forced to consider, again and again, how I know my friends. First there is the original experience, but even at that stage, before interpretation or memory, so much is unobserved, unrecorded. A few moments of colour and sound are partially registered and then all that is left are the neurotransmitters floating from axon to dendrite, hopefully creating a neural pathway. The lovely, faulty, biochemical science of friendship.

And yet, my recollections may bear little relationship to the facts – the facts being what my friend said and did, and what I said and did, in a particular location on a certain day. All the rest is interpretation. And sometimes it can all be contradicted by a photograph, a piece of paper.

Out of the blue Elizabeth emailed me two old photographs, along with letters I had sent her years ago. The scanned letters in my scrawly hand were written in my late twenties: I complain that with work and kids I'm not getting enough time to write, I suggest Elizabeth use the diaries of Anais Nin for a one-woman show, I'm still searching for inner truth and I've side-stepped Marxist ideology, I offer advice about an affair Elizabeth is having with a married man, I mention the difficulties of buying a house, I confess my desire for acknowledgement – 'I still want the world to say I'm a good, clever girl.'

The attached photographs were of the two of us sitting with my second child, Patrick, on the back step of the small house Anthony and I had just bought in the Blue Mountains more than three years *after* I believed our friendship had ruptured.

The timeline of events is evidently incorrect in my version. Although it's disconcerting, in fact worrying, to have misremembered events, I still want to present the version memory has retained, however poorly recorded it is.

It's easier to remember what happened with Gina when I arrived back from the farmhouse in France; the first split, not definitive, but still distressing.

After the farmhouse sojourn, I had taught classes in Paris before returning to Sydney. Cathy was still there, staying on by herself. Anthony had already returned to Sydney, as had Gina. After recovering from jet lag, I texted her for a catch-up coffee. Despite a sinking in the pit of my stomach whenever I thought about it, I had persuaded myself that the strange atmosphere in Lacapelle-Biron had been entirely in my own head and had not been seen or felt by anyone else.

Gina texted that she was busy. A job had come up. It might have been a television advertisement. She rarely did ads, but they paid the bills.

I waited another week then sent another text.

She was still busy. She might have some time in a couple of weeks. Her brother needed help. She would text me.

No texts came. Perhaps the atmosphere was not just in my head. She had made that half-audible remark at the train station in Fumel. But surely it was forgotten by now.

I waited a couple of weeks then texted again. She agreed to a coffee, probably next Friday. I breathed. All was well. She was not avoiding me.

On Thursday another text came, cancelling our catch-up. She had to take her brother to an appointment. I understood. Naturally she had to put him first. There was no question. I ignored the slight clenching in my stomach.

'Should I text yet again, or should I wait for her to be ready?' I asked Anthony. 'She might be trying to avoid me.'

'Why would she be avoiding you?'

'There was the weird atmosphere at Lacapelle.'

'What atmosphere?'

Really? I explained the convoluted somersaults I had performed there; not wanting anyone to think I minded his close friendship with Gina.

'But you don't mind, do you?'

'No, you know I don't. I love how open you are to everyone. It's just that, you know, I am ridiculously conscious of what people think. I didn't want anyone to think I minded, so I was kind of self-consciously relaxed.'

'You are weird.'

'I know. But now I want to sort it out and she won't let me see her.'

I waited another couple of weeks. My mind flipped back and forth; I was in the wrong, she was angry with me; there was nothing wrong, I was imagining it all. I texted again, lighthearted cheery: *Ca va? Ready for a coffee?*

Yes, she said. She named a café around the corner from her place. I relaxed; my shoulders loosened. All was well. It really was that she'd had other things to do.

She was sitting outside when I arrived. We kissed on both cheeks as we had done when we were Winter-Monet and Clarissa, but this time there was no laughter with it. I sat down. I talked. Gina responded briefly. Something was wrong. I kept talking. I asked after her brother. She answered, but her body was held back, her eyes somehow flat. I acted relaxed. Everything was fine. I kept talking. I was still working on my manuscript. It was a bright sunny day, our coffees arrived, all was well. I kept talking. I said Cathy had sent some beautiful photographs of Lacapelle, of the chooks from next door looking like humble angels in the light, of the long wooden table, of the back door framing the garden. I talked about Matt and how he was progressing with the film he was trying to get up. Gina responded each time and offered a few comments, but I was feeling more and more rattled. There was a disinterest bordering on coldness. I had never seen or felt her like that. It felt as if the usual warm light she shone on me had been turned off and nothing I said would turn it back on.

We stayed at the café for an almost decent length of time, then Gina had to go. She had a meeting to get to. We kissed on both cheeks again, said *au revoir* and walked in opposite directions.

About halfway home tears sprang. They weren't rolling down my face tears, just a wet stinging. I tried to pinpoint what had happened. I had tried to connect, but had been blocked. I hadn't been received.

'How was it?' Anthony asked when I walked in.

'Weird,' I said. I wasn't crying by now. 'I don't know if it's because of me at Lacapelle, it probably is, but it could be something else.'

It ran through my head for several days, churning interminably. My shoulders had tightened again, my neck was stiff. My brain replayed events at Lacapelle, and then our meeting at the café, over and over again. Finally, I sent another text.

Look, I know something is wrong. Your friendship means a great deal to me. Can we meet and sort it out?

After I sent it I wondered if I had imagined everything. Perhaps she had not noticed anything at the farmhouse and perhaps I imagined the terrible strain at the café.

I waited. Nothing that afternoon. I went to bed, not knowing what to think. Is no answer an answer?

A reply came the next day.

There is something wrong. I don't see what can be done about it.

I wasn't imagining anything. I walked around the apartment, wrote and corrected and sent my reply.

We can meet. I do want to sort it out. Whenever and wherever suits you. As long as it takes.

All right, I'm free next Thursday.
Would Rushcutters Bay Park be okay?
I knew unaligned space all around us might help.
Yes. 11 am next Thurs then.
I tried to discern the tone. Was it conciliatory or dismissive?
I had a week to mull it over.

The wording of the texts we exchanged is to the best of my recollection, not from record. I usually keep cards and letters and texts, and up until several months ago, I believed I had all our exchanges. I didn't delete any, not even accidentally, but one day when I was checking messages and dates, I discovered that nearly all of them were gone. I didn't know that phones could sometimes prune information to free up memory. I felt robbed and bereft, almost as if I couldn't go on. I had been relying on the factual reality of one particular message, a piece of evidence that, looking back, marked the end of our friendship. In a sea of self-doubt and uncertainty, it was clear and definite – something had happened, I wasn't making it up. But it was gone.

Then I found out there was an App for rescuing disappeared messages. It was expensive, but I bought it right away. I followed the instructions screen by screen – it was clear I could retrieve messages from anyone I wanted to. It turned out there was a time limit, so that the early messages about making arrangements just after the sojourn in Lacapelle-Biron were missing, but it looked as if all the later texts were there. I clicked through them, relieved and ready to copy and print out the particular text I wanted, to have it incontrovertibly on paper.

It wasn't there.

I checked and re-checked. I looked up and down the hundreds of messages. I smiled at the lovely arrangements we had made – to meet in cafés, to go to a show – I have some with comps to have a drink in a bar. The texts before and after the one I wanted were there; there were threads of texts, but not the one I needed – or my reply to it. I don't have any explanation for this and whenever I mention it to anyone they shrug. Everyone knows electronic memory can be just as erratic and selective as human memory. It doesn't even have the concept of salience to guide its selections and brutal deletions.

~

It turns out that even a story fixed in clay is not the last word, is not immutable. Among the 40,000 clay tablets found by the Americans in southern Iraq in 1889, there were a small number with older versions of *The Epic of Gilgamesh*, inscribed in Sumerian. Most of another version was found in Anatolia and parts were found in Turkey and in Palestine. Each time new fragments are found, the story changes. Or sometimes an old fragment is read more carefully, and another element of the story is revealed.

In 2018, researchers at Cornell University Library were looking at a fragment that had been overlooked from the 1889 haul. It didn't look that impressive, just sixteen broken lines, another version of how Enkidu was transformed from living like a wild animal to living as a human through his week of sacred sex with Shamhat. But it turns out this fragment was describing another whole week of sex and female influence. After the first week he could think and speak as a human, motivated by the desire to challenge and dominate; but after the second week he saw that skill and cooperation as part of a community were more important. To be fully human, Enkidu had to learn first to see himself as a thinking individual aware of his own strength and then take another step to see himself as a contributing part of his community. The newly interpreted fragment has given a whole new insight into what the early Sumerians thought about what it was to be human.

More than 4000 years after it was first pressed into clay, The Epic remains a work in progress. There are different versions in different languages, some have been destroyed or lost, some are in fragments, some are blurry, poorly imprinted in the first place, some are interpreted differently according to who is reading them. Neither the story nor its meaning have remained the same.

Is it too obvious to say the story of the clay tablets is the story of memory?

~

Seen from this distance, the friendships I made in the Blue Mountains give the impression of a Brueghel village painting, highly detailed and many coloured, people all over the place. It takes time to slow down and look at what is happening. It was the crowded middle period of life, busy with kids and Anthony, with writing and earning a living, and nineteen friends at regular Sunday lunches. Most friends came via our kids' school, an alternative school in the bush near Leura, then later from the community that gathered around Varuna, a writers' centre in Katoomba. But there were also two old friends from the Spofforth Street days who moved to the Mountains around the same time as I did.

Beth and Miriam had met at art school before they both arrived at Spofforth Street. Beth made steel sculptures and Miriam was a potter, but they shared a common sensibility and obsession with particular artists, mostly Matisse, Rodin and the abstract expressionists. Although I had known Beth first, from Auckland, for several years I was a third wheel in their friendship. But because we were in the same geography – friendship can be a matter of geography, sharing houses, streets, pathways, shops – over time I found an individual connection to each of them.

Beth offered more of herself more quickly, which made her easier to get to know. She was tall, big-boned, with long chestnut pre-Raphaelite hair and a round rosy face, often laughing. She came from England and was married to a young Englishman she had met at art school in London, whom she had left behind by the time she came to Sydney. When I first met her in Auckland, I was an artists' model for her small life-drawing group.

In Auckland we had seen each other every now and then outside of drawing class. One day, the artists I modelled for decided to drop acid together and invited me as well, so we all went to Paul's house. He was one of the artists and lived in the Titirangi Hills just out of Auckland – we all agreed it was better to have our 'trip' in the country. We were floating around in the trees and orchards and green fields, feeling blissful, when Paul suddenly said, 'Let's all take our clothes off.' Normally, it was easy for me to take my clothes off – I did it for this group every week – but there was something about Paul that put me off. I looked at Beth, thinking, 'Don't say yes, Beth, Don't.' She looked back at me with the same intensity.

We didn't take our clothes off and a few days later Beth told me, laughing, that she had been thinking, 'Patti, don't say yes, don't,' because she too thought Paul was weird. It's inconsequential, this memory, in that Paul was probably harmless, but we sometimes re-tell the story to each other, because it affirms that our shared past was true. We were both there, we knew each other when we were young, wandering, tripping dreamily through the fields in our floating dresses.

In the Mountains Beth wore overalls when she worked with her welding torch making steel sculptures in the backyard of her father's house. She was always surrounded by odd bits of steel she'd found in a railway yard or factory.

'Look at these beautiful shapes,' she'd say, pointing at some rusty cogs or keg hoops.

We talked for hours about how we made things. One day I asked her how she started to make a sculpture. Did she draw it first, work it out? Surely when there was a welding torch and solder involved she had to draw it beforehand.

'Not at all,' she said. 'I have to throw some things up first and see what I have. You can't sculpt in thin air. I weld a few bits together and then see what's happening.'

Ever since then, whenever I've started to write a book, I remind myself, you can't sculpt in thin air.

She made cut-outs in paper as well, influenced by Matisse's dancing cut-out figures, as well as painted abstract washes of colour and fierce, wild drawings in charcoal. She could draw with great accuracy – years later she was employed as a botanical artist – but I was puzzled when she said, 'I despise the easy line I can draw.'

'You are lucky to be so talented,' I protested. I didn't understand the trap of facility, I suppose because I didn't have any. Now that I can write a presentable line at times, I know it's an easy falsehood to make it look like I know something when I don't.

We circled often through the psychology of family and love – and laughed a lot. She had an ironic sense of humour that leavened my literal country mind, and she was clever at taking off characters and reproducing accents. Nothing slipped by her. Of any friend, she is still the one who makes me laugh.

She had a job in a plant nursery in the Mountains and came around to my place most afternoons after work to have a cup of tea and talk and laugh. She was passionate and open about everything; art, the state of the world, her friends, her loves. She fell in love easily, but hard, often with someone who was not available. Before coming to the Mountains, she had been passionately in love with a well-known sculptor who was married, and most conversations were about him for a while, the depth and impossibility of their connection.

But her art and her friends were just as important. In fact, everyone she met – everyone she meets – is of intense interest to her. I noticed that no matter whether she was talking to me or a celebrated artist or the girl serving her in a dress shop, she asked questions and laughed and listened in the same open-hearted way. It made me realise that my attention was selective, angled towards 'sensitivity', a kind of snobbery. I confessed it to Beth one day and told her that I wanted to be like her, to have her heart open to all. She looked embarrassed.

'I'm not doing anything. I'm just here.' To her it was unremarkable.

She began going out with the brother of one of her co-workers at the nursery. He was the manager of the Paragon, a local historic café, and at first Miriam and I disapproved of him. It wasn't personal, he was a friendly, steady man and we liked him, but he didn't seem a match for Beth's intensity; he wasn't an artist. It turned out we were wrong, or perhaps we didn't realise that what Beth needed was steadiness, not volatility.

One cold Mountains day when snow threatened, they married on a clifftop at Wentworth Falls, and then moved to Adelaide to start their life together. After that there were the infrequent but intense meetings that happen with friends who live halfway across the country. Beth returned to the Mountains and to Sydney to visit and I went to Adelaide to give writing workshops and visit her.

One year I was at the Adelaide Writers' Festival and was involved in a literary-political stoush on stage. Even though I'm one of eight kids and used to sticking up for myself, I'm not someone who enjoys a good fight and was rattled and trembling afterwards. Beth was in the audience and loyally reported how it had looked from there.

'We all were on the edge of our seats when she started attacking you,' she said. 'The atmosphere was electric. You were brilliant, you said exactly what needed to be said.'

I felt electrocuted rather than electrified, pumping with adrenaline and grateful for the utter loyalty of her friendship, no matter what I had said or done. She came with me to the pub for after-drinks with the publisher and dissected the whole on-stage attack and defence to the finest degree. She said. I said. She said. Beth loved this kind of analysis of events. It mattered to her because it mattered to me, but the natural inclination of her mind was to observe and fully understand whatever or whomever she came across. If she disagreed with me, she didn't argue back, but asked me questions. It was from her I learnt, though not very well, the futility of opposition, the wisdom and the expansion possible in leaning back and asking questions.

She had two daughters by now, but children were not the focus of our conversations. It was the state of our hearts and mind, the state of the world. Beth was not making steel sculpture anymore, but drawing beautifully detailed images of petals, stamens and leaves. Later, she became an art therapist, working especially with sick children.

'I let them paint their anxiety and fear. The things they cannot say,' she said. I thought they were lucky to have her, her largeness of heart, her love of painting.

She also became interested in Christian spirituality, a turn of her mind that troubled me as I had gradually moved from being a spiritual seeker to an unbeliever. I hoped she wasn't becoming 'religious' and worried that she would lose her open-heartedness, but I needn't have been concerned. She is still the friend who has shown me what a heart can be like.

'It's not about doctrine,' she said. 'It's about how to be with yourself. In silence. And how to act in the world.' And then she laughed at her own seriousness.

Her long, rippling chestnut hair is now grey and curls around her head in a tousled bob; she has survived cancer, and it seems to me, has lived every moment of her life with intensity. Last time I saw her, earlier this year, we talked about friendship. She was an only child and for her, friends were her family.

'I wonder now whether I haven't been too much. Too intense. I have wanted family and maybe other people have just wanted a friend.'

I told her I liked that kind of intensity and that it wasn't possible to always have that in a biological family. It has to be under the surface in families for safety's sake. But Beth has become part of my birth family – she is friends with two of my brothers and with one of my sisters, and although we didn't share a childhood, she knows at least a selected highlights of all our stories. She helped look after my younger brother's teenage daughter when she was living on the streets of Adelaide, she listened to my sister's pain after her boyfriend left her alone with her new baby, she talked art with my older brother Tim, the one who is a painter.

When we talked online not long ago, she told me she had opened a copy of *Poppy* by Drusilla Modjeska, which I had given her thirty years ago, and found a card I had written. First, she read out a paragraph from the page the card had been left in:

> Yet these connections between women are taken for granted, a backdrop to the real business of life: husbands, children, jobs. It takes only the slightest change of focus to see that these neglected intimacies, independent of more passionate demands, can offer the terms on which we learn to be our best selves. Equality, acceptance and free play are required for friendship to flourish. 'I do not wish to treat friendships daintily,' Emerson writes, 'but with roughest courage. When they are real, they are not glass threads or frostwork, but the solidest thing we know.'

Afterwards she photographed and emailed the card in which, all those years ago, I had written:

> I threw the I Ching in the hope of finding something special for you and all (all!) I found was an account of your life thus

far. It was 61, Inner Truth – I will leave it to you to read. This sounds a very esoteric way of saying, happy birthday, but there are no words to adequately encompass a shared history except to say, it is always there, not past, but here and now. All love and honour to you.

Beth added in the email:

With so few family, my friends have been my formation, identity and belonging, both men and women. But it is the women through my life who have shown me myself and abided. To them, the first tribute.

Our shared history *is* always there, not past, but here and now. Sometimes, when we talk, fragments of the past surface; Beth dyeing my hair with henna and washing it off in the sink at Spofforth Street; painting our faces black and purple before going to an anti-nuclear march in the city; all of us at Spofforth Street reading *The Vivisector* and *A Room of One's Own*; her being annoyed because three-year-old Matthew accidentally peed in her room one night, me being annoyed with her because she intervened when he answered the phone in his childish way – memories from forty years ago. Our friendship has abided.

~

'Memory is the seamstress and a capricious one at that. Memory runs her needle in and out, up and down, hither and thither. We know not what comes next, or what follows after,' wrote Virginia Woolf. She says that nature has provided a 'ragbag' within us so that 'a piece of policeman's trouser [lies] cheek-by jowl with Queen Alexandra's wedding veil', but it's clear these days that memory is no ragbag. It is already highly structured, we know now that the trouser and the veil lie together because we saw the policeman and the queen on the same sunny afternoon, or a photograph of both in the book we were leafing through at the library. Memory seems a capricious seamstress, but she has a pattern, just not one that can be smoothed out and seen all at once. It's only in the writing of it that it starts to 'come back to me in all the right order'.

I don't know what other pieces are there in the dark seahorse of the brain, but I do have a fierce urgency to find and connect the pieces. I want to see how, in the end, these friendships have made me, the ones that have abided and those that haven't. It's not an absolute truth, nor an attempt to influence anyone else's version, only an attempt to know what I have felt and observed.

~

Miriam was shy and reserved and more difficult to get to know. At Spofforth Street she befriended three-year-old Matthew first. She let him slip into her bed, golden-haired and tousled, with *The Bunyip of Berkeley's Creek* or *Dinosaurs and All That Rubbish* under his arm for her to read in her gentle voice. She also taught him how to make coil pots from clay and showed him how to shade with crayons. I have a memory, backed up or replaced by a black-and-white photo, of both of them sitting on the grass in the backyard with two large pots they were each burnishing with the back of a spoon. They have rounded solemn faces and Miriam's dark hair is pushed back from her creamy face, a style which doesn't suit her. Soon she would dye it black and have a fringe and suddenly become strikingly pretty.

In the Mountains when my second child, Patrick, was born – an angel who wouldn't sleep – Miriam was also there, picking him up, cuddling him, rocking him. When she could see I was worn out, she took him from my arms without a word and walked around the garden with him, softly humming. She was his other mother, always there for him. When he was a little boy she made pots with him as well, and for birthdays and Christmases gave him delicate presents; a paper Balinese puppet, a plaster copy of a Donatello cherub, which he loved better than any of his other presents. It sounds Jane Austenish to say it, but they both had a natural delicacy of feeling which made me feel as if I were made of coarser stuff.

Sometimes, I could feel Miriam's eyes on me, looking me up and down, deciding whether I was simply all show. Or perhaps she was assessing what I was wearing. My clothes were a bit louder and skimpier than hers, I'd wear coloured singlet tops and she would wear blouses with long patterned sleeves. 'You don't want to keep dressing like a teenager,' she said one day when we were shopping together. She pulled out a loose and sensible cotton shirt for me to try on that I knew would make me look frumpy. Then – and now – she wore intricate Middle Eastern and Asian ethnic jackets and loose pants made of natural fabrics and crafted silver jewellery, which always suited her perfectly.

She was physically strong and practical, getting up at dawn to do yoga and then heaving wet clay and heavy pots around, building a kiln, making her own fine glazes, green-blue celadon and iron red. She gave me bowls, plates, a large platter, a vase, all of them with the same earthy Japanese aesthetic.

Without seeming to, she cultivated my visual sense with her unwavering sensibility. I learnt to notice the fineness of a pot's shape, the quality of the glaze, the expression of the variation of nature through earth and fire, and most of all, the concept of beautiful imperfection.

'It's the craft of throwing and shaping, and then the nature of the clay, and the fire. And the chemistry of the glazes. But after that, you can't know what will happen.' She was happy to explain the process and showed me the chemical equations for the glazes and how she stacked her kiln, all the practical skills she had developed. From her, I understood that in creativity you can only set up the conditions for it, not control it.

Our friendship developed more after Beth moved to Adelaide. Without Beth's golden light to revolve around, we paid more attention to each other and the spin-off from our friendship with Beth began to take on a life of its own. She had been a country girl like me, although from the tropical north coast rather than the dry west, so we understood the lack of sophistication in each other. We began talking books and family and politics, and then when a series of boyfriends came along and tried to shape Miriam to their own needs, we talked about the psychology of relationships.

She has a rigorous mind under her gentle manner and reads books more closely than anyone I know, focusing on the fine detail in one novel, say, of Milan Kundera, or later, Cormac McCarthy, rather than reading vast numbers of books. She is a writer's Ideal Reader, although she didn't respond to my writing with that kind of attention. I wonder now if friends, like family, don't really know what to do with the writer part of me. It probably feels extraneous, a bit of baggage that I cart around with me for inexplicable reasons and about which I seem unaccountably sensitive. They tolerate it because they care for me, but it would matter little to them if I let it go.

In her thirties Miriam moved in with a new boyfriend who was already the father of a three-year-old boy, Harry. For the third time, she had a small boy in her life, this time as his stepmother. She immersed herself in his care, and loved him dearly, teaching him to read, knitting him jumpers, getting him ready for school. His mother had walked out on the family before Miriam arrived and swept in every now and then to create havoc. At that time, the complications she created took up Miriam's time, and our conversations, for several years. Later, the boy became a troubled teenager and there were brushes with the law that looked like he might end up in jail, but Miriam, it turned out, was also a fierce defender under her gentle exterior.

One day she told me how she had sat on her now teenaged son who was metaphorically and physically flailing and ready to cause damage he could not go back from. She held his arms down like a wrestler and screamed at him, 'Listen Harry, I love you. You have to stop doing this. I won't let you end up in jail.' I could hardly believe quiet and shy Miriam wrestling with and screaming at a flailing boy, and I thought how narrow my frame of her had been.

I haven't had a tempestuous life, thus far, but I like listening to hers. I see more and more that from early on in my friendships I have enjoyed being the audience for other peoples' dramas. I do not want a complicated life, but I do need friends who dive, or who are pushed, into the storm. I don't think it's vicarious, but I admit it is a bloody kind of nourishment. I suspect Miriam thinks my life has been too smooth and that it has been to my detriment.

'For some people everything goes well, and they don't know what it is like for other people. Their children are healthy and happy, their relationships are good, their job is rewarding. But I don't think they understand damage,' she said one day. She didn't direct it at me, but I felt accused.

Her storms settled, her son grew up and she went back to art school in the city. She lives on the northern peninsula in Sydney, and I live in Woolloomooloo near the city, but we regularly meet in the city at a flash pub, the Sir Stamford hotel. The bar is like a nineteenth-century men's club with deep lounges and old landscape paintings – we feel like interlopers and we giggle like the country girls we are. We started going there because there is a fire in winter and because it's always quiet enough to talk. Miriam is not making pots anymore because a car accident damaged her back, making the necessary heavy lifting too difficult. She does paint though, and teaches painting and drawing at Julian Ashton, an old-style school dedicated to the craft of art.

Like a couple of colonial ladies, we order a gin and tonic each. Like me, she too is an unbeliever, perhaps always has been, and I know she shared my worry about Beth becoming a believer, but we don't talk about it. We discuss our families and books, which, with Miriam, are the same thing. In our friendship, there is no distinction between literature and our lives; the conversation about family and emotion is exactly the same whether it is happening in our lives or in books. The unfaithfulness of Tomas in *The Unbearable Lightness of Being* is dissected equally with the narcissism of an ex-boyfriend.

The one thing I've never said to Miriam, but often thought, is that I wish she'd had a child of her own. I wish she'd had the experience of carrying a baby inside her, the stretching weight of it in the belly, because I know how deeply she would have felt it. I don't say it aloud because she might hear it as lessening the value of her mothering of her stepson, as if it were somehow less than being a 'real' mother. The truth is, of anyone I know, she has the most natural ability for the patient loving a child requires. The integrity and purity of heart she offers to children is an essential quality to me – I don't think I could be friends with someone who could not love a child. It seems a too specific criterion for friendship, but there is something limitless demanded by a child, an endless extension of the capacity to imagine and understand and simply deal with everyday life that makes a person's heart atomise and reconstitute as both raw and enduring. Such a heart can be relied on. If I needed her, she would not let me down.

~

Gina was already there, sitting on the grass in Rushcutters Bay Park, when I arrived. Her posture looked friendly – it's hard to sit on grass in a closed way – and we greeted each other with the usual two kisses, but her manner was cool and resistant. I tried to smile as I sat down opposite her, but it wasn't reciprocated. The sea was glittering behind her, masts clinking, boats bobbing.

I had a speech ready in my mind. I had experience with such a meeting, with my younger sister after a long period of difficulty in our connection with each other. The details of it don't matter here – under Montaigne's 'no other traffic' rules, dear sisters are also excluded from the definition of pure friendship – but I did learn that two things mattered. One was that both people must want a reconciliation and I wasn't sure if

Gina did, but at least she was here – and the other was to start with what was right rather than what was wrong. So I told her what she meant to me. It was hard speaking into the coldness.

'I just want to say your friendship has meant the world to me,' I said. 'I love your openness, your passion for everything, our conversations, your care for everyone in your world. It has been one of the joys of my life.' I observed a slight thaw as I spoke. Then I said that I had a few thoughts about what might be wrong. 'I've thought of nothing else for weeks, but maybe it would be better for you to speak first.'

Her manner became cold again. She spoke tersely. She really had nothing much to say. She didn't see there was anything to say. She didn't see the point.

My heart contracted. A twisting pain. Does it really contract? It feels like muscles squeezing the heart inwards. I had walked down to the park with such high hopes, very nervous, but with a steady belief that we would sort it out. I hadn't really considered the possibility that it wouldn't work. It was unthinkable that we wouldn't return to our old ease and delight. I tried again.

'Well, I guess I could say what I think could be the matter. I think something went wrong when we were down at Lacapelle, at Vicky's place.' I stopped.

Gina nodded.

'I think I was behaving weirdly there,' I said.

'Yes', said Gina. Her voice was still cold but there was a flicker of light in her eyes.

It felt too hard to go on. I wasn't being received; it was as if I were talking to a rock. Then suddenly Gina began to speak.

'You were so dismissive. Treating me as if what I said didn't matter.'

'When?' I replied. 'At Lacapelle?'

'Yes. That night at the table.'

What night? I felt panicky. I couldn't remember any night. I couldn't remember anything I'd said that could have been hurtful. I didn't know what she meant.

'I'm really sorry. When was it? What did I say?'

'I said, it was at the table. I was talking about my mother. And you said I should get over myself.'

'I really don't remember saying that. I can't imagine saying it. I certainly don't think it.'

I pictured the room and the table, trying to bring back the memory. I started to remember a conversation about her mother, but nothing about what either of us had said.

'We were at the table,' she said again, 'after we had finished dinner. I was talking about Mum, you dismissively said something like, "It will be all right. She was probably just trying to help." Completely undermining my reality.' Her voice was still cold but angry now as well.

Suddenly the scene sprang into clear focus in my mind. I could see not just the long wooden table and the remains of the meal and the yellow angular teapot on the dresser behind, but what Gina had said and what I said. It had come into memory from blank spongy nothingness, not gradually back into detail, bit by bit, but all at once. I think it was because Gina had said the exact phrase I had used, 'She was probably just trying to help.' It meant that I could even remember what I was thinking when I said it.

'I'm really sorry,' I said again. 'I didn't mean at all to undermine you. I can remember what I was thinking – I was thinking of myself as a mother and trying to do my best and failing. I just transferred that over to your mother. I really didn't mean that you didn't have a right to be upset by what she said. I can see now that's how it sounded.'

'You sounded just like my family dismissing me,' she said, but visibly loosening for the first time. She shifted her body on the grass, tucking her legs to the opposite side. We kept talking, going over the details of the conversation that evening. Gina's coldness began to melt but she was still angry. I felt relieved that it wasn't my generally weird behaviour and apologised several times for not properly listening. I could still feel the tightness in my stomach though, the worry I'd had for all those weeks that the rift was my fault. I knew I had to confess, even if Gina hadn't noticed my strained behaviour at Lacapelle and even if it made her angry all over again.

'It's curious because I had thought it was something else altogether. I thought it was me acting strangely around you and Anthony.'

'That too. What the hell! What was that? Who do you think I am? That you would think I was the kind of person who would steal someone's husband!' Her voice was coldly furious again and I wished I hadn't said anything.

'I don't think that!'

I tried to explain my strange behaviour; that I was so concerned with showing that I didn't mind and wasn't threatened by their friendship, that it made me 'act' not minding. She found it incomprehensible – who wouldn't? – but I persisted. I felt like crying. I was a ridiculous human being; even Anthony thought I was foolish.

'I've always been over-concerned about what people think of me. I think it comes from being left out when I went to high school. I didn't know how to be. That whole first year.' I hadn't talked about any of that for years, maybe ever, except to

Anthony. I had always made out that I had friends like everyone else in high school. But perhaps it would have happened anyway. Ever since I'd lost my childhood unselfconsciousness, I'd been concerned with the construction of myself.

As I talked, I realised the split I'd always felt because of it. There was always the sense of being a construction, even in my warmest and most intimate relationships. I might be found out to be nothing. Just a relatively well made shell. It was why I was a writer. It was the only thing that made me feel real and solid all the way through. No, not quite the only thing, the physical reality of body and babies and children and the love I felt, that was real, but now that those children were adults, even that was starting to feel imaginary. I poured all of this out, a flood of the absurdity behind my well-made facade. As I spoke there was a core of certainty about who I was. I was the one observing all this. I felt a wash of relief at my words, my body softened, an old dry split started to melt into shadow.

I could see Gina understanding, knowing what I was talking about. It wasn't what she had come to talk about, but she understood. Her warm light was shining on me again.

We talked more about her mother and her father and his death and her brother and sister and the way she was seen by them, or not seen. We talked for hours on the grass, I think it was near to three hours, until we both felt emotionally spent.

We finally stood up, but it was still not time to part.

'I think we deserve a champagne,' I said.

Gina smiled and said yes.

We walked out of the park and up the hill to a corner café. We sat outside and ordered a glass each. We toasted each other and then we shifted the conversation to the ordinary things of our lives. Gina's work, she had another show coming up, my manuscript and how I wanted to weave the French memoirists I'd been reading into the story, and then how her bedsitter was too small and she thought it was time to buy a studio if she could, and about Anthony and I wanting a place with a garden which we couldn't afford. It was re-establishing the damaged ground of our friendship, the mind and heart connection and the ordinary banal details of everyday life, a re-stitching and reconnecting of threads, making sure they were all still there and would hold.

Afterwards, when I arrived home, Anthony asked me what happened.

'It went well,' I said.

But even when there has been a stormy emotional resolution, things that have been damaged don't necessarily work in the same way anymore. 'I think it's okay now. We'll see.'

Ten

When our hippocampus puts together a memory using stored fragments of scenes, pre-existing knowledge, beliefs and expectations, and then layers in the environment in which the memory is being put together, we don't notice its editing work. I already had images of Rushcutters Bay Park which, no doubt, were edited into the scene of sitting in the park that day, plus an expectation of the goodwill of others formed in my childhood that shapes my interactions with the world. It's a kind of pre-recorded movie into which current scenes are spliced, but I can't always tell where the original movie was shot. Many errors of memory apparently come from flawed 'source monitoring', that is, our neural pathways are not so good at telling where the stored information came from – dream, film, real life – but I have full faith in my memory of that day, what was said, how I felt.

The rift and the reconciliation were in 2010, seven years after the beginning of our friendship. It was the first cut, more an accidental slip than a deliberate pruning and not so deep that it could not repair itself. It is also when my email record and retrieved text messages both start. I still want to rely on my memory of our friendship, whatever is stored in my frontal cortex, but our electronic exchanges seem an extension of memory, or at least a back-up storage compartment with the title *The golden years: Part two* scrawled on it. The difference between hard data and memory is that electronic records are not re-written and re-saved with changes from later events, they present only what was said and done at the time. There is some relief and reassurance in their unmarked freshness.

There are eighty or so emails from Gina, and around one hundred and forty texts. They have become a shorthand record of what we did together, although they don't reveal the first few months of over-compensating carefulness I felt after the first rift. I didn't want to ruin our newly restored trust. The emails and messages are limited evidence, but they at least sketch in events. We went to plays together – Gina often had complimentary tickets and gave one to me, and to films, especially French films – we went to the French Film Festival together; met for coffee at the Bar Coluzzi and Dov or for drinks at The Fountain and the Old Fitz; had dinner mostly at our place; made plans about meeting up in Paris again; loaned each other books; and we read together in Rushcutters Bay Park, Anthony, Gina and I.

Because we lived in an apartment then, without a balcony or garden, Anthony and I sometimes longed to sit outside and read. We bought a couple of ten-dollar fold-up chairs and, on Sunday mornings, got in the habit of taking them down to Embarkation Park at the end of our street, or the Botanic Gardens, or Rushcutters Bay. We would unfold our chairs, then sit and read silently, not talking, just reading. I mentioned it to Gina one day when she asked what we were doing on the weekend.

'Oh, that sounds perfect. I love it! You know I have been looking for ages for someone to read with,' she exclaimed. She still lived in her small bedsitter in Darlinghurst then and while she had a rooftop to sit in the sun, it wasn't the same as a garden.

'Do you want to come too? You can if you like. You'll just need a chair, and your book. We don't talk though.' As I said it I felt uncertain. Not everyone can read silently with other people. It takes a degree of ease to sit with someone else for a long time, each of you absorbed in your own world. I had only ever done it with Anthony and our sons, all of us comfortably silent as we read.

But Gina knew exactly how to do it. She arrived at the appointed time, we selected a spot down near the seawall, we each unfolded our cheap director's chair, chatted briefly and then headed off into our own books. For a short while I felt self-conscious reading in her company, but within ten minutes I fell into the silent reading of perfect companionship, a delicious place. Occasionally one of us looked up and made a remark, or read out a line, and one or other answered, but there was no conversation. Occasionally one of us shifted our chair into the sun, or out of the sun. After an hour or so Anthony walked over to the café and bought us coffees and we talked then, mostly about what we had been reading. Gina said again that she had been looking for someone to read silently with for ages, that it was one of her favourite things, but she didn't know anyone else who liked doing it. Anthony and I both glowed; we were the chosen ones, the creators of the reading circle in the park.

I'm wondering now if Gina realised how honoured she made me, probably all her friends, feel in her friendship. Perhaps it was an unconscious gift, the glow she bestowed on others. I thought for a long time that I was the one who felt chosen by her, that I was gaining more from our connection than she did, but one day after she returned some books she sent a text.

She thanked me for the books – I don't remember which ones they were – and said they were brilliant and perfect. She was working on the editing of a play, sifting and trusting. It was so important, she wrote, to have artist friends who were close. That I was one of those for her. Then she added that she hoped I experienced the exchange that she always felt with me.

I felt a rush of warmth – we were back on the open, loving ground of our friendship. The world had righted itself, the truth of our open-hearted connection flowed between us. At the same time, I realised she might not have felt as powerful in the friendship as I thought she had, that I wasn't the only one who needed reassurance. Perhaps I had projected wholeness and power onto her when she was in fact as fragmented and vulnerable as I was.

Vulnerability was the first thing I noticed about Marguerite – not Marguerite from The Land, although she too was vulnerable – but Marguerite in the Blue Mountains. She was a nodding acquaintance from school events, but I first talked to her when she dropped off her older son to play with mine. She was neatly dressed and very pregnant, looking beautiful but fraught, her dark eyes anxious.

'When are you due?' I asked.

'Next month. Still four weeks to go.'

'It's a bit scary, isn't it?'

She shot me a piercing look. Later, when we were friends, she told me how surprised and grateful she was that I had acknowledged her fear. I don't know why I did. I was more inclined to say safe words, more inclined to ignore worries. Just get on with it. Perhaps it was the memory of my last birth, so hard and emotionally rattling, that had left me more tender than I had been before.

We stood outside my house, talking openly, although we'd only ever exchanged greetings before. She told me she was from South Africa, which was apparent from her clipped and earthy accent anyway. She was dark-haired and dark-skinned; if she still lived there she would have been designated as 'Coloured', a category which limited where she could go to school, which hospital ward she could be sent to, where she could live, where she could swim, where she could sit. She had left South Africa and married Paul, a white Englishman she had met on the boat to Australia. I could tell from our first conversation that we were going to be friends.

A couple of weeks later, on a day pouring with rain, she rang me. I was in the middle of work at home, preparing a class on Early American Literature about which I knew nothing. I had to spend all week reading and taking notes to stay a step ahead of the students.

'The baby is coming,' she said. She sounded afraid.

'Where's Paul?'

'He's at work in Sydney.'

'So you've rung him? He'll be home soon.'

'No. Yes, he is coming. But he's not going to get here in time.'

'How far apart are the contractions?'

'Five minutes'

'They often stay that way for ages.' I thought she was panicking, the thing to do was to soothe her.

'No. It's coming.'

'Do you want me to come around? I can wait with you.' I didn't want to drive anywhere in the pouring rain. I hardly knew her.

'I need to get to the hospital,' she said, her voice urgent.

'Where are you booked?'

'Penrith – it takes forty minutes to get there. And Paul will take over an hour to get home. I haven't got time.'

I suddenly realised I had to let go of what I was doing. I grabbed my keys and dashed out through the rain to the car. It would take two minutes to get to Marguerite's house and with me there, she might settle down and wait for Paul.

When I arrived, Marguerite was at the door with her hospital bag, bent over, waiting for a contraction to finish. There was no question that I had to drive her to the hospital right now. It was before mobile phones, so she scribbled a note and left it on the kitchen table. We headed down the Mountains, the rain bucketing down, Marguerite breathing through fierce contractions, me breathing with her and driving as fast as I dared in the deluge. We passed Paul heading up the Mountains, but there was no way to let him know. I could barely see in the driving rain, the road was awash, and my heart was thumping too hard.

'It's coming, drive faster.'

'Hang on, I'm driving as fast as I can. I don't want to kill us all.'

We arrived at Penrith hospital and I left the car out the front where ambulances normally parked and, leaving Marguerite, ran inside. The nurse in reception responded calmly, no doubt used to panicky arrivals, but as soon as they had her inside and checked in the admissions office, they hurtled her off to the delivery room. Five minutes later, a beautiful baby girl was born.

After that beginning, our friendship seemed destined. Marguerite said if I hadn't made that remark about birth being scary, she would never have thought to ring me and, as there was no-one else to ask, she would have had the baby alone at home, and who knows what would have happened. She asked me to be her daughter's godmother. Marguerite, like me, was brought up a Catholic, but, unlike me, was still a believer. I said yes, but explained that I was unlikely to give any of the religious guidance required from godmothers.

Marguerite didn't mind. 'So long as you are there,' she said.

We visited each other, but I think I mostly went to her place. We talked about work – she was a high-school teacher and I was just beginning to teach writing classes – and about our families, about children and how to bring them up, about parents who would come and stay for too long, about complicated sisters.

One day when I was visiting, she told me a story about her restless teenage brother. 'You never know how kids will turn out,' she began. He had been beaten up in the streets one night in Johannesburg, then taken to hospital where, according to a secret phone call to her parents from a Coloured doctor, he had been left to die so that his heart could be used. It was during the era of the first heart transplants in South Africa. Her parents rushed to the hospital and demanded their son be looked after, and now, said Marguerite, he's an accountant in Canada.

She told the story as an illustration of how her risk-taking brother was now a steady and respectable member of his community, but I heard it as a story of brutal racism. I tried to write it several times over the next year or so, a story about the 'black heart' of racism, but it didn't work until one day I remembered what I had felt when she had first told me. The inadmissible truth was that I had been jealous of her having such a powerful story from her childhood when my childhood was so uneventful. I realised my first emotion, even before shock and compassion, was story-envy – I wanted her story. So, I wrote a story instead about growing up in Australia where the suffering of others was treated as a story to take and use; it became an account of my own black heart. That story was published in a literary magazine, and I proudly gave a copy to Marguerite.

She invited me around for a coffee a couple of weeks later. When she opened the door, it was obvious something was wrong. She was terse and cold; it wasn't at all her usual warm and loving welcome. I have never been able to handle coldness, the withdrawal of love. I become instantly a frightened child, trembling – which makes me realise it must have been how my mother disciplined me. I don't think it happened often, but often enough for me to fear it. I will do just about anything to win back love from coldness.

I had remembered her anger as being a reaction to my confession of story-envy – and perhaps it was underneath. Confession never guarantees absolution. But just now I re-read the story in a dusty magazine from over thirty years ago and the phrase I had remembered upsetting her is not there. The fragments start coming back to me. Her accusations were about Paul. It was something I'd said rather than something

I'd written. I had used a phrasing the previous time I visited her, 'You nabbed Paul', which for me was a lighthearted way of saying she had seen he was a good man and how lucky they both were to have found each other. But that wasn't how Marguerite heard it.

'You said I had grabbed Paul, used him as a way out. A way out of being Coloured. That I was lucky he picked me.' She was speaking quietly but intensely. 'I love Paul, we fell in love.' I was so afraid of her coldness I could barely find the words to answer. We talked for ages. I apologised over and over for the wording, until I convinced her that 'thinking she was lucky that a white man wanted her' was the furthest implication from my mind.

'In fact,' I finally said, 'I think the opposite. You are beautiful – I think Paul is the bloody lucky one.'

She allowed a very small smile at that. I eventually went home, still feeling ambushed but believing that we could still be friends. We did keep seeing each other, but soon I had more work on at university and she moved to another town, so the visits became less and less often.

I hadn't seen her for a long while when she rang up out of the blue and asked me to come and visit her. After I knocked on her door, she took a while to open it, and when she did she was wearing a t-shirt with some liquid spilled down the front of it. She had always been neatly dressed, much more so than I was. I felt unsettled.

The disturbance increased as she talked, somehow more loosely than usual, until I finally realised she was drunk. I stayed for a couple of hours, disconcerted but acting as if everything was the way it had been. Her daughter, my god-daughter, came home from school and treated her mother coolly, going about her business as normal. It was evident she was used to this.

After that Marguerite contacted me a few times and each time I fobbed her off. I felt guilty but I didn't know what to do. I have never known how to relate to anyone who has had too much to drink – except when I also have had too much to drink. My mother's father was an alcoholic and she created in our family the feeling that any drinking of alcohol was not a good thing. I can remember my father only ever having a glass of beer at the end of harvest – just one glass once a year. Although I like having a glass of wine or beer in the evenings, and theoretically have no problem with intoxication, I have a pinched-mouth attitude to actual drunks. I try to hide it, but it's there. I remember driving up the Mountains one day, and in a kind of reverse movement of the rainy birth drive down the Mountains, I decided I wouldn't respond to Marguerite's calls.

It was another few years before I received an email from her. She was dry and wanted to say sorry for anything that had happened before. I was the one who should have said sorry, but I didn't. We exchanged emails, she sent me photos of her new grandchildren, but I had moved to Sydney by then and we didn't meet up.

One day she turned up in a writing class I was giving at Varuna Writers' House in the Blue Mountains. It was the first time I had seen her in years. We were changed, not young mothers anymore, but there was an intense recognition as we looked at each other. I felt relieved that she had forgiven my neglect; I wondered what we had in common now that our children had grown and our parents had died, but there was ease between us as we talked during the class break. We stood by the fire at Varuna and I felt the warmth of her gaze and a kind of steady strength that she had not had before. She had been through the crucible of addiction and come out the other side, steady as a rock. We talked in the breaks over the next few months of the course, mostly catching up on what our children were up to, not talking about what she had been through.

As it's happened, we haven't visited each other since, partly because we live in different parts of the country – she moved to Queensland – but we still connect on social media. With some people, it is just staying in touch for the sake of it, but with Marguerite there is a loving connection, perhaps because we have seen each other's frailties, my greedy insensitivity and her drowned sorrows. Whenever we exchange news or comments, I feel warmth for the times that we shared, and some guilt.

~

Not long ago, I sat by a river staring at the fast-flowing water. It was a snow-fed river, rushing over boulders and tumbling down rapids then swirling into pools and onwards into the sea. At first, I thought of Hermann Hesse's Siddhartha sitting by the river, finding enlightenment after parting ways with his friend, Govinda. Then I thought of Gilgamesh and Enkidu bathing in the river, reconnecting themselves to the gods. (I like the way the natural world lives in books and then books live in the natural world.) And then I became absorbed in watching the flow of water, eddies and tiny whirlpools, striations and glassy ovals directly in front of me. The varying depths of the riverbed and the rocks and holes caused the miniature maelstroms, a trailing bush created the striations, each constantly shifting and changing shape. But what fascinated me was the sheen of surface tension on the water, sometimes disturbed as little waves formed and broke, but always re-forming. It was almost a fabric lying on the water, holding it together on the surface, an undulating silvery silken skin. Like people, I thought dreamily, mesmerised by the water, each of us holding together under the surface tension, a smooth covering over the rocks and holes. A friend sees beneath the surface tension, sees under the smooth skin to the deep, uneven undercurrents. A friend 'searches the depth of your heart to know your needs', as La Fontaine wrote in *Les Deux Amis*. How restful to feel that your murky vulnerable heart has been seen and accepted as it is. No need to hide, no need to impress. It's a rare enough relief.

~

I met Paula soon after I moved to the Mountains. She was the mother of one of Matthew's friends from school, as most of the women who became friends at that time were. The almost daily process of dropping off and picking up our sons at each other's houses gave a natural framework and rhythm to the unfolding of friendship, but at first I didn't think Paula would become a friend.

The people I met through Korowal, an alternative school in the bush near Katoomba, were all living on the fringe in some way, through their work, gender, colour or spiritual beliefs. They were artists, actors, other writers, gay couples – both Matthew's friends in kindergarten had two female parents – people building their own mud-brick houses, natural therapy healers, political activists. Most lived on very little – we were living on welfare supplemented by Anthony's taxi driving – and didn't want more, not materially anyway.

With Paula, as with Jane, I remember the first moment I met her. It's as if the brain knows someone will matter to you and it clicks a mind-photo of a face and body, clear and geographically located. With Matthew standing by my side, I knocked on the door of her neat suburban house in Springwood. The moment she opened the door I had an immediate impression of a self-contained middle-class woman, fine, blonde-streaked hair, observant blue eyes, about ten years older than I was. She doesn't live in the same world as me, I thought, based purely on my (mis)conception of her as conventional and well off.

But our sons remained friends, so I saw Paula regularly at drop-offs and pick-ups and we started talking. I learnt that she was recently divorced, that she hated her suburban brick house and almost everything about the social structures of Western life, that she had an English working-class background and had put herself through university, that she used to be a radio journalist and now lived on a single-mother's pension and odd editing jobs – and that she wanted to write.

Our sons started going to Zen Chi Ryu martial arts on Friday afternoons. The dojo was nearer to Paula's place, so I collected the boys, dropped them off at the class and came back for a cup of tea with her every Friday. We talked about writing – both of us were unpublished except for a few short stories and articles – and I sometimes showed her my work but I didn't see any of hers; she wasn't really writing anything much at the moment.

'I'll get started soon,' she said. 'I just need to sort a few things out first.'

I took it all at face value but after a while I began to realise that nothing ever happened. There was always a reason why she couldn't start now; she was always going to get started soon. When friends started to get computers – I hadn't been able to afford one yet – she said she had to get one before she could start. She just had to get that sorted, then she would be fine. I started to feel critical. Just sit down and write, I thought. I had no real idea of the emotional trauma behind her inability to sit down and do it.

It's not that she didn't tell me, over and over, but when I try to recall it now, I realise I must not ever have listened properly – all I can remember are vague fragments. A disapproving mother, Methodist, narrow, judgemental; a thwarted love when she was a teenager; a passionate sensuality that got her into trouble with men, a disconnect with the soullessness of contemporary life. She researched psychological therapies, read all the latest healing books, went to therapists, and 'worked' on herself, as she called it.

She had a hungry analytical mind, which sometimes wore me out. 'Now that I have it sorted, I can get started with my life,' she said one week. I felt relieved and happy for her and agreed with her full analysis of what had happened in her past. The next week it was all unpicked and the premises I had agreed to had disappeared. The second and third time she understood and sorted everything, I felt relief and happiness for her again, and then again, the confusion of having all the insights I had agreed to dissolved by the next week. It continued, the fourth and fifth and sixth time, week after week. There was a pressurised feeling in my brain as last week's definite resolutions were treated as if they had never existed. It felt like an endless merry-go-round, and I started to feel like getting off.

One day when I felt more than usually impatient with the latest labyrinthine analysis, I decided to point out that everything she was saying was the opposite of what she had said the week before. We were sitting on a bench, I'm not sure why or where exactly, I only recall that it was somewhere outdoors in the street. We were sitting side-by-side, and she must have been able to sense my lack of sympathy because suddenly, before I'd pointed out anything, tears started rolling down her face. There was no containment of her anguish in analysis, only a pure outpouring of her emotional pain and loneliness. Her existential grief. She was a woman crying on a public bench. I sat there, shamed in my emotional privilege, knowing I should ask for her forgiveness, but not knowing where to start with the extent of my hard-heartedness.

I said nothing, but it was a silent turning point as I saw how little I knew about other people's lives. Paula, like everyone, was an archipelago of small islands visible to others, the rest, the drowned depths could only be sensed. It was the job of a friend, surely, to sound those depths, to listen to the echoes coming from them. Why had I thought it my work to judge when Paula gave me only encouragement and support, especially for my writing?

She read widely about politics and environmental catastrophes, encompassing the 'big picture' easily with her wide-ranging mind. I remember sitting in her tidy lounge room – my first impression of neatness never changed – a pot of tea, sunlight coming in through a window. She had just finished reading a book on the history of money, its imaginary value, the nature of trade and economic structures. As she ranged across an analysis of the world's current ills, I was forced to recognise that I had a 'small picture' mind, one that was absorbed by the endless scrimshaw detail of inner and outer lives. She saw what had made the details happen, the large forces. Time and again, I came away from our conversations feeling as if my brain was exploding with the vastness of her conceptions.

But we also discussed relationships, especially with men. Her ex-husband was a dreamer, she said disparagingly. 'He grew marijuana in our back garden. We had a baby! He wanted to be a writer and wasn't earning any money to support us.'

'It sounds like Anthony,' I said, laughing.

She looked at me, hurt.

Another afternoon we were walking up her street in Springwood, and I told her that I had enrolled in an MA at a university in Sydney.

'You're lucky that Anthony said yes to that,' she said.

I looked at her in astonishment. 'It didn't even enter my head to ask him!'

She laughed, realising what she had revealed about herself. She was only ten years older than me but between my youth and hers the Western world had started changing for women. By the time I left school I believed I could do whatever I wanted, that choices were all mine to make. Paula often repeated my response word-for-word, laughing each time; 'It didn't even enter my head to ask him.' It made her re-think her sense of accountability to men, she said.

She had several lovers over the years. I listened avidly to her psychological analysis of each relationship, sometimes throwing in a few stories myself, but mostly devouring hers. She had a sexual aura and attracted men easily, but I wondered sometimes if they weren't afraid of her wide-ranging mind. And then one day, Michael, my friend from university days, turned up in need of a home and stayed with us for a few months. As soon as he and Paula met, the sexual energy between them was obvious. I remember watching Paula at a Sunday lunch on my back veranda, leaning forward, elbow on table, flirting and laughing, sensuous in her every move.

'Michael has a sensitive soul. He's affectionate – and clever,' she said. I silently bridled. He was my friend.

Michael moved in with Paula and I found myself resenting it. The old judgement of Paula as not belonging in my world surfaced. She couldn't walk around in my alternative world and cherrypick my friends. I knew it was an absurd possessiveness, but I couldn't shake it off.

Michael was a drinker though, a needling drunk, and one night Paula turned up at my place shaken and in tears. He had physically threatened her. She stayed the night and asked him to move out the next day. I was relieved, not just for her, feeling my world settle back into its proper distinct parts.

It wasn't the end of their relationship, it was too passionate to end with one storm, but they eventually went their separate ways. I never admitted my guilty possessiveness to Paula – or anyone else for that matter – but I suspect she saw it anyway. I hide a lot, but I am not very good at it. My feelings slip out in a quick glance, or in the sheen of my eyes, or the way I walk across a room, all of which Paula is gifted at observing.

Paula moved to Byron Bay on the far north coast and immediately felt at home in the subtropical warmth and fertility, enfolded by tangled rainforest and cultivated fields. 'It's the first time I have felt I belong in a landscape,' she said. It was before emails and text messages, but she rang, and we had long conversations on the phone.

One summer holiday I drove north with Anthony and our boys to visit her. We stayed in her sunny house not far from the beach, sand on the bare floorboards, open and relaxed. She gave us an air mattress to sleep on in the living room, but it

209

kept going down all night and each time one of us turned, the other was bumped down onto the bare boards. In the morning we were sleep-deprived and ill-tempered with each other. Later that day as Paula and I walked barefoot along the beach, I told her that Anthony and I had had an argument because we didn't get much sleep on the dodgy mattress. A curious look came over her face, one I still can't pin down, but it had something of the caught-out, defiant child in it.

'I know it's a terrible mattress,' she said. 'But I thought, you have each other in bed and I have no-one. I'm going to keep the comfortable bed for myself.'

I burst out laughing. 'You gave us the horrible bed on purpose? To punish us and make us fight.'

She nodded.

'I love it!' I said. I meant that I liked that she had told me. It would have been so easy for her to say, 'Oh dear, I'm so sorry, I didn't know that mattress was like that.' In her confession, I felt absolved of some of my own history of less than good-hearted thoughts. We kept walking along the beach a long way, just the two of us.

It was several years later when Paula told me that she felt she had to let go of what was holding her back, that she was ready to start her life. This time it sounded different. There was calmness and humour, not the desperate insistence of earlier statements. In memory there is no setting for this conversation, no tables and chairs, but the sense of it has stayed with me, along with some of the exact words. 'And I want to thank you for all the years you have listened to me sort out my life,' she said, smiling.

I admitted that I had wanted to walk away several times and she smiled again. 'Don't be too hard on yourself,' she said. We talked then about our friendship, our failings, and our care for each other. It can happen sometimes that the right words can be said, that people can reach each other across the abyss.

When I last visited Paula in a tiny village in the hinterland behind Byron Bay, I confessed to her that I was writing a book about friendship.

She smiled. 'It's the most extraordinary thing, friendship, that anyone can reach anyone else is a miracle. To stretch out across the vast space and be at one with someone else,' she said.

'You'll be in it,' I said. 'Or at least, my construction of you.'

She laughed. 'Say whatever you like.'

Of any of my friends, I know she means it. When I think of my friendship with her I am reminded of Toni Morrison's words, 'She is a friend of my mind. She gather me, man. The pieces I am, she gather them and give them back to me in all the right order.'

I like to think I do the same for her.

Eleven

In making a distinction between the 'flames of passion' and friendship, Montaigne says 'the love of friends is a general universal warmth, temperate moreover and smooth. A warmth which is constant and at rest, all gentleness and evenness, having nothing sharp nor keen.'

It's evident that my friendships have not been 'all gentleness and evenness', but neither have they been tempestuous. I have had unspoken judgements, occasional irritations, some needling in the way Gilgamesh needles Enkidu in the forest, but not the 'feverish fire' of passion, the uncontrolled battles at the top of my vocal range that I've had with Anthony at times. Nor have I had, with friends, the exquisite tenderness I've shared with him.

When Montaigne distinguished between the heightened 'true' friendship he had with de la Boétie and 'common friendship' he also noted that common friendship can be shared, there is no exclusivity in it, it is 'bound by chance or some suitability', and it can rest on one aspect.

'In one friend one can love beauty, in another, affability, in another generosity ... and so on.' The unique friendship he is talking about loosens all other bonds, there is only one another, it is exclusive.

I'm content with sharing friendships with others in the same circle, and accepting the delineations of each friendship – 'loving affability in one, in another generosity', and in another a passion for creativity, the sacred ground. That ground was the territory of my friendship with Gina. We talked about the making of things endlessly. There's not so many of my friends who have wanted to do that, perhaps that's why I've felt its loss so keenly.

~

Gina arranged to come around to our Victoria Street apartment a few months after our reconciliation to do a reading of her Simone Signoret script. She emailed that it was a second draft, and her plan was still to do the third 'Signoret' draft in Paris. She had read through the previous one after about ten days away from it and thought it was thready (lots of loose ends), and that it would benefit from feedback from Anthony and me.

'Maybe Saturday night?' she suggested 'Takeaway and a read through? I'll buy us dinner.'

She arrived with the script printed out, looking fresh after walking in the cool air. She was nervous so we sat down with a glass of red wine and talked for a while. Anthony was making dinner despite Gina's offer – he always cooked – so we decided to eat first and then have the reading. We didn't sit at the table, just balanced plates on our knees, ready to focus on the job.

'I think we should listen without interrupting at first,' I said.

'Yes, but stop me if there's anything that just seems incomprehensible.'

'I'll take notes,' I said. 'I don't know if I have a good sense of theatrical structure so I might not be of much use.'

'Structure is structure,' Gina said. 'You'll be able to see it – or not.'

We finished dinner quickly, Gina picked up the script, settled herself back in her lounge chair, pulled a wry face, and began.

'Signoret.'

Her face and body changed as she concentrated, relaxed and focused at the same time. Her head was bent slightly so that her thick hair swung forward but she pulled it back with one hand and lifted the script. She glanced quickly over at me, aware that I was watching her rather than listening. I sat back with my notebook.

She read with absorption, but I could see her critical faculty hovering like a guiding spirit somewhere above or behind her voice. These were her words, but she was both writer and actor. I understood the writing part, what it was like to see my words on the page and not know if they conveyed the colour and light of the day, but I didn't know about the acting part, the losing of voice and body and self in another character.

She had done an enormous amount of research on Signoret, watching her films over and over, and taking notes from biographies and academic papers. She was fascinated by the way Signoret had become each character so fully that no-one really knew her outside of the sexy, earthy characters she played. The script was a series of short scenes exploring her life and work, a play for one actor. Each of the scenes was like a small jewel, poetic and insightful, but after a while I realised that they were sprawling outwards like a loosely made mandala. I glanced over at Anthony, and I could see he was ready to call a break.

I made tea and put the cake she had brought on plates on the low Afghani table. We talked about structure. We were only three-quarters of the way through, but it was time to talk. Gina already knew it was too loose. It was her process to put everything in at first, and then cut away. Anthony, who has a good editing mind, said paring back was needed; he liked to start with less and build. 'It's going in too many directions at once.'

Gina started reading again. She was tired now, but even here in our lounge room, she gave her all. I realise now that it was central to her, that nothing could be done half-heartedly, that it was impossible for her not to give herself fully. It was what made her acting so powerful and her friendship so rich. All or nothing.

In the last section it was clear that the play was too long. It was nearly three hours since we had begun. My attention wandered. Some of the material seemed, if not repetitious, then running parallel to what had gone before. The momentum had been lost. We were all tired by the end of it, but we started in on the structure again. What could go, what needed to stay? What are you really wanting to say? Then an image triggered a connection for Anthony, and he jumped up and grabbed Ferlinghetti's *A Coney Island of the Mind* and read part of one of the poems:

> we ogle the unobtainable imagined mystery
> Yet away around on the far side
> like the stage door of a circus tent

is a wide vent in the battlements
where even elephants/ waltz through.

Suddenly, we were excited again, happy with the connections we were making. We buzzed for a while, rejuvenated, working productively.

'This is what I love,' said Gina, 'working with friends. It's the best.'

It was late, around midnight by the time we finished, or at least called a halt. There was more to say, more to do, but it was enough for one session. The second wind that poetry had blown through us had faded and we were all hit by weariness at the same time. Anthony asked if Gina needed him to walk with her home through Kings Cross, but she said she was fine.

The next morning Gina sent another email, thanking us for making space for her. She said it was terrifically useful, that the first attempt at getting the words from her mind out of her mouth, in a space so trustworthy, was essential. She thought she still had a long way to go, but was more confident of getting there. She thanked Anthony, too, for bringing her back to some poetry, it had been ages.

The golden age was fully restored. It felt as if the rift had not even left a scar.

I do know continuity is an illusion, in the sense that it doesn't exist outside my mind. There is the illusion of unity between past and present whenever I recall memories of my friends even though each memory is made of separate fragments. Every time I think of them, I put them together without seeing the gaps, so I have a continuous walking-talking cyber-memory of Jane or Paula or Gina, almost like the real thing. Science tells me each of them are made of two different kinds of memories, one to do with facts, what each friend said and did, and the other to do with the process of being a friend, knowing how to 'be' with each one.

Memory researchers identify the two kinds of memory as declarative and procedural. Declarative memory is explicit and is further divided into semantic and autobiographical memory; semantic contains facts and definitions; autobiographical contains experiences and their emotional charge.

Procedural memory is mostly implicit, not conscious. It's about knowing how to do things. In the moment of writing, I don't think about how to write a sentence, the nouns and verbs know where to go, and in the moment of acting, Gina strode like a detective without consciously directing each of her limbs. Procedural memory is the sacred ground. It draws in its unseen way on semantic and autobiographical memory and makes something new. It is that part of memory that resists analysis, and if I do analyse it, become conscious of it, I become awkward, I lose flow. Knowing how to be a friend comes from procedural memory, but thinking about it after it has ended, is autobiographical.

~

The Mountains years are crowded with autobiographical memories and, specifically, with memories of bountiful friendship. I had turned thirty the year before we bought the small concrete-block house in the mountain village of Hazelbrook. We still lived on very little; Anthony drove taxis in Sydney on the weekends and I was teaching part-time at the university in Western Sydney, but there was a bush-filled backyard with a creek at the end of it, a room for writing, and Sunday potluck lunches on the back veranda. Friends called in often, mostly school parents.

Cathy, who came to Lacapelle-Biron with Anthony, Gina and me, was, at first, only 'Ben's mother'. She was small and slight like me, with short dark hair and a boyish air – no dresses, no lipstick – and had a reserved manner. She was practical – she and her partner had built their own mud-brick house by hand – but without the bustling air of a practical person; rather the opposite, restless, almost discontented. She had studied at art school but was teaching English to migrants full-time so she rarely had time to make art of any sort. I found it difficult breaking through her reserve, but I was drawn to some shadowiness in her, a curious feeling of grievance. Something wounded. I became determined to make her like me.

I don't remember first meeting her, but I do recall first walking into her mud-brick house, impressed that she had made the curved wall and the angular kitchen and all the bedrooms with her own hands. I couldn't even put up a bookshelf on my own. On the smoothed mud walls there were landscape paintings she had done some years ago, nothing recent. She shrugged when I remarked about them.

I saw a pile of books on her table. I don't remember what they were – it was the late 80s, so probably Elizabeth Jolley or Peter Carey, or maybe Bruce Chatwin – but I know we began talking books. For her, it wasn't about the story, or even the characters, but the moments of revelation, the lovely sentence or scene that had changed her, made her think. Later, when she read books I had written, she gave me precise notes about particular sentences she had liked, which was like giving me small carefully chosen presents.

I was just starting out as a writer when I first met her and so I talked about what I was trying to do. She listened but I sometimes felt her bridling against my enthusiasm. I was the empty pot making so much noise. 'Oh, Patti,' she said at times, implying that I really wasn't to be taken seriously. Or a glance and a remark about the way I was dressed – red lipstick, a leopard-print bolero, an outfit made entirely of tied scarves, always second-hand. It was a comment and a glance I recognised from my mother – you are all show, just settle down.

We talked about our families, the endless discussion about mothers and fathers and brothers and sisters, our partners, our kids.

'All I got from my mother,' she remarked one day, 'was that I was the wrong kind of person.'

We were sitting at the table against the curved mud wall, drinking coffee, the place we always sat if it was too cold to be out in her native garden.

'What kind of person did she want you to be?' I asked.

'Optimistic, I suppose. Full of relentless enthusiasms. Like my older sister.'

Like me, I thought. I wondered then if we don't seek out in friends the same relationships as in our family and try to do a better job of it than we did before. My mother was reserved, introverted, so is my younger sister.

When her children were older, Cathy went back to art school. She built a studio in the bush beside her house and started painting and taking photographs and making small sculptures and installations. New paintings and objects that she had made started appearing in her house. I remember one sculpture, a white egg in a framed cage, which she had placed in her living room and which I found very moving. Every time I looked at it, I wanted to cry.

'An egg should not be caged,' I said.

'No, it shouldn't,' she said wryly.

After she started her degree we began to argue about art, or rather about art education. It was a personal and emotional argument, not at all cool and intellectual. I had studied postmodern literary theory at university and come out with a head full of ideas and very little craft. Now I was devoted to craft, to the right words in the right order, nothing fancy; writers should know sentences, painters should be able to draw and understand colour and structure. Cathy had already learnt craft years before at school and now was lapping up postmodern art theory; we were at opposite stages. The extra and unspoken layer was that I had a brother who was a painter, mostly self-taught, who made beautiful, highly skilled paintings, and who disdained the often ill-made conceptual work of contemporary painters. I knew Cathy thought I was defending my brother, but she didn't say so.

When our sons left school, we each took off in different directions, she to Hong Kong, where her partner was teaching English, and I went to France. Our sons didn't see each other anymore, but we emailed each other regularly and once I stopped off and stayed with her in her high-rise apartment for a few days. She showed me around Hong Kong and then, back at her apartment, spread out the pictures she had been making. She had started a Master's degree in art and was now focused on photography instead of painting. At first it was because photographs were easier to submit for assessment from

Hong Kong, but she became fascinated with their possibilities, their relationship to memory and to the construction of a self.

We stood in her tiny workroom in Hong Kong – I was sleeping in it – looking through her images and I loved how they revealed her questioning, observant eye on the world. Each image conveyed clarity and simplicity, but at the same time, an acceptance of the complex nature of even simple things: incense sticks, shadowed walls, dried squid hanging in the market. Looking at her still plainly dressed, unadorned, blending in, I thought, she is in camouflage; no-one would know she is watching so closely. A spy in the house of art. I admired a particular image of an ironing board and a reflection of underwear pegged on a hanger, cut in half dramatically by a dark corner. When I was leaving, she gave it to me. It hangs in my kitchen now in the lovely light that comes in, and whenever I look at it, I'm looking at the world through her eyes.

One day after we had both returned from our long sojourns – she lived in Hong Kong for four years – she visited me in Kings Cross. We were walking back from the café at the El Alamein Fountain, down Orwell Street towards my place, when the art argument started again.

'Why should artists have to theorise in words about their artwork?' I said. 'Making visual art and words come from two different parts of the brain. I don't have to make paintings about my words, why should artists have to write words about their paintings?'

'But visual artists shouldn't be excluded from the intellectual work of theory. We should be able to critically theorise our work,' Cathy countered.

'Of course you can, that's not what I mean. I just mean you shouldn't have to. Not everyone can and it shouldn't diminish their work or mean it doesn't get noticed. Making art and theorising about it are two totally different things.'

'Is this really about your brother?'

I looked at her. She had finally said it.

'No,' I said. 'It's about people who paint and draw and sculpt not letting word-people like me take over their territory. We already control the world. Keep us out of painting.'

'You think just because someone paints they can't think?' She was heated now, much more than I thought was warranted. It felt very personal, hurt, as if she thought I was attacking her. I sensed then, and can see now, that we were each defending a secret fear, an opposite anxiety about our work. I feared not being creative enough, unrestricted by theory, she feared not being intellectual enough. We were poking at each other's hidden sore.

We haven't had the art argument again. Sometimes we go near it, but one of us veers away. We talk about our work still, specific projects we are working on – she is just now working on layering photographs of vegetable flowers to create textured images.

'It sounds painterly,' I said.

'I don't like people saying my images are painterly as if it were a compliment for a photograph to be like a painting. As if painting is real art and photographs are not.' She was prickling.

'But some people admire a painting because it looks just like a photograph,' I said.

She laughed then. 'That's true.'

Cathy has moved back to the country now, to the north coast, so we don't see each other as often, every few months instead of every few weeks. We send each other messages and when we meet we talk about the books we have read, and discuss the practice of art, carefully, and exchange stories about our family, and we occasionally, but not very often, mention mutual friends.

~

In recounting my friendship history, I feel a chronicler's concern for the facts, for every friend and everything that happened. But it's futile, because it's impossible to include all the detail of even one friendship, let alone include every friend. The Brueghel painting is becoming crowded with characters spread all over the village on the day of the fair; playing, arguing, eating, gossiping, drinking, sleeping, performing, arriving and leaving. And still, dear friends have been left out altogether or unfairly truncated. The whole shifting crowded scene is not background, but the actual subject of the painting, every figure matters. Brueghel was able to look from above, to see the whole pattern and hold it together with flashes of red dress and red banners and red fire, but I'm down there in the village in the general chaos, most likely in the audience watching the travelling players on the stage in the centre of the picture. I cannot properly see what the whole village looks like.

~

Connie was a mutual friend. Cathy, Connie and I often met at the same time, and occasionally Gina joined us as well. I've never been in a shiny group always having coffee together, like *Friends* or *Sex and the City* – but friendships have eddied and gathered at times, especially in the early days of Sunday lunches and going to each other's places every few days to pick up kids. Connie and I met because our sons, Patrick and

Merric, were best friends even before Korowal School – they had met at childcare when they were three – so I saw her, or her partner, James, every other day for years.

In the spectrum between reserved and expressive, with me as a shifting middle point, Connie was at the opposite end to Cathy. She had flamboyant red hair and a voluptuous body, which in those days she hid behind colourful, loose clothes. She was an actor and was warm, outgoing, generous, exuberant. She talked openly and laughed loudly; she ate life up in large mouthfuls. She still does.

Connie and James lived ten minutes' walk from our place in a log house with a wild and fruitful garden that James had created. Anthony and I became friends with James as well, in one of those coupled friendships where there is nearly as much exchange with one as with the other. Steady and gentle, James dropped off and picked up the boys, took them to shows and outings we couldn't afford, let them play in mud until they were totally covered from head to toe, smoked joints with Anthony on the back veranda, told us about Connie's exploits when she was on tour with a show. In many ways our lives appeared to run in parallel; we were at the same stage of life, we lived outside a mainstream working life on very little money, our sons were at home in each other's houses.

The boys were important in our friendship. In fact, I think my friendship with Connie grew out of our shared pleasure in *their* friendship. We both delighted in the way they created worlds for each other to inhabit for days on end. After school and on weekends, Patrick and Merric lived in a Tolkien-coloured universe: dragons and potions and orcs and dark forests grew around us as we sipped tea on our back verandas. We each still have a photograph I took of the boys, their concentrated faces bent over a row of tiny phials of coloured water – red, yellow, blue, purple, green – as they made magic potions one sunny afternoon. It seemed to us a picture of their true beings – and even now when they are grown men with children of their own, we know this is who they truly are.

Every summer, both families went on bushwalks down through the scribbly gums to the damp tree ferns of nearby Terrace Falls, had picnics by creeks and pools and watched our boys play in the water, pale against the prehistoric rocks. On weekends, Connie stood on the side of soccer fields and yelled encouragement with an abandon I couldn't match, we saw each other at school fairs, concerts, at the shops, at other people's parties, and every year we holidayed at Wamberal on the Central Coast with a house-load of boys and other parents.

I remember one year at Wamberal, Connie stitching together a quilt for Dolly after she had suffered the brain haemorrhage. A fundraiser concert and auction had been organised at the Belvoir Street Theatre and Connie asked us all to make squares for a quilt. She sewed with her machine at the table and afterwards hand-stitched pieces together as the rest of us talked and came and went from the room. It was methodical work, the kind that I have never been any good at, and although I knew Connie made quilts between acting jobs, I realised I had not seen that quiet and orderly part of her before.

Connie and I had years' long conversations about our boys and about the families we had grown up in, and most of all, about the state of our own souls. We both at that time believed in some sort of undefined higher power – perhaps all mothers need access to magic spells to protect their children – and understood life as a process of becoming our best selves, so we examined endlessly the nature of our relationships, our judgements, our failures, our insights. I wondered if it was because we were both brought up Catholic, trained in examining our consciences – it's a habit impossible to let go – but then Cathy, too, was brought up a Catholic and it wasn't part of my friendship with her. It was, and is, the particular quality of my connection with Connie that even now, when I have given up on higher powers, we share our self-examination, a couple of dusty travellers to who-knows-where.

Connie was, and is, generous. She often gave me 'with comps' to the shows she was in at Belvoir Street, the Griffin, The Wharf, The Q, never making me feel as if I owed her, but I was able to go to the theatre only because of her thoughtfulness. I watched her act, but I didn't share in the process. Even though theatre was central to her life – she had wanted to be an actor since she was six – she didn't discuss her acting in the way Gina did. She talked about whatever play she was rehearsing with boundless enthusiasm, but was uncharacteristically reserved about her creative process. Our connection was on a more blood-and-turmoil-of-life level, tied to emotion rather than art.

We were always pleased to see each other, but Connie was more expressive about it, thrilled when my books were accepted for publication, admiring of any successes, sympathetic about failures. She bought me little presents when books were published – a brass bee brooch when the book with bees on the cover came out – and gave me huge, warm hugs. She was like that with everyone; intensely excited, intensely sympathetic, passionate. Every now and then when I was feeling low, her warm, excitable energy felt like something I had to resist.

How glossy that life looks from here, memories burnished by long handling to an impossible sheen. It all happened, of course it did, and the times were good and golden, there was real sweetness, but the memory editor can be romantic and lazy. And self-interested, finding only those memories that fit the preferred version, the one already selected. Every time I sit down, I fight the urge to write only the golden moments, preserved in an amber glow.

Connie knew Dolly before I did, through her partner Kris, another actor. I had met Dolly at one of Connie's parties in their log house on the edge of the bush. The day after Dolly died at the end of a year of pain, Connie said, 'I saw Dolly yesterday and I told her that she didn't have to hang on. She didn't have to keep suffering; she could let go.' We were both standing outside my house; Connie was on the steps leading up to the road, another location-snapped memory.

I nodded, feeling a surge of resentment. How could she claim credit for releasing Dolly from her hell? I felt possessive; I was the one who looked after Dolly's little son, Teddy, three days a week. I was the one who drove to the ends-of-the-suburban-earth to visit Dolly in hospital every week. I didn't say anything, just stewed in silence as I do, and realised later that Connie had only meant to connect herself to what had happened, an ordinary human need. In my proprietorial grief and fear I had misread her.

One night Anthony and I came down from the Mountains to see her in a play at the Griffin. We had arranged to meet with her afterwards for a late supper, so Anthony went down the street to grab a table and I waited for Connie in the foyer. She came out pulling a wheeled suitcase behind her.

'You look like you are running away from home,' I said, joking.

'Funny that,' Connie said, with a look I had never seen on her face, wry and pained.

I stared at her, puzzled.

'I'll tell you down the road. I have to see someone first. I'll be there in a tick.'

I just had time to tell Anthony that Connie had said something puzzling, when she arrived, bag still in tow. She told us then that she had left James. We talked about it all evening of course, and for a long time to come. It was a shock and something I resisted approving of for months. It felt wilful – as if Connie was making something happen for the sake of drama – but I realised my reaction was because I was afraid. Our boys had just left school and were ready to make their own way in the world and who could say what would happen now. If Connie and James could break up, then anything could happen. I wanted everything to stay the same forever; I knew it was the beginning of the end of the shiny part of life.

After Anthony and I moved from the Mountains' house and bought a one-bedroom apartment in Kings Cross, Connie came to see me. I was buying a new rug that day because everything from the Mountains' house was too shabby and dusty. I thought a rug, grey-green like the bush, would look good.

'You need something red, like a waratah,' Connie said, standing in her red coat, leaning on the railing that ran around the walls. I bought a red rug.

Not long afterwards, she moved to a small apartment, ten minutes' walk away on the other side of William Street. I strolled down to her place with a bottle of Bombay Sapphire Gin and we sat on her rooftop looking at the city and toasting our new city lives with gin and tonic. Our boys were grown, and we were not young anymore but we were still friends.

When I left and she hugged me goodbye, I felt enveloped by her, and was aware of my own small, slightly stiff body.

Since leaving James, Connie had begun wearing more flamboyant and sexy clothes. She had always worn striking earrings, beads and colourful outfits, but now they revealed her curvaceous figure. She had dresses with red roses on them, a fitted leather jacket, and ankle boots and swirling skirts with little tops. She was nearly sixty by now, but she always pulled it off, drew an admiring gaze. It was as if she had finally released herself into her body.

One year, Connie and her new boyfriend turned up in Paris for my birthday dinner. I was often alone for my birthday and would just have a drink in a local café after a writing class, trying to look as if I didn't care. Back in Sydney I had joked, 'It's a big one for me this year, why don't you meet me in Paris for my decade celebration.'

Neither Connie nor her boyfriend had any money, but they looked at each other, and said, 'Yes! Let's do it!'

A couple of months later, I booked a table at a Belle Époque restaurant – domes, painted tiles, etched glass, a Parisian dream of a place – and bought a new dress. It was dark purple and tight, and I wondered if I was too old for that kind of thing. I walked into the glorious restaurant feeling self-conscious. Anthony was there, with Vicky, Trish and Gabrielle, friends who lived in Paris. And then Connie arrived in a short black net skirt, a tight scarlet bodice which pushed her always wonderful breasts up into magnificence, torn fish-net stockings and lace-up boots. She was steam-punk perfection at sixty. She strode through the Belle Époque elegance and the waiters stopped what they were doing and watched. All the diners looked up and admired her progress while her boyfriend at her side glowed with pride. As Gabrielle said later, the French dress discreetly, but they love anyone who breaks all the rules.

'To celebrate your birthday!' Connie said, giving me one of her big, warm hugs.

It was a brilliant evening, the food was elegant, the waiters sang happy birthday and I felt properly celebrated. When we walked out of the restaurant and down the street towards the Métro, all eyes were on Connie, and we all smiled and laughed at her causing a sensation in Paris.

A few days later, a small unnoticed child in me thought, everyone in Paris who saw us that evening would remember my friend, Steam-Punk Connie, and no-one would recall the small woman in the tight-fitting dress beside her whose sixtieth birthday it was.

When Connie broke up with her boyfriend a few years after the Paris trip, I reacted in the same way I had when she broke up with James. I wanted her to stay with him, for them to work out their differences. I haven't been like that with my other friends, but with Connie, it was as if I insisted she be a model of coupled happiness. It was partly my 'happily ever after' fantasy – I really do want everyone to live happily ever after – but I realise now it's also that I have a tendency to think I know other people's lives better than they do. During the break-up, I know she felt my lack of support and after each time I met with her, I resolved to do better next time. I think, although I am not sure, that she forgives me each time.

I saw Connie this week and she gave me a present. 'For your birthday,' she said. It was a glasses case with bees printed on it in my favourite green.

'It's beautiful! I love it. But you know it's not my birthday,' I said. 'It's nowhere near it.'

'I know, but I saw it and it called out to me, Patti, Patti, Patti, so I had to get it.' She said 'Patti' in a sweet tiny voice as if the present were speaking.

And then I mentioned the bee brooch she had given me five years earlier, and the bee honey pot that she and her former boyfriend had given me, and we wove our history together again. Then we talked about our sons' babies and showed each other photographs on our phones and we each let the other show all pride and delight, the glow that you must not show others for fear of making them feel left out. She is the friend who allows me to be excessive about those secret joys, and, when I am with her, it never feels like excess.

Twelve

During the golden years, I saw every production Gina was in. There was a major film, a television series, a few readings, including Chekhov – she was a passionate admirer of Chekhov – plus several contemporary plays – *and* at least three Shakespeare's, including a powerful Desdemona.

Othello was performed in an outdoor theatre in the grounds of a grand house in the Blue Mountains. The theatre had a raised grassy stage with a wooden structure providing different levels for the action, high hedges for wings and a freshly mown lawn area below for the audience. There were several rows for blankets and cushions, and then rows of bring-your-own chairs. Anthony and I had brought the directors' chairs we used for reading at Rushcutters Bay.

It was a warm mid-summer twilight, the smells of mown grass and food mixed as people unpacked their picnic dinners and balanced glasses of wine on their knees. Looking along the rows, I saw my sons' former high school teacher, and parents from Korowal School days, people from my writing classes,

and a few of my sons' friends, grown up, but still looking like
boys to me. We were all older and it felt like the past, but it was
a past that didn't feel claustrophobic.

Then Gina was on the grassy stage and the evening centred
itself around her. She looked beautiful in the way everyone
expects of Desdemona, her hair, which she had been letting
go grey, was dyed black, and she was gorgeously costumed in
a red and gold Moroccan-style dress.

She understood Desdemona as she understood every
character I had seen her play, from the inside. It wasn't just to
do with her knowledge of Shakespeare's language, or being in
tune with the rhythm of each speech, or even of the meaning
of the narrative, but a physical knowledge of a living being.
Without self-consciousness, she emanated a calm dignity. If
she tried to persuade Othello, it was an entreaty where she
kept her sense of innocence. It was evident in her every move
that she knew who she was, an intelligent, aristocratic woman.
I felt awed by the transformation of her body and breath as the
story unfolded and she became more desperate, devastated by
Othello's dangerous jealousy.

Afterwards, Anthony and I waited in the warm dark until
she appeared in her t-shirt and jeans. She looked distracted.

'You were superb!' I said, and hugged her.

'Thanks.' she said tersely. 'But I'm furious. Emelia, my
maid, talked to me out of character just before the scene where
I'm killed. I can't believe it. She's done it before.'

'How? I mean, when? We didn't see anything.'

'When I was high up on the set. You wouldn't have been
able to see it. That's not the point. I had told her not to do it
before. What the fuck is she up to? Bloody hell!'

'It must be hard to be suddenly jerked out of character.'

I was trying to understand, not really knowing what it takes to be in character, the almighty concentration.

'It's high-school drama stuff. You don't break character like that.'

'It didn't show though. You were great. Better than Othello I thought.'

Gina nodded briefly.

We had planned to have a late-night drink together, but that obviously wasn't going to happen.

'No drinks at the Ritz, then?'

Gina didn't smile. She was tired and pissed off and needed to go home. Anthony and I gave her a lift back to her place, a house shared with some of the other actors, and said goodnight outside. We both felt deflated but didn't say anything to each other.

The French connection, the Ritzy thread in our friendship, was beginning to fade. I packed up each September, walked for several hundred kilometres – I had become obsessed with long-distance walking – presented the writing workshop, then returned to Sydney in November, always with a small present for Gina. She couldn't afford to go to France as often and when she did go, it was at a different time of year.

Then, one year, less than a month after I had returned home, there was a terrorist attack in central Paris. The Charlie Hebdo newspaper offices in the rue Nicolas-Appert were stormed and twelve people, mostly writers and cartoonists, were killed.

It felt personal, much more than yet another violent news story. I had been wandering in those streets so recently, I was familiar with Charlie Hebdo and its aggressive satirical cartoons – I had a sneaking admiration for its attitude of

offending everyone without distinction – but most of all it was
that people who used words and drawings to earn their daily
bread had been massacred. It felt like a murderous attack on
the people I knew.

'Have you seen it? They are killing us,' Gina texted.

We printed *Je suis Charlie* in large letters on posters and
walked down to the demonstration at Martin Place, not far
from the shootings at the Lindt Café hardly a month earlier.
We stood with mostly young French travellers, shocked and
bewildered, and listened as the French ambassador spoke.
There are photos of both of us, me smiling (at what?) and
Gina serious, both of us holding our home-made placards. I
remember the warm Sydney summer evening, the milling
about, the palpable shock, the sombre mood, the sense of
angry helplessness in young faces, as well as the strength of
shared hurt and outrage, the feeling of solidarity.

It was futile, I suppose, and our outrage was subjective given
the endless, wide-ranging horrors inflicted all over the planet.
But it has made me wonder how much friendship requires a
shared sensibility about the state of the world, shared politics.
It was a given in my friendship with Gina that we had the same
political views and, when I think about it, with all my friends.
I've noticed lately that when I meet someone who could be
a friend there's an unscripted checking of attitudes about the
wider world – on both sides. If we judge for and against the
same issues in the same way, then there's more chance of a
friendship unfolding. More than affirming we are looking at
the same world, we make clear we interpret it in a similar way
and whether we talk about it or not it becomes part of the
ground beneath our friendship.

~

Politics was central to Vicky, whom I met in Paris not long after meeting Gina for the first time, but it was not central to our friendship. Vicky 'came with the apartment'. Having found out I was there to write, the Australian owner of the apartment I was renting had left the telephone number of her friend who loved books and who lived nearby in the 18th arrondissement. 'You will like her,' she said.

One day when I was lonely and desperate for someone to talk to in English, I overcame shyness and rang the phone number. Vicky invited me around. I remember her welcoming smile as she opened the door to a stranger. That and the wall of books behind her. I have written before about our connection during the time I lived in Paris, but after I left, our friendship continued from either side of the world.

As soon as I had arrived back in Australia, I moved from the Mountains to Sydney. Anthony was still in Paris finishing up work and was staying with Vicky. They had become friends as well and had more in common, in fact, than Vicky and I. The three of us shared a love of books, but Vicky and also Anthony shared an avid fascination with, and knowledge of, politics. When they started talking detailed politics I, not having any up-to-the-minute developments to add, faded away. I didn't mind disappearing – I don't always want to be present even in company – but it made me more aware of a side to both of them where I was quite irrelevant.

A few years ago Anthony stayed at Vicky's farm at Lacapelle-Biron for three months long-service leave. 'Come and write here,' she had invited. 'No rent.' She knew Anthony had published many short stories when we were first together and I suspected she felt he had given up his dreams for me. It was true that his work covered the gaps in my patchy income, allowing me time to write. He spent his time in the farmhouse writing, watching spring arrive and looking after Vicky's garden until I joined him there for a few weeks. Vicky came down to see us both and I saw her glow with delight to see Anthony so content there.

We exchanged emails and came up with a plan for an annual writing workshop in Paris. She would be my assistant, organising apartments, meals, Métro tickets, outings. We began the workshops the following year and found we worked well together. Vicky is one of those people you could leave the running of the world to – capable, ready to laugh and ever-so-slightly bossy when it is required. She has an upper-middle-class English accent which she was happy to use to good effect when she wanted something done, although mostly she would do it herself. On the morning of the very first workshop, she ran all the way from the Île Saint-Louis to the rue de Charenton beyond Bastille and back, a distance of three kilometres, to collect my teaching notes when I realised I had forgotten them. She didn't suffer fools gladly, especially impractical fools who dithered and left their notes behind, but she suffered me.

I sensed her being impatient with me at times, with my generally impractical nature. Why couldn't I just turn the key in the impossible French lock and open it? Hadn't she just shown me how? Why didn't I remember the way to the café? Hadn't she pointed it out to me earlier? I bridled childishly each time, knowing I didn't have her command of the practical world, and sometimes answered back, muttering like a powerless little sister.

When there were difficult or troubled writers in the group Vicky looked after them without question. One older woman refused to take the bus or Métro alone and Vicky organised one of her young Algerian cleaners to be her nursemaid; another woman's boyfriend broke up with her by text from Australia and Vicky spent the day walking around the streets with her, listening. It was part of her job, but it was also her open and generous heart – it was natural to her.

I always felt the need to be aware of not exploiting her practical generosity: she had given me the use of her apartment in the rue Labat and her farmhouse in the Lot-et-Garonne, she took me out to dinner on my birthday if she was in town, she bought me beautiful presents – Japanese plates and individually designed earrings – and gave me woodblock prints she created herself. I could not repay any of this generosity.

I was aware, too, of needing to keep her trust. After I had known her a few months, she told me that a dear friend, a woman she had loved and trusted, had accused her of theft. It had cut so deep that it had damaged her trust in others, perhaps forever. I could see the hurt shadowing her grey eyes as she told me the story. It had happened decades ago. I wanted to say, 'You can trust me,' but there's no way of saying those words without sounding dodgy.

And then there was the issue of class. Vicky told me once that when she was a child, her nanny went with her to birthday parties. She said, 'Each girl had her nanny standing behind her chair at birthday parties.' The image has stayed in my mind, beautifully dressed little girls with beribboned hair, sitting around a birthday table, with a row of nannies on either side, standing, watching.

She had fled to France to escape her class and lived a life similar to mine; group households, growing vegetables, doing menial jobs, finding time for writing and painting, bringing up and supporting her children alone, and refusing any help from her parents. She still went back to England and visited her parents and sisters, but she lived in a different world on the other side of the Channel.

One day when I was staying with her at the farmhouse, I met some English friends of hers. After they left she said, 'You know, if I had stayed in England, I would never have been able to have friends with accents like that.' I realised, with a sense of shock, there were all kinds of class signals going on that went entirely over my colonial head. We talked then about class, its privileges and its controls, and how from opposite directions we had escaped to the same place just outside the rules. Sometimes, just for a tiny moment, the rules of her native class flashed out, phrased as, 'My mother wouldn't like ...' As in, 'My mother wouldn't like the way you pull grapes off the bunch instead of snipping the cluster.' I would blush and feel how badly brought up I was.

Vicky, in fact, has lived further outside the rules than I have. For most of her life she has had lovers, once for a few years there was a ménage à trois, and then for decades she was the mistress of a married man. She didn't talk about him often and didn't see him often enough, but it was clear how passionately she loved him even though she sometimes took other lovers. 'You ought to take a French lover,' she once told me. She was in her sixties by then, ten years older than I was, and I could feel the glowing hidden pleasure in her words. I thanked her for her advice but primly explained that I was quite happy with Anthony, thanks. I remembered finding some photographs of her in the farmhouse when I was staying there once. She was young in the photograph, with beautiful grey eyes and lovely breasts, and I realised that she was a far sexier woman than I was.

I introduced Vicky to Gina and to Trish and she was

friendly, but didn't develop any further friendship with either of them. One's friends are not necessarily friends with each other. Whatever spark is fired in each other doesn't always catch in someone else. There is an attraction in friendship, a drawing towards something essential, a feeling of being valued because of it, but it's not always the same essential thing in each friendship.

In Vicky, the essential thing seems to be our shared love of books, but, on my side anyway, it's more to do with her warm heart. If I look closely, I can feel myself being drawn to her warmth. I always have dinner at her place several times when I am in Paris to do the workshop, and the rest of the year we email and talk online. She tells me about her new boyfriend, I ask her how her painting and etching is going, she holds up her work to show me, we talk about our various dud politicians. We still talk about books. She reads the books I have written and makes comments about them, including whether the latest one is better, or not so good, as the last one. Because she reads so much in English and French I value and fear her opinion.

'Come and write at the farmhouse,' she often says. 'You can use my painting studio. Stay as long as you like.' She dangles heaven-on-earth in front of me and would love nothing better than for me to accept it.

'Soon,' I say. 'I can't get there right now.'

Each year when I go to France, she welcomes me with a warm hug and shining eyes, and each year when I leave there are tears in her eyes. I suspect there are things about me that still irritate her – the way I pull grapes off bunches leaving sticky twigs, and my inability to put a key in a lock without fumbling – but I feel loved by her and that is what matters.

~

Political discussion and intellectual exchange is one of the threads in my connection to women friends, but in identifying that I can now see in my friendships with men it has been the only one. I only show them my mind; emotional frailty and intimate revelations are not part of it – perhaps I appear stronger with men because of that. If I talk about emotions with them, it is with an un-messy detachment, a thoughtful analysis. It makes me realise my friendships are much more gendered than I had thought.

It's not that it's been complicated to have male friends, not in the expected sense of erotic disturbance anyway. There has been attraction at times, a frisson, certainly when I was younger, but not to an unnerving degree. Or am I being evasive, unwilling to notice erotic undertows?

Some readers of The Epic suggest that the friendship between Enkidu and Gilgamesh was erotic. Before Enkidu first arrived in the city, Gilgamesh dreamed of a meteor, which, for him 'held the attraction of a woman'. And then he dreamed again of an axe, which he picked up and wore at his side, again feeling an attraction towards it as if it were a woman. His mother interpreted the dreams, saying the meteor and the axe were signs of the comrade who would come in his strength from heaven and that Gilgamesh would 'love him as a woman and he will never forsake you'. Enkidu, too, longed for 'a comrade who would understand his heart'.

It does seem they were more than just a couple of mates, which could disallow their friendship under Montaigne's 'no other traffic' rules, but I tend to think that no friendships are disembodied. Holding hands, an arm around a shoulder, linking arms, kissing on cheeks, hugging. Just not for too long; that is, if you don't desire other traffic.

But I suspect my friendships with men are more shaped by the fact of having five brothers than erotic tension. As a child, I played cricket with my brothers, explored the creeks and hills, wrestled and argued, did homework at the kitchen table, and jostled over doing the washing-up after dinner with them. Thanks to fair-minded parents – and a mother who didn't like housework – I wasn't made to feel I should look after or serve my brothers. The boys had to do as much washing-up as the girls, although they did more wood-chopping than we did. And in the evenings around the fire after our parents had gone to bed, the long conversations about life were with my brothers. There was, still is, an ease and directness and an unquestioned sense of equality with men which, I think, comes from being surrounded by boys all my childhood – all my life, in fact, as I went on to have two sons. I have always been attracted to men and can behave foolishly in their presence, but the default position is equal and brotherly.

Still, they have been left out of the story. It is not because they do not matter. Michael the journalist, Alan the poet from university days; Kris with whom I became a substitute parent after Dolly died; Phil the cartoonist who deserves honour as the only friend of mine who came to my mother's funeral; ethereal Peter who hears whole symphonies in his head and who makes my head explode with light – they have all been 'friends of my mind'. They are another story, not just another tangle of figures in the Brueghel village, but on a different canvas altogether.

Thirteen

Life in the burnished village in the Blue Mountains had ended even before I went to Paris, or at least the fair had moved on. Children grew and friends moved away. Some friends died.

That stops me in my tracks. Friends who have died. They are gone but they live a crypto existence in my mind, without flesh or blood, but still breathing. A sight or sound in the present awakens them and they flicker into my memory, a poor, shadowy place to exist, then there is impossible yearning. I stand there in another time, willing them back in living detail. Life is transient, but I hold on with my nails digging in, half-moon cuts in flesh, until long after the last minute, making a song and dance about it.

Starting right back with The Epic, when people have died, when relationships are over, there has been the urge to make them live again. To me, the most moving part of The Epic is when Enkidu dies and Gilgamesh is distraught with grief. He felt the whole world, even the earth beneath his feet, was weeping for his friend: 'Like a mother mourning /Weep, all the paths we walked together.'

He cried for him and would not let him be buried until 'the worm fastened on him' – Enkidu's body was visibly decomposing before he could let him go. Then he set off to find the secret of everlasting life and arrived at the Mountains of Mashu that were guarded by the man-scorpions.

'Why have you come on so great a journey, for what have you travelled so far, crossing the dangerous waters? Tell me the reason for your coming?' asked the man-scorpions.

'Since my friend went, my life is nothing,' answered Gilgamesh.

Does that mean friends stand between me and death? That friends give me not only a delineated self, but the reassurance of a living self? When I am with a friend I see myself reflected in her eyes – I exist and death is hidden, at least obscured. When my friend dies, I am left to face the dangerous water, the mountains, the thornbushes and darkness alone.

Friends who have died: Dolly, who became Dina in the book that led Gina to me; Helen, a writer, who died of cancer; James, Connie's ex-partner, and then there was Michele.

Michele was an actor I met at one of Connie's parties. At first, I was in awe of her. I had seen her already in films and television shows and especially at the theatre – *The Three Sisters* and *Uncle Vanya* – and knew her expressive face and warm eyes in the close-up intimate way we know actors' faces.

It took me a while to recover from my fan-girl-chattering-too-much – but we became friends.

She had grown up in England and studied acting and then came to Australia and starred in *Jesus Christ Superstar*, which, I realised years later, was when I first saw her. And then again in the two Chekhov plays at Belvoir Street Theatre, although by this time I was familiar with her name. I was still a young mother in the Blue Mountains and I'd take a train to Sydney to go to the half-price matinees on a Tuesday. In one of the plays she was a plain young woman – Sonya in *Uncle Vanya* it must have been – and in *The Three Sisters*, a pretty sister, I don't know which one. I was stunned to see how she transformed her face from nondescript to pretty, as if she were inhabiting a different body.

She had been married and divorced when she was young and then had met Jeff when they were both in the same show in Melbourne. Jeff said he had decided when he saw the cast list, even before they met, that he was going to marry her. He was younger than she was, handsome and boyish and easy to like. It was obvious that she was the rock in their relationship, perhaps in every relationship she ever had, even in her own birth family.

I remember her talking about her mother who had died when she was in the middle of a show and how she kept on playing.

'I wish I hadn't,' she said. 'I was too young to know the show doesn't have to go on.'

And about her father, who was currently slipping into dementia. For several years she had to make sudden dashes to Sydney after he had escaped from his nursing home to be found wandering streets or suburbs away. Then he started taping everything in his room with masking tape, to 'fix it'.

His lights, his chair, his walking stick, pictures on the wall, everything was taped. He had been an alcoholic most of his life, but now he had forgotten all about it, all the pain he had caused. I can see her face so clearly, her wryness, her compassion as she talked about him.

Michele drank too much herself. It feels like I am 'speaking ill of the dead', but I don't think she would mind. She was piercingly self-aware – and aware of others – she knew how I felt. I think I behaved slightly better than I did with Marguerite – I didn't abandon her – but I still muttered irritably when, after a midday lunch, she was still at our place at midnight, always the last to leave, a maudlin drunk resisting Jeff's pleas to go home. A few times I swore I would not invite her to my place, only go to lunch at hers so I could leave when I wanted to.

I remember dinners at her house, Jeff cooking risotto, she and I sitting, elbows on the table, drinking wine; reading with her on the veranda at Wamberal – although I think she only came there once; the two of us going away for a week up the coast to Coffs Harbour to teach workshops on writing and acting. We shared an apartment near the beach and talked and laughed and drank wine every evening until late. She had a peerless insight into human behaviour – her acting training partly, but also her gift, her heart knowledge of what motivated others. At the same time, she also made me feel as if whatever I said mattered.

There's a photograph of Anthony, Jeff, Michele and me sitting at a table in her garden. We each have a glass of wine and there's a bowl of salad between us. We all look so young, apple-cheeked, that a wave of nostalgia washes through me. I remember that day, the warmth of friendship and the laughter.

I remember going to see Michele in plays after she became my friend, *The Summer of the Seventeenth Doll* and *Beach Blanket Tempest*, and how, like Gina, she always disappeared into character. It wasn't until I heard her sing in *Beach Blanket Tempest*, that I suddenly realised I had seen and heard her as Mary Magdalene in *Jesus Christ Superstar* twenty years earlier. After she died, I listened to her sing 'I Don't Know How to Love Him' on YouTube and couldn't believe she wasn't alive anymore.

She told me a couple of times that Jeff, who was ten or twelve years younger than her, wanted a baby, and so did she, but she was forty-seven years old, too old to have any chance. They had both accepted the fact and adopted a dog. And then one day when I was visiting, she offered me a cup of raspberry-leaf tea.

'No way. Sorry, but raspberry-leaf tea is horrible. I'd only drink it if I was pregnant.'

'But I *am* pregnant,' she said.

I have an image of where she was standing in the kitchen, half-turned towards me, teacup in her hand, the embarrassed delight on her face. She hadn't been quite ready to say it. After the shrieking died down, we took our cups of raspberry-leaf tea and sat on her veranda. She had a dainty, neat English garden, the opposite of my messy bush backyard.

'I am afraid I will die before she is grown,' she confessed.

'Don't be silly. You will only be sixty-seven by the time she is twenty. Of course you will live.' I was ten years younger than she was and already had two teenagers. It was easy to be relentlessly optimistic.

'But I think I *will* die,' Michele said.

She asked me to be at the birth, which, since she had many

lifelong friends, I felt as a great honour – I still glow when I remember it. The birth turned into a hasty Caesarean, I ran down the corridor with the nurses and doctor and then Jeff skidded into the operating theatre at the last minute. I held her hand as a neat, perfect girl's head popped up through the slit in her belly.

Because she was an actor and because she had a baby at forty-seven, a women's magazine did a cover story on her. She had it all – a handsome young husband, a baby coming after a brilliant acting career, a pretty house in the Mountains. In the cover image, she and Jeff and her baby daughter looked perfect.

But Michele did die when her daughter was sixteen, not quite grown, and I couldn't believe she was gone. She had moved to a small town near Melbourne, and I flew down to see her two weeks before she died. We had lunch together in the restaurant where Jeff was a chef. She sat opposite me in an elegant turban, her face thin and her head bald from chemo that was never going to work, still so intensely alive.

I still find it hard to believe that she is no longer in the world. I don't believe in an afterlife, I don't believe we will meet again anywhere, any time. She is gone.

~

Gina came to dinner after Anthony and I moved. We had found a terrace house just down the steps from our old apartment, and she had already left her bedsitter and bought a small apartment in Kings Cross, no more than five minutes' walk away. When she first moved, it felt like a new affirmation of her friendship; I was the person she wanted to live near.

It was a casual, disorganised dinner. There were still boxes of books stacked all around the room, no bookshelves yet, no pictures on the walls, saucepans and plates were in unfamiliar places, the stove was an enigma, but Anthony had cooked up a tagine that filled the place with spicy smells. And then, just before Gina arrived, my brother Tim, the landscape painter, and his university student son, turned up unexpectedly. Outdoor chairs were dragged in and squashed around the table.

'A tagine can always be made to expand,' said Anthony as Tim started to protest that he would buy some takeaway.

Gina's bottle of champagne was opened and we all sat around the table, laughing at the general chaos and toasting the new house. Tim, who can be awkward, relaxed as Gina asked him about his painting. She had admired his pictures hanging in our former apartment and had also been to one of his exhibitions. I could see him starting to unwind. And she asked my nephew about his studies; he had just begun a PhD in chemistry.

'Oh, so you can run the ice lab for us,' she joked.

He laughed and they talked about *Breaking Bad*. She is so good at this, I thought. She makes everyone feel as if they are smart and funny and that everything they say is interesting. I sat there, proud of having such a generous friend.

That was the last time Gina ever came to my place.

There's a scene in *The Prisoner* where Proust's narrator talks about not being able to recall the details of a turning point or a last time, because he didn't know its true nature while it was happening. As usual, he elaborates on it at some length as he trawls his memory trying to recall an exact phrasing, an exact expression. Oddly though, I do remember this last time in my friendship with Gina in detail, possibly because it was also the first dinner in our new house. I don't believe I had any presentiment, and yet I do recall there was some relief in Gina coming to dinner, which suggests I had sensed an already occurring shift in our friendship. It's impossible to know now if that sensation has been sketched in by the memory editor or it was really there that evening.

~

I remember in some detail the evening I first met Trish, right down to the 50s second-hand dress I was wearing – it was a summery cut and colour, large red flowers, but the material was too thick, too warm for the summer heat. I didn't know then if Trish would become a friend or not, and at first she was only an acquaintance, someone to talk to in English. She became friends with Gina more quickly, in fact she was the only person I met in Paris who also became friends with Gina, making us a threesome in the early days.

After we met, we started to rendezvous for drinks every now and then. Trish had lived in France for years, first as a singing student in Strasbourg and then had moved to Lyon as part of the Lyon Opera and eventually to Paris. The sense of not being able to match her – I have always been in awe of musicians, their ability to enter the heart without need for words – gradually shifted. I don't know if she was aware of my awe, perhaps she was – she is perceptive about how other people feel.

Soon after meeting her, I saw her in a 'Best of Mozart' show at the Theatre du Tambour Royal in the 11th arrondissement. She had a rich alto voice and an unsuspected comic touch – I have never seen anyone have such fun with Mozart as she did. After that I saw her performances whenever I was in Paris, finding myself drawn into a world of opera I had known little about. She also composed her own songs and shows. She wrote one song, 'Wolves', inspired by the same book that had led Gina to introduce herself to me, and sang it at my reading at The Red Wheelbarrow Bookstore in the Marais. The audience was impressed, or stunned, when Trish went on to sing in her powerful operatic voice another song she had written, 'Who the Fuck Are You?' She effortlessly stole the show with her glorious bel canto 'Fu −u- u- u − uuuck' vibrating around the bookshop.

She had been married to a Frenchman but had left him because 'I couldn't sing when I was with him'. She had two sons, two tumbling dark-haired puppies when I first met them. Each year when I went back to work in France I'd see her and the boys as well, although sometimes they were at their father's house. She performed in concerts and opera choirs and gave singing lessons, riding her bike around Paris even in the wet and cold, zipping through the traffic from lesson to lesson.

I remember going to her place for dinner one year and Terry, her new Australian boyfriend, a rock guitarist, was cooking dinner − stuffed capsicums as I recall. Her eleven-year-old son, Nico, was there, playing riffs on an electric guitar. Trish was focused on what her son was doing and made suggestions about the music, which he listened to, acknowledging her expertise. Her gaze was loving, proud, but also attentive like a teacher. I watched them together, thinking of my own boys and how I shared what I knew of reading and writing with them. Part of our friendship has been that we have both been the mother of two sons and we each allow our sons to know us as something other than a mother.

Some years later when Nico was at university, I met with Trish for a drink at a café near the Gare de l'Est and he turned up as well. He took out an art notebook and started showing me beautiful and original drawings and small constructions – a page made of pink autumn leaves sewn together – that he had been making. After he left Trish smiled. 'I loved that he showed you that. He hasn't shown me. I love that he feels open and trusting with my friends.'

'It was a way of showing you what he does,' I said.

Trish moved out of the city to a country house in Nanteuil-sur-Marne, and I'd take the train out to see her. One year we walked along the Marne under an avenue of walnut trees, gathering fallen walnuts. Another year she met me at the train on her bike and pushed it back to her house, in tears, tossed about by her relationship with her boyfriend. Every year she showed me her garden, the fruit trees she had planted, the mountain of compost, the bountiful piles of carrots, broccoli, tomatoes on her kitchen table. She always took a bag of vegetables for her sons on her weekly visits to Paris to teach singing lessons.

Once when I rang to arrange a visit, Trish said she and Terry would be rehearsing a new show, but we could go for a walk afterwards.

'I'll listen to you rehearse,' I said.

'Oh, we are just putting it together. Just scratching around. We're only fit to play for the chooks yet.'

'I'll be a chook,' I said. 'I'll love it.'

When I arrived, I sat in the corner and disappeared into the clutter of leads and speakers and instruments. I watched and listened. I saw the glances between them as they played, the starting and stopping, the repeating of phrases of music, the adjusting of instruments, the suggestions for a change of approach, but most of all, the exchange of energy between them as they worked. I have little musical knowledge and an under-developed musical sensibility, so I couldn't share in the process, but I loved watching it.

It took longer to get to know Trish and not just because of my awe of her as a musician. I think I felt inadequate in her presence at first, ungifted certainly, but also somehow sexless, no fun. It wasn't anything she was doing, it was an awareness of a lack in myself. But gradually she talked – and I listened – about the secrets and distortions in her complicated family back in Adelaide, about her Australian boyfriend – how he wouldn't learn French and was too dependent on her – and about our lovely boys. There is a sweetness in being the mother of sons that has woven itself into the fabric of our connection, a secret thread that no-one else sees.

Whenever Trish returns to Sydney we catch up and sometimes she stays with me. Last year, while I was walking in France, she and her younger son, Damien, stayed in our house for a month. When we came back, I remember walking with her around the foreshores of the Botanic Gardens towards the Opera House. Moreton Bay figs spread their extraordinary green skirts, the harbour glittered, the Opera House settled swan-like in front of us. 'Why on earth do you want to come to grey Paris when you have all this!' she exclaimed.

Before she returned to France, Anthony and I went to see her sing French *chansons* in a pub in Newtown on the other side of town. She wore a fitted dress and her hair was piled up so she looked like a French cabaret singer in the nineteenth century. She played the piano standing up and with a mischievous air sang the working-class songs in her glorious voice. I sat in the audience, proud of my tuneless self for having a friend who could sing so beautifully. It made me realise that admiration is part of all my friendships.

~

Gina started to turn down or pull out of arrangements. She didn't come to my book launch, the first one she had missed since I had known her, she didn't have time for a coffee or to come to dinner. I did go to a show with her at the Eternity Playhouse, an Irish play which we thoroughly dissected on the way home. The only other time I saw her during this period was for a few minutes after a play she was in. There were three or four other friends of hers present and we exchanged only a few words. I had a sensation of being moved to the side.

At first I didn't notice anything. We were both busy; she had the flu and then had a show to rehearse, and I was getting ready for two months walking across France before the Paris writing class. I made one last effort to see her before I went overseas but she had 'stuff to do' and 'we can schedule when you get back'. I did try again as soon as I got back, when I was still jet lagged according to my texts, but there was no reply.

It was a hot, humid summer, a relief from the grey chill of a European autumn. One afternoon I went to Shark Beach at Nielsen Park and read in the shade of the Moreton Bay figs. I swam around the shark-net, stopping a couple of times to regain my breath, then dried off and lay briefly in the sun. I thought about Gina and me walking along the road in Darlinghurst years earlier, laughing at ourselves. Something was wrong but I hadn't admitted it yet.

It was six months since the dinner. I began to think there might have been some evasive texts even before then. The sequence felt the same as the rift after the Lacapelle debacle, the same stretching uncertainty. A week after I got back, I sent another email, hoping she was well, filling her in about my travels, telling her I had seen Trish, how she was doing lots of gardening and singing, and then gathered up my courage and wrote: *Also, I'm unsure now whether there is something causing you to not want to rendezvous for so long (even before I left)? Perhaps not, perhaps I'm just worrying. Whatever the case, I will still be here with an open heart for you. Let me know if/when you feel up to meeting. Miss you.*

The next day she replied, saying she was under a lot of strain, some under her control, some not, both family and financial stuff. She said she did not have the energy to discuss anything whilst being in the middle of it, that's all. I felt some relief – it wasn't something I had said or done, not like the mess I had made last time – but also mildly rebuffed. Why couldn't I be of use to her when times were tough?

I replied, saying I understood. I sent two more texts in the two months before Christmas, one answered, one not, and then, remembering she had vowed to stay away from her family's Christmas, sent her another text inviting her to our Christmas dinner, which was answered a couple of weeks later on New Year's Eve. She said she was busy looking after her mother and that she was 'just trying to ride out the times'. The feeling of uncertainty persisted, but I told myself that she had other things on her mind, that it was self-absorbed to think I was being sidelined.

Fourteen

Early in the new year, a distressing text arrived from Gina. She was seriously ill in St Vincent's Hospital. She had been there for four days and, she said, was being well looked after.

'Oh no! Can you have visitors?' I texted immediately.

'Yes. But not in the mornings, they are full of appointments.'

'I'll be there this afternoon.'

I should admit my first emotion was relief that she had contacted me. Then anxiety about the sudden illness. As I walked along Victoria Street to St Vincent's Hospital, time stretched in the weird way it does when bad news comes out of nowhere. I told myself I must be quiet, attentive, not talk about writing or ideas, just listen.

I found my way through the labyrinth of the hospital – medical smells, shiny floors – finally arriving at the room Gina shared with three other patients. She was just getting back into bed with the help of a nurse, so I greeted her with a smile and a wave and waited to one side until she was propped up on pillows before taking a seat in the blue bedside chair. She nodded and I smiled again, not wanting to be too expressive, conscious of how low her energy must be and how large and bright my good health could look. I felt the tension of someone who is acting relaxed.

'So, what happened?'

Gina headed off into the story of the last few days. She had been feeling tired and was walking home along Victoria Street after seeing a doctor, when she suddenly felt the strength go from her legs. She stumbled and nearly fell.

'Oh my god! That sudden!'

No-one took any notice, nothing unusual about a stumbling woman in that part of town. She thought she would collapse completely. Luckily, she was near a pharmacy so she staggered in and bought a walking stick. She walked slowly back to her apartment building and managed with huge effort to get up the stairs. Soon after she arrived home, an actor friend rang and Gina told her what had happened.

'Get a taxi straight to the hospital. Right now,' her friend had said. 'Right now.'

'Thank God she told you what you needed to do,' I broke in.

'Yes. I don't know why I couldn't see what I needed to do. It was obvious.'

'But you were already too sick to know what to do. Sometimes we need someone else to tell us.'

Gina nodded and continued. She wasn't smiling or animated, but she seemed to want to tell the story that she must have already told several times. She rang a taxi but as she started down the stairs, she realised she could not make it by herself. She texted the taxi driver – or perhaps she had told him to come up the stairs, I can't remember this part – and he helped her down to the cab, then drove her to St Vincent's Hospital where she was immediately admitted. A series of specialists examined her and after several days she was diagnosed with a rare illness where the immune system attacks the peripheral nerves. The doctors didn't yet know how serious it was for her, but they were hoping that she might recover in a few months, that she would walk and be able to work again.

'How weird that it happened so fast!'

'I know. From one moment to the next. Now my life is totally changed.'

We talked for more than an hour, but only about the illness, the hospital, the care she was getting, whether she needed anything else. That night when I got home, I researched the illness online. Anthony was travelling in India for work so I sent him an email telling him what was happening. I couldn't admit, even to him, how relieved I was that Gina had contacted me.

I visited her as often as I could over the next couple of weeks. Every time I arrived, a friend was leaving, and when I was leaving, often another friend would arrive. We laughed when we bumped into each other in the lift or corridor – how many friends she had! Gina texted me to bring her some earplugs as there was a snorer in her room and I felt privileged, like a child, to have a job to do. The next time she asked me to get her a soy chai latte on my way to the hospital, and again I felt childishly pleased.

Each visit she updated me on the details of the illness and treatment, which she must have done with each other friend, and I wondered if that was tiring. But then I remembered when my mother died a couple of years before, I had wanted to talk about it over and over, so I thought it was probably what she wanted to do. It appeared the illness was not as severe as the doctors first thought, and they expected that she would be able to walk again soon.

She talked about the other people in her room. One of them was a Patrick White character, she said, and I immediately thought of his story 'A Cheery Soul' and squirmed. I have always guiltily worried that I might be a cheery soul – it's the anxiety of an optimist.

I took in a story I was working on. 'I don't know if you are up to reading, but if you are?'

She accepted the story, but the next time I visited she gave it back, saying she couldn't concentrate. I wished I hadn't given it to her. She could have felt I was urging her to be well for my own needs. I sat in the blue chair, still acting relaxed.

She started physiotherapy and one day when I arrived she was ready to do a practice walk up and down the corridor. I walked by her side, not holding her. She used a frame like my mother had in her last years, pushing it slowly in front of her over the shiny linoleum.

'They are talking about me going home,' she said. She sounded worried.

'Really? That's good, isn't it?'

'I don't know if I can manage. I told them that, but they said they will help. They will send someone to do my shopping and do housework and check how I am.'

'And I can help. We can help. Anthony is still in India, but he will be back soon. We can bring around meals. Take you to appointments.'

'Yes. Everyone has offered to help.' She was circumspect but I put it down to her independence. She was good at looking after herself, but she also knew how to ask for help if she needed it.

'We can collect you and drive you home if you like?'

'Thanks, but that's already arranged,' she said. It was an old friend of hers from school days. That's natural, I told myself. A friend who has known you when you were young is what is needed when you are in extremity.

When I have been in extremity – giving birth, my mother's dying – it has been Anthony I have turned to. He has known me since I was nineteen years old – chubby-faced, gold-red Botticelli hair – and he still recognises me in my altogether different body. I cannot include him in the catalogue of friends, but through him I understand the need for a friend from long ago. When your body or heart has shattered, there must be someone you don't have to be anything for; not clever, not beautiful, not charming, not consistent, not wise, not interesting, not even good.

~

After seven years as my workshop assistant, Vicky decided to quit. She wanted to paint and make woodcut prints and spend more time at the farmhouse at Lacapelle-Biron. I would have to find someone else to help me keep the show on the road – which was how Gabrielle became my friend.

I had previously met her when I was looking for new apartments for the writing class. She was about my age, slim with fine dark hair and creamy skin, reserved and discreet in manner and appearance in what I'd come to think of as a typically French way. She was wearing narrow black jeans and delicate jewellery the first time I met her, and she walked with a limp. I later found out she had a club foot.

We started working together the next year. She was still reserved but when I discovered she read widely in French, English and Italian, I made a conscious effort to draw her out. I wanted her to like me. I imagine it's obvious that I've always wanted people who read a lot, whose life is about reading, to like me. If you have stepped through that door into the vast world of thinking, creativity, insight, and every field of human experience and, if inhabiting that world, you still think well enough of me, then I must be all right.

Through Gabrielle I realised too, that a new friend can be made at any age and that a new friendship can be as rich and affirming as an old one. There is a different quality to a new friend, a freshness of discovery, the foreignness of an unshared past, the excitement of warmth and openness offered and received. It doesn't have the reassuring quality of remembering each other's glorious young faces – which is why I was thrilled to see a gamin-haired picture of Gabrielle when she was about twenty with the sort of elfin face boys fall over themselves for – but it has the rewards of novelty.

Gabrielle was born and grew up in the 11th arrondissement, at that time a working-class suburb, and for her, the city, history and literature were a series of permeable tapestries, each soaking into the others, each layered around her. 'Henry IV was killed here,' she said suddenly, looking down the rue de la Ferronnerie one day. Another day she took me into a church to show me the hand-written names of the soldiers from that arrondissement who had died in the First World War. When she found out I could read in French, albeit slowly, she started introducing French writers I hadn't come across. Patrick Modiano was a favourite of hers, at that time not translated. I took my time reading him in French, and found him fascinating, the way he pinned down the world of streets, of place, but left everything else, memory and storytelling, in the air, able to change at any moment.

I knew she had lived in California for twelve years, which was why her English was perfect and colloquial, but it took me a few years to find out she had been married to an American, a rock'n'roll singer who was trying to make his name.

'I got tired of being the cute French girl,' she said.

'Most women would love to be the cute French girl,' I said.

She shrugged. Her shrug and her moue were so perfectly French they made me laugh.

I didn't find out more about her Californian life until a few years ago when Gabrielle started writing. She sent me her manuscript and there on the pages was everything she had never told me. She painted, she designed t-shirts, she supported her husband's faltering career; he found someone else. That was years ago in the 70s. She has not told me about any boyfriends she has had since then. It's not that they haven't existed, but as with Merril, it's not part of our conversation.

She lives on very little money, but she manages to buy books and music and small gifts for me. One day after I had known her for a few years, she invited me to her place for lunch. She lived in suburban Paris just outside the *périphérique* in Nogent-sur-Marne. It was cheaper there; she couldn't afford to live in the city anymore. I felt honoured, aware that the French only invite family or close friends to their homes to eat.

She had put on a spread of seafood. 'I noticed you always have oysters when we take the writing group out to dinner,' she said. There was far too much food for the two of us, an absurdly generous amount. Knowing how little money she lived on, I was embarrassed.

Her living room, as I expected, was lined with books, in bookcases, on the piano, on side tables, on the floor. I remembered her disdain when we had visited an Australian writer in Paris. 'For a writer, he doesn't have many books,' she remarked, and I knew that writer was forever damned. Here in her cavern of books I felt the richness and complexity of her being and had a strong sense of entry being offered to a closer level of friendship.

She began to loan me books when I was there; the poetry of George Seferis, Fernando Pessoa's *The Book of Disquiet*, everything by Stendhal; always Europeans, and I, sometimes with pleasure, sometimes dutifully, read them. Mostly I had to bring them back to Australia to finish them and emailed my responses. 'Pessoa reminds me of a highly intelligent, depressive teenager,' I wrote. 'Going around and around in circles about the pain of existence.'

'We all have our own preferences and affinities with writers,' she responded.

For my part I have tried time and again to read Céline's *Voyage au bout de la nuit* because so many people say it is brilliant, but no matter how hard I try, I just can't hack it. There are writers that I like but have trouble reading, like Zola. I enjoy what he writes about (like *Le ventre de Paris* about Les Halles), but I can't stand his vulgar style. Same with Rousseau, too whiny for my taste.

When I recall our conversations and look back through our email exchange, it is almost always about books, writing, reading. Once, when I was back in Australia, I emailed her that John Berger was speaking at Shakespeare's bookshop and asked her to go to the event for me. She did, and sent me pages of notes about everything he said:

> When asked about his current reading he mentioned Andreï Platonov whom he praised as an exceptional writer akin to Spinoza in his establishing a direct connection between the materialist and spiritual world, and the Greek poet Yannis Ritsos.

And then she added some 'trivia' as she called it:

> I have bought a couple of books by Philippe Lejeune: *Le pacte autobiographique*, and *La Mémoire et l'Oblique* about Georges Pérec. I'll read them soon, once I am done with *Montaigne à cheval*, which I'll send you with the Annie Ernaux compilation. About Stendhal: If you can get your hands on his *Journal; Henry Brulard* I think you won't be disappointed.

'Gabrielle is scary,' I said to Anthony when that email came. How could I send her my Australian offerings from a thin transplanted culture when she was coming from the width and depth of European literature?

When one of my books was published, shortly after we first worked together, she sent me a list of memoirs she loved: WG Sebald's *Vertigo*, Stefan Zweig's *The World of Yesterday*, 'and of course the incomparable Giacomo Casanova'. She also said she had just read Annie Ernaux's *La Place* and even though she didn't like her tone, she liked her 'dry style, devoid of sloppiness', which I felt as an implied criticism.

I have given her my books though. At first she contented herself with remarking about the typos, just as Merril had. But this time I was able to say, 'Don't tell me about the typos. I know they are there. I have found them all already.' She sent instead notes on things she liked in it and a list of factual errors, each identified with page numbers and explanations.

The next book I sent her, I again said it wasn't necessary to find the typos, and added, nor errors. This time she sent me reading notes which began, 'I had some trouble getting into the book.' Wrong-footed from the start, I stumbled through the rest of her notes, which pointed out things she didn't like before she got to the aspects she did. I sent a pissed-off note back, saying, 'These are the kind of things one says to a writer before (underlined) her book is published, not after.'

'Wow!' she wrote back, surprised that I had taken her remarks to heart. After a few days, I realised it was a clash of cultures. To people of an Anglo background, such criticism from a friend is a personal offence, an attack; to the French it is a natural part of a friendship between equals. Australians, despite thinking of themselves as open and friendly, do not say what they really think; the reserved and discreet French do. I got over my hurt feelings and made an extra effort to be amiable in my emails. Gabrielle did, too.

Recently, when we were talking online she said, 'I think I'm a nice person, I try to treat others well, but people have said I'm scary.'

I jumped unseen on the other side of the world. 'You are a nice person,' I said.

Because I only see her in October, it is perpetually European autumn in our friendship. The leaves of the plane trees are just starting to turn, there are overgrown pink dahlias and roses in the Luxembourg Gardens, the streets are mostly grey and drizzly. The evenings close in, there is a turning inwards that increases day by day, we wear coats and scarves and gloves. Some days are bright and blue, startling, and I think of Australia on those days.

I would love Gabrielle to come to Australia so that I could show her some of the strange marvels on this side of the world; crimson waratahs in the bush, black swans, creatures that carry babies in pouches, red deserts, sunny carelessness, some good books. But she won't come. She doesn't have the money and her foot gives her a lot of pain. She is my friend from the other side of the world, the one who makes me realise that even though I think I know books, I have mostly stood in the English waves at the edge. She urges me to go deeper and further into other seas.

~

Anthony arrived back from India, and I texted Gina to ask if we could both visit.

'Tomorrow is good,' she said.

I asked if there was anything we could bring but she said she had everything she needed. We walked over to her place in the February heat, noting how long it had been since we had been to her place. We were both nervous, unsure of how fragile Gina would be.

She welcomed us at the door, leaning on a walking stick. I hugged her, carefully, and so did Anthony. She looked a little more slender than before and her air was circumspect, but she seemed welcoming. Her thick auburn hair was swept back and she wore make-up. I noticed the changes since I had last been in her apartment; the bookcase had been built, the little sitting-room area was now in the front corner of the studio, and she pointed out the new safety railings in the bathroom. She gestured towards the small lounge and chairs in the corner where there was a low table set with tea things.

We sat down, the two of us opposite her. The dainty matching teacups were fine china with a delicate ivy pattern. There were some pastries on another plate, éclairs, I think. She poured us each a cup of tea and handed it to us. It was so measured and well-presented, as if we were in another more elegant era.

'So, what have you done to yourself?' Anthony asked with a wry smile.

Gina launched into an account of what had been happening, going back over the last three weeks of drama. I had filled him in, but he wanted to hear it all from her. When she was finished, I asked about leaving the hospital and coming home where there was no-one to look after her. 'What was that like?' I was aware of managing my energy, not wanting to use any of hers.

'I'm doing okay.'

Anthony was relaxed and warm, asked all the right questions. Do you have what you need? Have people been to see you? Can we do any shopping for you?

She was fine. She had everything she needed. Her friend from Melbourne, the one she had stayed with in Italy before coming to Lacapelle-Biron, had been to see her, but she had sent him away.

'It was all about him. He had no awareness of my needs.' She sounded angry and disgusted with him. 'I don't have the energy for it. The doctor said my nervous system was *fried.*

That's the word he used. *Fried.* I just can't deal with people who want me to be something for them. Fuck them.'

'Oh, that's no good. You think he would get it.' I was sympathetic, understanding, but later, after the text came telling me to stay away, I wondered if he had been trying his inadequate best.

Gina asked Anthony about his trip to India and he filled her in briefly. I sat back and listened. I was conscious of holding back.

'What do the doctors say now?' I asked.

'They don't know. Everyone is different. But they are happy so far, hopefully I will be able to function perfectly well again. And it's not my grandmother's illness. That's what I thought at first.'

'It might never come,' I said. Uselessly. Afterwards I told myself it was a good visit, that everything was fine. We were all reined in, not ourselves, yes that was true, but it would be okay. It would just take time.

A couple of days later I sent a message to Gina asking how she was and whether she had a French Film Festival program. If not, I could call in with it.

We can pick you up and drop you off if you want to go.

She replied saying she had someone else calling in so it would need to be another time. I texted again a week later, saying I had a program and could drop it over. She responded, saying that the process of recovery was uneven. She was on pain management still, and had physiotherapy appointments.

Not up to a visit now and prefer to surface when I have the energy to be social. This is not a reflection on you. I've made the same request to other friends as well. Thanks. I have to make clear boundaries in the interests of my own recovery.

My first reaction was a combination of 'fair enough' and a feeling of being rebuffed. Other friends had been told not to visit too, but some I knew were allowed to see her. I wasn't one of the chosen ones. I checked my hurt. Gina had more than enough to deal with. Her nervous system had been shot to pieces, of course she had to take it easy. I would send her a text every now and then to reassure her I was here for her. I could wait.

I sent a message once a week. *Ca va?*, it said, a nod to our Paris connection. And a small note about what I was doing and to *please ask if you need anything*. None of them were answered. That's fine, I told myself. It's just so that she knows she is cared about.

The interval between texts shifted towards two weeks. It wasn't that I was less concerned for her, but I started to think once a week made her feel crowded when she was so fragile. I was worried. How was she being looked after? Would she call if she fell? I made my texts light in tone. No-one when they are ill needs to be burdened with other people's worries.

The texts were still not answered. Sometimes a quick jolt of anger flashed through me. It wouldn't take a minute to say, *All good*. I squashed the anger down. Gina had nearly died, and she was conserving her energy for a recovery that had no guarantees. All I needed to do was affirm that I was still there for her.

And then the text came from her, one of the two texts that stayed on my phone for a couple of years and then disappeared without warning. I have tried the text restoration app again, but the messages still stubbornly resist electronic recall. Now I can only rely on my own memory, with all its flaws of layering and mixing of details. I am sure I remember the meaning conveyed, but I am not sure of the exact words. This is what I recall from four years on:

You have disregarded my instruction to not contact me. Your trite messages serve only yourself and are a burden to me. It's not about you. I would appreciate it if you do not keep sending me messages.

I'm not certain she used the word 'instruction', it could have been 'requirement' or 'request' and I have remembered a colder word out of hurt feelings. The word that leapt out and did the most damage was 'trite'. But now I wonder if the word wasn't 'banal'? Both words terrify. The other word that went in sharply was 'burden'. My friend had said my messages were a burden.

I re-read the earlier message about not being up to visits to see if it had said not to contact her. It didn't. My instinct was to argue, *that's not what you said*. I waited until the next day. I wrote and re-wrote a reply – that reply has also disappeared. This is the 'bending over backwards' gist of what I wrote:

I am sorry to have been a burden. My heartfelt texts were only to let you know you are supported. I shall respect your wishes. I am still here for you.

And that was it. I was not allowed to see her, nor contact her. Incomprehensibly, when I think about it now, I still didn't think our friendship was over forever. I was being shut out for now. That was all.

Fifteen

The writing note I made for the period after what was, in hindsight, the end of the friendship, says 'the long bewilderment'. All the hurt feelings, the spurts of anger, the thwarted desire to help, the impulse to understand and accept, the hope that in a month or two all would be well, the confusion about why I was considered a burden, the memories of how close we had been, the suspicion that I may have imagined our closeness, all helplessly summed up as 'the long bewilderment'.

After the initial shock of being pruned – the still sappy, discarded branch lying on the ground – I tried to be philosophical; it was temporary and in a few months when she felt better, Gina would be in contact. She was struggling with a frightening illness and had to do whatever was right for her. I had drinks with Connie and Cathy, I visited Paula and Miriam, I emailed Jane and Vicky, Trish and Gabrielle.

But there were sudden outbursts of raw hurt that I didn't mention to anyone except Anthony, who was as puzzled as I was. Why was I one of the branches cut away? Why was I of no use? A burden? She had said that 'it wasn't about you', which meant that it would be utterly self-centred to take it personally. Not only was I judged to be superfluous, I had no right to feel hurt about the judgement.

Tracking things back to the exact moment they changed has always been an obsession. When I'm long-distance walking, I sometimes lose my way and spend ages mentally tracing my steps back to the moment I took the wrong turn, sifting through memory images of paths dividing, and painted red and white signs on posts and rocks, trying to identify the precise location of the deviation. It seems important to identify what I missed, what led me onto the wrong path, but because it wasn't registered as a deviation at the time, it is often difficult to locate. Sometimes it's been because there was a branch obscuring the sign, other times because Anthony and I were talking and didn't notice it, sometimes it's been because the sign was missing.

With my best efforts, I can't make all the connections, nor can I locate precisely where the friendship with Gina changed. The quality of friendships, the texture of being in the world, is like a mirage or the light of a film on a screen, attractive but always in flux. A few months after the 'no contact' text I broke the rules. It was Gina's birthday, impossible to forget the date – fireworks at the Eiffel Tower and cocktails at the Ritz. I sent a Happy Birthday text, which was not answered.

And then, within a few days of each other, I heard from Connie that Gina had had a small acting job, and from Trish, that she had been to Melbourne to see friends, her first trip away since her collapse. The reassuring stories in my head shredded; she had the energy to go to work and to get on a flight to Melbourne but could not see me when I lived five minutes away. I think now, that was the moment that I realised I was no longer worth any effort. There is a peculiar pain attached to recognising that you don't matter, a humiliating sting.

Still, in my wilfully blind and optimistic way, in a few days I picked up the story that all would be well again soon. Perhaps it was because I lived so close that she couldn't afford to reconnect just yet. Friends further away were less demanding of time and energy. Perhaps she thought I would expect too much. I thought about how I would react when I saw her in the street now that I knew she was out and about again. It must happen, living so close to each other.

Then, one Friday evening, Anthony and I were walking home from town along William Street and stopped with a few others to cross the road at the lights. Suddenly Anthony stepped forward and hugged one of the waiting people, who in that instant became Gina. I rushed forward and hugged her too, careful of the walking stick she was leaning on. We all talked hastily – the others standing at the crossing were young actor friends of hers who waited amongst the scuffled greetings. Her friends were going in an opposite direction and Gina said she was catching a taxi so I held her elbow, clutched it in fact, to help her over the road.

'I can walk a bit further,' Gina said once we were on the other side. I was still clutching her arm and didn't feel able to suddenly let it go. The three of us walked up the hill together. Gina talked about her sister, whom she always said judged against her, and how it hurt that she was prevented from seeing her sister's children. I also knew that her husband had been ill with cancer for the last couple of years, but Gina hadn't been allowed to help.

'Her husband has just died,' she said. 'I've been forbidden to go to the funeral.' Her voice and face were strained.

'Shit! How can she do that? You're part of the family.'

'Apparently not. He forbade it before he died. He said he didn't want me at his funeral.'

I felt the full weight of such a command from the grave. A twisting punch to the heart. I could not say anything about my own confusion. The dark pain of her banishment seemed to radiate from her limping figure.

'I knew she was shutting me out. I knew it wasn't my imagination!' she said bitterly.

As we reached the steep part of the hill I asked if she wanted me to hail a taxi for her. She said no, she thought she could make it home. Anthony and I walked with her to the door of her apartment building and left her there. I felt a disturbing mix of distress for her pain and awkwardness at my own, but knew there was nothing I could do about either.

It was the last time I have ever seen her.

Anthony saw her once a couple of weeks later. She was in the café he habitually called into for a coffee on his way to work. He told me they talked briefly and then she started to cry. He hugged her then stayed with her as she talked again about her sister shutting her out, her brother-in-law banning her from his funeral. Truthfully, I felt relieved it was him and not me who had bumped into her.

~

Even though we had bumped into each other, the ban on contact wasn't lifted. Before leaving for a couple of months walking and writing, I broke the rule for the second time and texted her to say I would be away. Again it wasn't answered.

I broke the rule for the third and last time at the end of the first year, texting a Christmas greeting: *Hoping you are healing well and enjoying life again. I have missed you in my life. I'm not expecting things to change, but I'm still here if you want to re-connect. No need to respond, only when/if you feel like it. All best for Xmas.*

I received a polite, correct reply, which gave me, absurdly, a fluttering of hope. It thanked me for my 'kind wishes' – that was the phrasing. It also said she thought we might catch up in the New Year. Maybe all would be well, said my hopeful, can't-take-no-for-an-answer voice. Perhaps I had exaggerated everything. Despite the sharp pruning, our friendship could re-grow, cell by cell.

Of course, nothing happened. Gina didn't contact me and hasn't since. I held on for a little while, unclear about when, exactly, a new year lost its newness, but by March I understood it wasn't going to happen. I wouldn't break the rule again. It had become absurd sending messages into the void. I practised accepting that the friendship was over. I hadn't been as valued as I'd imagined and that still hurt; I wasn't permitted to be hurt, and that still made me angry. Short, sharp bursts which died quickly. Then bewilderment.

I didn't send birthday or Christmas greetings again, but each time it felt like a serious omission, like not wishing my own sisters a Happy Birthday or Merry Christmas.

Halfway through the next year my older son, Matt, had a film premiering at the Sydney Film Festival and we all dressed up for the Big Night. Family and friends came. I was aware of Gina not being there with us. I went to the after-party and talked to the actors and drank champagne and felt proud of my son who was in great demand.

A day or two later, Anthony received a text from Gina: *Congratulations on the wonderful film, Matt has done a great job. You must be proud of him.* Or words to that effect. Anthony doesn't keep his texts like I do, but I did read it at the time. It was the first text she had initiated to either of us in more than two years.

'Kind of strange, sending it just to you after so long,' I said. 'Not to both of us.'

'I know,' Anthony said. 'Maybe she thought I would just show you anyway. She didn't need to send you one as well.'

'Even so,' I said.

'It does seem a bit pointed,' he said.

~

I realise that all the way through this archaeology, I have avoided defining the exact nature of friendship. There's a risk of sounding like a 'wise' meme on social media: Friends are always there for you; friends accept you the way you are; friends listen; friends see your qualities and ignore your flaws. But it's also a reluctance to pin down its shifting and subtle nature. Even the long-ago and unknown author of The Epic understood its shifts; the power battle at the beginning between the friends; the union of their hearts immediately afterwards; Gilgamesh saving Enkidu from depression by suggesting an adventure; their regular arguments about how to proceed in their battle against Humbaba; defying the gods together;

listening to each other's dreams; the dreadful and long-lasting grief of Gilgamesh when his friend died.

More than half The Epic is devoted to the period after the loss of Gilgamesh's friend. He searches for what seems an endless amount of time, not for the return of Enkidu, but for the secret of eternal life and for eternal youth. Neither is possible, and in the end all that can be done is to write his story. The last line of the story in the edition of the paperback Epic I have on my desk is: 'He went on a long journey, was weary, worn out with labour, and returning, engraved on a stone the whole story.'

I have nothing as permanent as stone or clay, nor is it the whole story, but it is an engraving of a sort. It says: a true friend is a sweet thing – sometimes it lasts for a lifetime, but sometimes it's over and you don't know why.

These days, when I go walking there is a low-level frisson of anxiety that I will bump into Gina. As far as I know, she still lives five minutes' walk away. I am afraid I will not know how to behave. Will I say, 'This is awkward,' like a cool and clever woman in a film? Will I walk straight past her with the merest nod? Or will I find myself performing a charade, smiling as if nothing has happened?

And perhaps to Gina, nothing has happened. Much has circled through my mind about the ending of our friendship about which she is oblivious, and about which she naturally has an entirely different and equally valid story. I am certain that little I've written here will match her account of the last several years. I imagine that since the pruning I have not featured much at all, there has been too much else for her to think about. We don't have the same story in our heads anymore, although I still hope the story about our shared past is similar.

I don't want that to have been a one-sided story, a monologue.

The truth is that in all my circling, I still haven't arrived at why I was pruned. It still could have been an unwitting hurt I inflicted, something I don't remember, but given my relentless raking over of memory, I doubt it. I became burdensome, clearly, but why, I still don't know. It is embarrassing to express the pain of being considered a burden. It has a pathetic air, like an elderly aunt tottering in the lounge room, bumping into the coffee table with her cane, apologising, trying not to get in anyone's way. It's not the sort of pain anyone writes a poem or song about; there's little drama or passion, just humiliation. In four years, the pain has faded, or rather, seems like an artefact stored behind glass in a museum cabinet, all its ability to hurt gone, but I do still feel bewilderment at times.

The most likely explanation is not that I did something 'wrong', but that I was no longer worth the effort. Knowing Gina had time for others and not for me made me feel strangely ashamed. It's not that I felt guilty, but in a sense, outcast. An outcast, by definition, cannot share what has happened to them. It is not something to discuss with other friends – if I've been found unworthy by one friend, why would I advertise the fact to another? Somewhere in the neural pathways of memory, or perhaps further back in the DNA of our survival, there is the dark sliver of fear of being cast out of the tribe. I must not talk about the rupture in case it spreads.

And then I recall the lines from Emerson that Beth read out to me one day: 'When [friendships] are real, they are not glass threads or frostwork, but the solidest thing we know.'

I can see now that my friendship with Gina was made of glass threads, beautiful, but too easily broken. At the same time, other friendships have been the solidest thing I know, bending and swaying with the shifts in our lives yet remaining intact. For me, loving friendship is not a fusion with another, but it is a rickety swing bridge to a separate being, and even though I know it can fall away into the abyss, the urge to step onto it is always there. There is strength in that desire for connection, the possibility of being saved from invisibility. Even though I cannot really know anyone else, only carry a memory-picture of them around in my head, when I am with a friend, I am woven into the human mystery.

A recent memory returns. I am sitting on the grass in Rose Bay park with a friend too new to name, perhaps we are not friends yet. We are seated on a slight rise, looking towards the sea, a coppice of masts sway and clink in front of us and sunlight silvers the water in rippling splashes. Even though it is winter we are warm and sweaty – we have both walked five or so kilometres to meet here. We drink coffee, we put sunblock on, we adjust our hats. We talk about writing and family – we are still at the stage of offering pieces of ourselves – and I feel the steady flow of energy between us. Afterwards, as I am walking home, I feel lighter. Perhaps the swing bridge will hold this time.

Acknowledgements

The author and publishers are grateful to the following for permission to reproduce copyright materials:

New Directions Publishing Corp for lines from *A Coney Island of the Mind* by Lawrence Ferlinghetti, New York, 1958
Penguin Random House for lines from *Beloved* by Toni Morrison, London, 1987; and for lines from *Poppy* by Drusilla Modjeska, Melbourne, 1990.

I also acknowledge the following books and websites I have referred to:

The Epic of Gilgamesh, edited by NK Sanders, Penguin Books, London, 1972.
The Essays: A Selection by Michel de Montaigne, translated by MA Screech, Penguin, London, 1993.
The Autobiography of Alice B Toklas by Gertrude Stein, Penguin, London, 2001.

Essays by Ralph Waldo Emerson, viewed 6 September 2021 <https://emersoncentral.com/texts/essays-first-series/friendship/>

Selected Poems by WB Yeats, Penguin, London, 2011.

The White Goddess by Robert Graves, Faber & Faber, London, 1961.

In Search of Lost Time by Marcel Proust, translated by CK Scott Moncrieff and Terence Kilmartin, London, 2002.

Les Deux Amis by La Fontaine, viewed 3 September 2021 <http://www.la-fontaine-ch-thierry.net/deuxamis.htm>

Many thanks to all at UQP, especially Madonna Duffy and Jacqueline Blanchard for their faith in this book and for pushing me further with it, and designer, Alissa Dinallo. I am grateful too, to Carol Major for her clear insights and Delia Falconer for listening to my anxieties about writing friendship. Many thanks to Kristina Olsson, Ceridwen Dovey, Kathryn Heyman and Caroline Baum for their thoughtful reading.

I want to thank the friends from various times that I have not written about, in particular Linda, Sue W, Kris, Phil, Peter, Michael, Lyn, Anna-Maria, Alan, Douglas, Beth, Kathy, Julie, J-J, Ana, Annie C, Margaret, Boguslawa, Sylvie, Carol – and friends too new to name. Perhaps these friends are grateful I have not explored our connections, nevertheless, thank you for the gift of your friendship. And thank you to the friends I have included for trusting me, sight unseen, with my version of our friendship. Some names and a few details have been altered in the interests of privacy.

Finally and always, thank you to Anthony Reeder, my first reader and editor, and, despite Montaigne's criteria, my dearest friend.

THE MIND OF A THIEF
Patti Miller

When writer Patti Miller discovers that the first post–Mabo Native Title claim was made by the Wiradjuri in the Wellington valley where she grew up, she begins to wonder where she belongs in the story of the town. It leads her to the question at the heart of Australian identity – who are we in relation to our cherished stolen country?

Feeling compelled to return to the valley, Miller uncovers a chronicle of idealism, destruction and hope in its history of convicts, zealous missionaries, farmers and gold seekers who all took the land from the original inhabitants. But it's not until she talks to the local Wiradjuri that she realises there's another set of stories about her town, even about her own family. As one Wiradjuri Elder remarks, 'The whitefellas and blackfellas have two different stories about who's related to who in this town.'

Black and white politics, family mythologies and the power of place are interwoven as Miller tells a story that is both an individual search for connection and identity and a universal exploration of country and belonging.

'*The Mind of a Thief* deals with the big issues ... This is complex stuff but Miller sets it all out calmly and clearly, using the craft of storytelling.' —*Weekend Australian*

'This exploration of identity and belonging is brilliantly crafted, brave and full of love.'—*The Mercury*

'... a remarkably fluid, virtuoso piece of writing.'—*The Age*

ISBN 978 0 7022 4936 5

RANSACKING PARIS
Patti Miller

What does it mean to fulfil a dream long after it seems possible? When Patti Miller arrives to write in Paris for a year, the world glows 'as if the light that comes after the sun has set had spilled gold on everything'.

But wasn't that just romantic illusion? Miller grew up on Wiradjuri land in country Australia where her heart and soul belonged. What did she think she would find in Paris that she couldn't find at home? How could she belong in this city made of other people's stories?

She turns to French writers, Montaigne, Rousseau, de Beauvoir and other memoirists, each one intent on knowing the self through gazing into the 'looking glass' of the great world. They accompany her as she wanders the streets of Paris and talks about love, suffering, desire, motherhood, memory, the writing journey – and the joys and responsibilities of ransacking.

Exploring truth and illusion, self-knowledge and identity, and family and culture, Miller evokes the beauty, the contradictions and the daily life of contemporary Paris.

'A quietly persistent commitment to her craft has made Miller the foremost exponent of life writing.'—*The Sydney Morning Herald*

'The combination of literary history and domestic detail sets the book above its rivals.'—*Books+Publishing*

'A charmingly unconventional and personal journey.'—*Booktopia Buzz*

ISBN 978 0 7022 5339 3